Front Cover:
John Singleton Copley
Mrs. Daniel Sargent

Back Cover:
John F. Peto
The Cup We All Race For

… AMERICAN ART

*An Exhibition from the
Collection of Mr. and Mrs. John D. Rockefeller 3rd*

1976

AMERICAN ART

A Narrative and Critical Catalogue by E. P. Richardson

THE FINE ARTS MUSEUMS OF SAN FRANCISCO

*Exhibited at the M. H. de Young Memorial Museum, San Francisco
from April 17 through July 31, 1976
and at the Whitney Museum of American Art, New York
from September 16 through November 7, 1976*

*Managing Editor: F. Lanier Graham
Copy Editor: Ann Karlstrom*

Copyright © 1976 by The Fine Arts Museums of San Francisco

CONTENTS

Foreword by Ian McKibbin White

Preface by E. P. Richardson

Catalogue of the Exhibition by E. P. Richardson

- 15   I   The Migration of Painting to North America
- 21   II   The First Native-Born Talents
- 29   III   Major Talents Begin to Appear
- 49   IV   The Transition to the New Republic
- 65   V   The Generation of 1800: The First Romantics
- 83   VI   The Generation of 1825: Landscape, Portrait and Genre
- 125   VII   The Flowering of the Nineteenth Century: Before the Civil War
- 137   VIII   The Flowering of the Nineteenth Century: After the Civil War
- 219   IX   The Twentieth Century
- 245   Bibliography

Alphabetical List of Artists and Catalogue Numbers

Allston, Washington	22	Hartley, Marsden	99
Anshutz, Thomas P.	55	Hassam, Childe	100
Audubon, John James	23	Heade, Martin Johnson	48 and 49
Badger, Joseph	3	Henri, Robert	101
Benbridge, Henry	6-8	Hicks, Edward	26
Bierstadt, Albert	40-44	Homer, Winslow	69-73
Bingham, George Caleb	30 and 31	Hovenden, Thomas	74-76
Birch, Thomas	24	Hunt, William Morris	77
Blythe, David G.	32	Johnson, Eastman	78-82
Bricher, Alfred T.	56	LaFarge, John	83
Brown, J. G.	57	Lane, Fitz Hugh	50
Brush, George DeForest	58	Maynard, George W.	85
Bunker, Dennis M.	59	McCloskey, William J.	84
Burchfield, Charles	95 and 96	Moran, Thomas	86 and 87
Catlin, George	25	Mount, William Sidney	37-39
Chalfant, Jefferson Davis	60	Page, William	51 and 52
Chandler, Winthrop	15 and 16	Peale, Charles Willson	12-14
Chase, William Merritt	61	Peale, Raphaelle	27
Church, Frederic E.	45 and 46	Peto, John F.	88 and 89
Cole, Thomas	33 and 34	Rimmer, William	53
Colman, Samuel	62	Sargent, John Singer	90 and 91
Copley, John Singleton	9-11	Shahn, Ben	102
Demuth, Charles	97 and 98	Smibert, John	2
The De Peyster Painter	4	Stuart, Gilbert	20
Durand, Asher B.	35 and 36	Sully, Thomas	28 and 29
Eakins, Susan Macdowell	63	Trumbull, John	21
Eakins, Thomas	64 and 65	Ulrich, Charles Frederick	92
Earl, James	17	Unknown Massachusetts Painter	1
Earl, Ralph	18 and 19	Vedder, Elihu	93 and 94
Farny, Henry	66	Whittredge, Worthington	54
Feke, Robert	5	Wood, Grant	103 and 104
Gifford, Sanford R.	47	Wyeth, Andrew	105 and 106
Harnett, William Michael	67 and 68		

FOREWORD

John D. Rockefeller 3rd, in his book, *The Second American Revolution,* speaks of the democratic process:

> "For my part, give me the decision to become involved by more and more people, and I will gladly take my chances as to the quality of their choices and actions."

It is a nice statement that pertains to the development of this exhibition and the many events which it effected.

Mr. and Mrs. Rockefeller had decided to exhibit their collection of American paintings for the first time. Even they had never seen it all together because it usually is divided between a New York office, an apartment, and a country home.

The idea of the first public showing as a Bicentennial tribute to the city of San Francisco was appealing. California has fewer museums than the eastern United States, so there is less to see here of American art from earlier centuries. Inevitably the nation's celebration will focus on the historic cities of the East, but Bicentennial visitors also will come to San Francisco, many from the Orient. With their strong interest in Asia, Mr. and Mrs. Rockefeller felt it a fitting location for the collection to be seen before it moves on to be shown at the Whitney Museum in New York, the city where they live.

They were aware that The Fine Arts Museums of San Francisco have been committed to collecting, publishing and exhibiting American art for many years. When the M. H. de Young Museum and the California Palace of the Legion of Honor merged administratively in 1973 the American paintings in each museum were united to form a collection of considerable scope. A new suite of galleries will be completed in late 1976 at the de Young Museum to house the American collections of paintings and decorative arts adequately for the first time. Attracted by these activities, the Smithsonian Institution decided to locate its West Coast office of the Archives of American Art at the de Young Museum, near the strongest American art reference library in the area.

Perhaps more importantly, the Rockefellers' decision was influenced by the educational potentials that the presence of their collection could generate in the San Francisco Bay Area community. The news was announced to all the colleges and universities in Northern California and the response was enthusiastic. Several schools will teach American art courses during the exhibition. For example, in an improvement on the usual classroom lecture illustrated with slides and textbook reproductions, nearly three hundred undergraduates from Mills College and the University of California, Berkeley, will come to the Museum to study actual paintings. Special round-trip bus transportation and seminar rooms, with comparative European and American paintings from the Museums' collections, are part of the convenient plan. Ten of the most capable students will be trained to give talks in secondary schools and community centers to prepare visitors for what they will see in the exhibition.

General audiences will benefit from an eight-week series of humanities presentations, drawing on the Rockefeller collection for inspiration, which will recall the cultural, social, political and economic milieu of the times. Through the use of film, slides, live and recorded music, drama, dance and the spoken word it will attempt to provide an integrated view of the forces which shaped the artists and the works of art they produced.

Certainly one of the happiest adjuncts of the Rockefeller exhibition is an Archives of American Art exhibition of documents. Original letters by nearly a third of the artists represented in the Rockefeller collection will be on view in an adjacent gallery including a letter by John Smibert dated 1743, the earliest document in the Archives, and photographs of twenty-two of the artists, as a reminder perhaps of the immediacy of the American past.

On behalf of everyone who has been involved with this exhibition I can express our gratitude best in terms of Mr. Rockefeller's own statement. We are deeply grateful to Mr. and Mrs. Rockefeller for their extraordinary generosity in giving up their enjoyment of the paintings for so many months. They have taken their chances with all of us "as to the quality of our choices and actions" with regard to this exhibition. In doing so they have enabled more and more people to become involved in the appreciation of a precious part of our country's heritage.

Greatest credit for the preparation of this exhibition and our special tribute of appreciation go to Dr. E. P. Richardson who selected the works and wrote this unusual catalogue. It is a significant departure from a traditional exhibition catalogue in that it combines impeccable scholarship and warmly human narrative. No one could have been better qualified for the task than this distinguished historian of American art who has advised Mr. and Mrs. Rockefeller on the formation of their collection over the past decade.

F. Lanier Graham, Chief Curator of The Fine Arts Museums, deserves our special thanks for his role in the development of the exhibition since its inception four years ago, for his careful editing of this catalogue, and for his concept of a regional educational program.

We have been particularly fortunate in obtaining the services of Professor Wanda M. Corn, Mills College, Oakland, to design the educational programs. In consultation with Thomas K. Seligman, the Museums' Vice Director for Education, and assisted by Dianne Sachko, she has created an innovative and enriching experience for the students she will be teaching in the American Art program of the University of California, Berkeley, and Mills College. Working closely with Stephen Arkin, Wesley Chamberlin, Sister Mary Dominic, Paul Karlstrom, Bruce Merley, Charles Mills and Leni Sloan, she has produced a wide ranging program of dramatic performances in place of the usual lecture series. The concept for the installation was developed by Wanda M. Corn as Visiting Curator and Thomas H. Garver, Curator of Exhibitions. As never before, every single member of the staff assisted in the realization of this undertaking. It is only the limits of space which preclude naming all the individuals who contributed in so many ways.

A special note of gratitude must go, however, to William Woolfenden, Director of the Archives of American Art, the Smithsonian Institution, Garnett McCoy in the Washington, D.C. office and Paul Karlstrom in the San Francisco office for allowing some of the rarest documents in the Archives to accompany the exhibition.

Our appreciation also goes to Howard Lipman, President of the Board, and Tom Armstrong, Director of the Whitney Museum of American Art, in connection with the presentation of the exhibition at the Whitney Museum of American Art in New York City.

We wish to thank the following institutions whose generosity and support made possible the presentation of the exhibition and its enriching programs: Mills College and the University of California; Alcoa Foundation for grants to both The Fine Arts Museums and the Whitney Museum of American Art; the National Endowment for the Arts, The American Issues Forum of the National Endowment for the Humanities and The Museum Society of The Fine Arts Museums of San Francisco.

IAN McKIBBIN WHITE
Director of Museums

PREFACE

This exhibition is selected from a collection spanning three centuries of painting and sculpture in our country. It calls for a brief explanation.

Both Mr. and Mrs. John D. Rockefeller 3rd are collectors whose interests and tastes are distinct though overlapping. This exhibit is drawn only from American works of art acquired by Mr. Rockefeller. He came rather late to American art after an unusually wide experience of other arts and of the world. He grew up among great examples of mediaeval and renaissance European works of art at home. He watched at first hand the restoration of Colonial Williamsburg, and saw his mother form the pioneer collection of American folk art now housed in the Abby Aldrich Rockefeller Folk Art Collection at Williamsburg. His mother was also active in the founding and early years of The Museum of Modern Art, New York; in more recent years, his wife has also been deeply engaged in the affairs of that institution.

Mr. Rockefeller went to the Orient as a member of Secretary of State Dulles's mission to Japan and the subsequent peace conference at San Francisco in 1951. This was his introduction to the arts of Asia, of which he continues to be one of the great collectors. He has been chairman of the Rockefeller Foundation and of the Japan Society, founder of the Asia Society, the Agricultural Development Council, and the Population Council. These and other activities resulted in extensive travel over the world. He thus brought a wide acquaintance with other lands and arts to the exploration of the art of his own country.

His interest in American art came about in the following way. He found himself acting as host in New York City to visitors from all over the world: some acquaintances from his own travels, others whom he was asked to entertain by the State Department or by our delegates to the United Nations. He became discontented with receiving these guests in a home containing only oriental art and French impressionists. Thinking that his home should also offer something characteristic of his own country, he acquired two pictures, the Church (No. 45) and the Fitz Hugh Lane (No. 50). From that beginning American art has grown into an absorbing interest. This exhibition is drawn from the results of ten years of exploring the art of the United States.

Mr. Rockefeller has never, in my experience, acquired a work he has not himself enjoyed and found significant, often after long study. The exhibition thus represents a thoughtful, personal view of our art by an observer of unusual experience and perspective. The collection interests me both for the works of art themselves and for its choices. It passes by works representing a purely esthetic impulse or mode, in favor of those expressing a response to human life and to nature. Included are realists and dreamers, artists of only an artisan's skills and those of great sophistication, famous names and unknown or forgotten figures. All speak from the heart.

E. P. RICHARDSON

CATALOGUE

I

The Migration of Painting to North America

The art of painting came to America with the first permanent settlements early in the seventeenth century. The English in Virginia and Massachusetts and the Dutch on the Hudson and the Delaware (where the Swedes also settled) brought with them arts and skills of their homelands. Family pride was strong among these ambitious, strong-willed people, and they brought along with them a need for family portraits. There was an English painter in Massachusetts by 1635. A Dutch painter, trained at Leyden and Amsterdam, was in New Amsterdam before 1660. In contrast to painting in the French and Spanish colonies where the first requirement was for pictures to teach the faith and doctrines of the church, the first aim of painting in what was to become the United States was to record the people themselves.

By the early eighteenth century most of the little seaport capitals of the colonies from Massachusetts to South Carolina had a portrait painter of European training. These artists painted in the late baroque style typified by Sir Godfrey Kneller—formal, stiff, decorative, concerned more with giving a sense of dignity and social status than with characterization. In this form a great art first crossed the ocean to a new world.

Unknown Massachusetts Painter

The last after-glow of Elizabethan painting lingered in seventeenth-century Massachusetts Bay Colony long after it had been extinguished in England itself. A group of portraits painted at Boston in the 1670's are in a style characteristic of sixteenth-century English painting under Queen Elizabeth I and James I. How could this happen? Louisa Dresser, the leading student of seventeenth-century New England painting has published the record of two men of the town of Reading, Berkshire, England, who on March 4, 1634/5, took the Oath of Supremacy and Allegiance with the intent of going to New England (Dresser, 1966). One was Augustine Clement, painter; the other was his "servant" Thomas Wheeler, probably his apprentice. Clement arrived in New England aboard the *James*, June 3, 1635. He died there on October 1, 1674, leaving a "dwelling house & barns orchards & gardens & land" in Dorchester as well as "housing both new and old" in Boston. When Clement left England, Van Dyck was already painting at the Court of Charles I, but his High Baroque style had not yet spread beyond court circles. Clement, trained in the provinces, would have brought the older tradition of his craft to America. No documents connect him with *The Mason Children*; none have been found to indicate his activity in America. They do, however, show that a well-trained English artist emigrated to New England and lived until 1674.

Represented in this painting are the children of Arthur Mason and Joanna (Parker) Mason of Boston: David, born at Boston, October 24, 1661, died in 1724; Joanna, born at Boston, March 26, 1664, married first Robert Breck and second Michael Perry, July 12, 1694; Abigail, baptised at Boston, April 2, 1666, married Captain Benjamin Gillam. A likeness of a fourth Mason child, Alice (born 1668), by the same artist, is owned by the Adams Memorial Society, Quincy, Massachusetts. For a long time it was in possession of the Adams family, as it was then supposed to represent John Quincy, founder of the town of Quincy, as a child. A much restored portrait, perhaps representing an older sister, Mary Mason, is also in the Adams Memorial, having formerly been supposed to represent Anna Shepard Quincy (Dresser, 1935; Burroughs, 1936; Flexner, 1937).

The painter of these three children had a perceptive eye. Nine-year-old David stands very upright, holding gloves in one hand and a silver-headed walking stick in the other to show that he is the grown-up. His little sisters stand decorously still but are quite aware that, in their white linen caps, moss-green dresses with white pinafores, necklaces of red beads, and brown leather shoes with red laces and silver studded soles, they are looking their very best. Joanna holds a yellow fan, Abigail a red rose. As the saying goes, they are "pretty as a picture." Such a portrait, so decorative and human, shows how far from the whole truth is the dismal stereotype of puritan New England dominant in American popular memory.

The portrait remained in the family for just over 300 years, passing always by inheritance from Joanna Mason through family ownership until 1974. The line of descent is given by Louisa Dresser (1935).

Canvas: 39½ x 42-11/16 inches. Inscribed at the right of David's head: *Anno Dom.* 1670 and at the left *8*; at the left of Joanna's head: *6*; at the left of Abigail's: *4*.

1 *The Mason Children,
David, Joanna and Abigail 1670*

John Smibert 1688-1751

Of the European-trained painters who brought the art to America, Smibert was the most influential. Scottish born, he worked his way up from a humble beginning, painted in Edinburgh, Florence and London, and came to America with Dean Berkeley, arriving at Newport in 1729. He soon after left Newport for Boston, which was his home for the remainder of his life. His portraits, his "colour shop" where he sold engravings and artist's materials, his gallery of copies after pictures in the Medici collection, were a school of art for two generations of American-born artists.

Smibert's portrait of John Nelson was painted in 1732. Nelson was then seventy-eight years old. He had come out to Massachusetts at the age of twenty-three, prospered, and married a Boston girl. When in April 1689 the Bostonians rose against Sir Edmund Andros, governor for King James II of all the English colonies from Maryland to Canada (except Pennsylvania), Nelson led the party that made Andros prisoner. However, he was excluded from the subsequent government because he was an Anglican. On a trading voyage to Nova Scotia he was captured by the French and spent years in prison at Quebec and in France; he was finally released to rejoin his family in 1698. In the nineteenth century Samuel Adams Drake wrote a romantic novel suggested by these adventures, *Captain Nelson: A Romance of Colonial Days* (1879).

The seventeenth and early eighteenth centuries were a time of dignified formality in manners and in art. Smibert's portraits have the formality of his age, yet he gave us here a vigorous study of the firm, intelligent face, upright carriage and fine hands of a striking personality.

Canvas: 44½ x 36 inches. Inscribed at lower left: *Aet 78 1732*. The coat of arms in the upper left is said to be that of the Temple family. Nelson was a near relation to Sir William Temple, the diplomat, statesman and author.

2 *John Nelson* 1732

II

The First Native-born Talents

The practice of painting in both Holland and England was a subtle and complex skill, using the wide range of richness of tone and hue of oil paint to create effects of light, air, movement, solid forms in deep space. This was beyond the training or experience of many of those who were born with a bent toward painting in the new settlements of America. There were other skills nearer at hand. The centuries of settlement were those in which the decorative arts of Europe were in flower. A variety of artisan skills made cities like Amsterdam or London bright with color and gold leaf on inn and shop signs; heraldic glass in church windows and homes; color, carving, gilding on walls and furniture. Skills of eye and hand, drawing and color were required in all of these crafts, different from those of the artist but nonetheless real and admirable. Evert Duyckinck, glazier and glass painter, came to New Amsterdam in 1639 and practiced as an artisan but before the end of his life turned his skills to portrait painting. His sons and grandsons followed in his footsteps. The artisan turning to painting portraits, in the absence of the trained professional, was to become a characteristic phenomenon of the new settlements of America.

Joseph Badger 1708-1765

The last entries in Smibert's list of portraits were made in 1746 (Oliver, 1969). Failing eyesight caused him to stop painting, and for the next ten years (until an English migrant painter, Blackburn, arrived in 1755, followed shortly by the rise of Copley's star) most of the portrait business of Boston fell to an artisan painter of Charlestown named Joseph Badger. Although his skills were limited and his portraits of men often unbearably wooden, Badger's portraits of women or children could be pleasing and even evocative.

The portrait of Anna Porter of Wenham, Massachusetts, who married Nathaniel Brown of Salem in 1743, tells us a good deal about this serious, responsible New England housewife. There is no hint of a smile in the earnest mouth; the eyes are straightforward, her face plain; yet there is something attractive in this directness of character. One feels certain that her family was well cared for and her home quiet and orderly.

Canvas: 48 x 37 inches.

3 *Anna Porter Brown*

The De Peyster Painter

The Dutch who settled in the Hudson Valley in the seventeenth century came from a country where painting was enormously popular, artists were numbered in the thousands, and every home contained pictures. Thus it is not surprising that native-born painters should appear early among the Dutch on this side of the ocean. The De Peyster family brought family portraits with them from Holland and continued to have portraits painted in New Amsterdam. A group of portraits of De Peyster children in The New York Historical Society, painted about 1720-30, has given a name to the De Peyster Painter, whose style is recognisable here.

This is the daughter of a Dutch merchant, Herman Winkler, who came to the New Netherlands colony after service in the East India Company's trade at Batavia, Sumatra. He had two daughters, Maria Maytilda and Jacomina, whose portraits were painted as a pair. Maria Maytilda married Nicholas Gouverneur of Newark, New Jersey; Jacomina died in childhood. The artist painted Maria Maytilda holding a lamb, the symbol of innocence, borrowing the pose from a mezzotint by John Smith after Kneller's portrait of *Lord William and Lady Mary Villiers*. Jacomina was painted holding a snarling little lap dog, taken from a mezzotint of the *Dowager Queen Catherine of Braganza* (Belknap, *American Colonial Painting*, 1959, Nos. 50 and 51). The portraits descended in the family of Maria Maytilda until her portrait was offered to Mr. Rockefeller.

Canvas: 30½ x 25½ inches.

4 *Maria Maytilda Winkler* ca. 1720-1730

Robert Feke ca. 1707-ca. 1752

Feke is the most gifted American-born painter to appear before 1750. He is a shadowy figure whose activity can be firmly established only from 1741 to 1751 in Newport, Boston and Philadelphia. He was born at Oyster Bay on Long Island in the province of New York. In 1741 he painted and signed a portrait group in Boston. He was married in 1742 at Newport, Rhode Island, which became his home. He was painting in Philadelphia in 1746 and 1749-1750, and at Boston in 1748. The last record of him is at Newport in 1751; he appears to have died or disappeared before January, 1752 (Mooz, 1971). An artist of natural gifts but little training, he learned what he could from the portraits of Smibert in Boston and Hesselius in Philadelphia and from studying English engravings.

Grizzel Eastwick (1709-1796), the subject of this portrait, married Charles Apthorp on January 13, 1726. Her husband was paymaster and commissioner of the British naval forces which had their headquarters at Boston, where he became a wealthy and prominent merchant. His portrait by Feke is in the Cleveland Museum of Art.

The eighteenth-century ideal of stately dignity was translated in the art of painting into a formal, idealized, decorative portrait that was a symbol of one's status in society rather than an intimate record of personality or a glimpse of a person in the setting of life. Feke painted this formula of status and dignity with skill, making a handsome decoration of the upright figure and the billowing folds of her gold-brown satin dress. Mrs. Apthorp sits, serene, elegant, untroubled, holding a copy of *Paradise Lost* open on her knee. We know from other sources that she was the mother of eighteen children.

Canvas: 50 x 40 inches. Signed and dated center right: *R. F. 1748*.

5 Mrs. Charles Apthorp *1748*

III

Major Talents Begin to Appear in America

In the eminently social eighteenth century, portrait painting was a great art practiced by artists of the greatest talents who found in it a high road to fame and financial success. On this side of the ocean, European painters who had migrated had led the way until about 1750. Soon after, in the third quarter of the century, a generation of native-born painters appeared to give the colonies an art of their own. Benbridge, Copley and Peale were American-born, mature artists, capable of giving us notable insights into the men and women of their day. We are fortunate that the generation which won independence was recorded for us by artists of such stature.

Henry Benbridge 1743-1812

This big man with the strong, intelligent, pugnacious face was one of the heroes of the eighteenth century. Lamartine spoke of Paoli's fame as out of all proportion to the smallness of his country: Corsica, he said, is a mere province but Paoli takes his place "among the ranks of great men." Dr. Johnson, to whom Paoli was introduced by Boswell in 1769, said afterwards that General Paoli had the "loftiest port" of any man he had ever seen.

The Corsicans chose Paoli in 1755 to lead their revolt against Genoa, as his father had done before. Successful in that war, he was an enlightened ruler of the island. In 1768 Genoa ceded the island to France, whose armies overwhelmed the Corsicans in 1769. Paoli escaped to England, where he lived until, in the euphoria of 1789, Louis XVI appointed him Lieutenant-General of Corsica. After the execution of the king, he refused to obey the Convention, defeated the forces sent against him, and arranged a union of Corsica with England. The union was short-lived. Napoleon conquered and annexed the island to France, and Paoli spent the remainder of his life in England. He is buried in Westminster Abbey.

James Boswell, visiting Corsica in 1765 at the end of his tour of Italy, met and conceived a great admiration for Paoli. Boswell's *Account of Corsica* (1768), translated into French, Dutch, German and Italian, brought its author a European reputation. Through an intermediary, Boswell commissioned a portrait of Paoli from a young colonial painter from Philadelphia then completing his studies in Italy. Benbridge went to the island in 1768 just in time to meet Paoli before the French army overwhelmed the Corsicans. This portrait was exhibited in London at the Society of British Artists in 1769 with a collection box before it for aid to Corsican refugees. It aroused great interest, was viewed by the royal family, and was engraved in mezzotint for Carington Bowles (1769). This provided an admirable introduction in London for the young artist, but after about a year there Benbridge decided to return to America.

The portrait hung in the Boswell house at Auchinlech until sold in 1973 to help pay for necessary repairs to the house. The elaborate rococo frame is presumably the one ordered for it by Boswell in 1769.

Canvas: 85 x 50 inches.

6 *Pascal Paoli* 1768

Henry Benbridge

After his return to America, Benbridge's style changed; his drawing grew crisper, his chiaroscuro more dramatic. The change is seen in the sharp definition of these two portraits which, looking out from their circular frames, seem almost startlingly real.

The subjects are a young Philadelphia shipmaster, Robert Shewell, junior, and his wife, Sarah Boyer. There was reason for the artist to do his best. Robert Shewell's sister, Elizabeth, was the wife of Benjamin West. Another sister, Mary Shewell, married one of Benbridge's cousins. The two artists considered themselves cousins, and Benbridge had lived as an intimate of the West household in London. These are family portraits, warmed by a sense of kinship and spurred by Benbridge's desire to show his family what he had learned in Europe. The costumes indicate that he painted them in the early 1770's immediately after his return from London.

The portraits descended in the family through five generations. In 1942 William Sawitzky, a pioneer student of eighteenth-century painting, published them as the work of Matthew Pratt. But in 1948 Anna Wells Rutledge put together the work of Benbridge in two articles that established his role in the middle colonies and the south. Mr. Rockefeller acquired these portraits in 1967 as characteristic works of Benbridge, and the exhibition of his work at the National Portrait Gallery in 1971 made it clear that they are among his finest works.

Canvas: diameter, 26 inches each.

7 Robert Shewell, Junior   ca. 1771

Henry Benbridge

8 *Mrs. Robert Shewell, Junior ca. 1771*

John Singleton Copley 1738-1815

Most of Copley's early portraits were of young people whose fresh, smooth faces and handsome clothes were proper subjects for portraits of elegance. His interest in character developed as he came to paint older people whose faces were marked by time and experience. This is one of his earliest portraits of an older woman.

Katherine Stanbridge married Rufus Greene in 1728 in King's Chapel, that stronghold of the Church of England in Congregationalist Boston. She and her husband and children belonged to the Anglican minority, from which, in the troubled years ahead, came many of the New England Loyalists. One of her daughters, Mrs. John Amory (whose portrait by Copley is in the Museum of Fine Arts, Boston) went into exile when the Revolution came, sailing to join her husband in London on the same ship that took Mrs. Copley and her three children to England. In Mrs. Amory's diary in exile she spoke affectionately of her mother, whose sweet, pious, courageous character Copley painted with great understanding.

The portrait has been cut down from a larger size because of damage by fire at some time in the past.

Canvas: 24 x 20¾ inches.

9   *Mrs. Rufus Greene   ca. 1760*

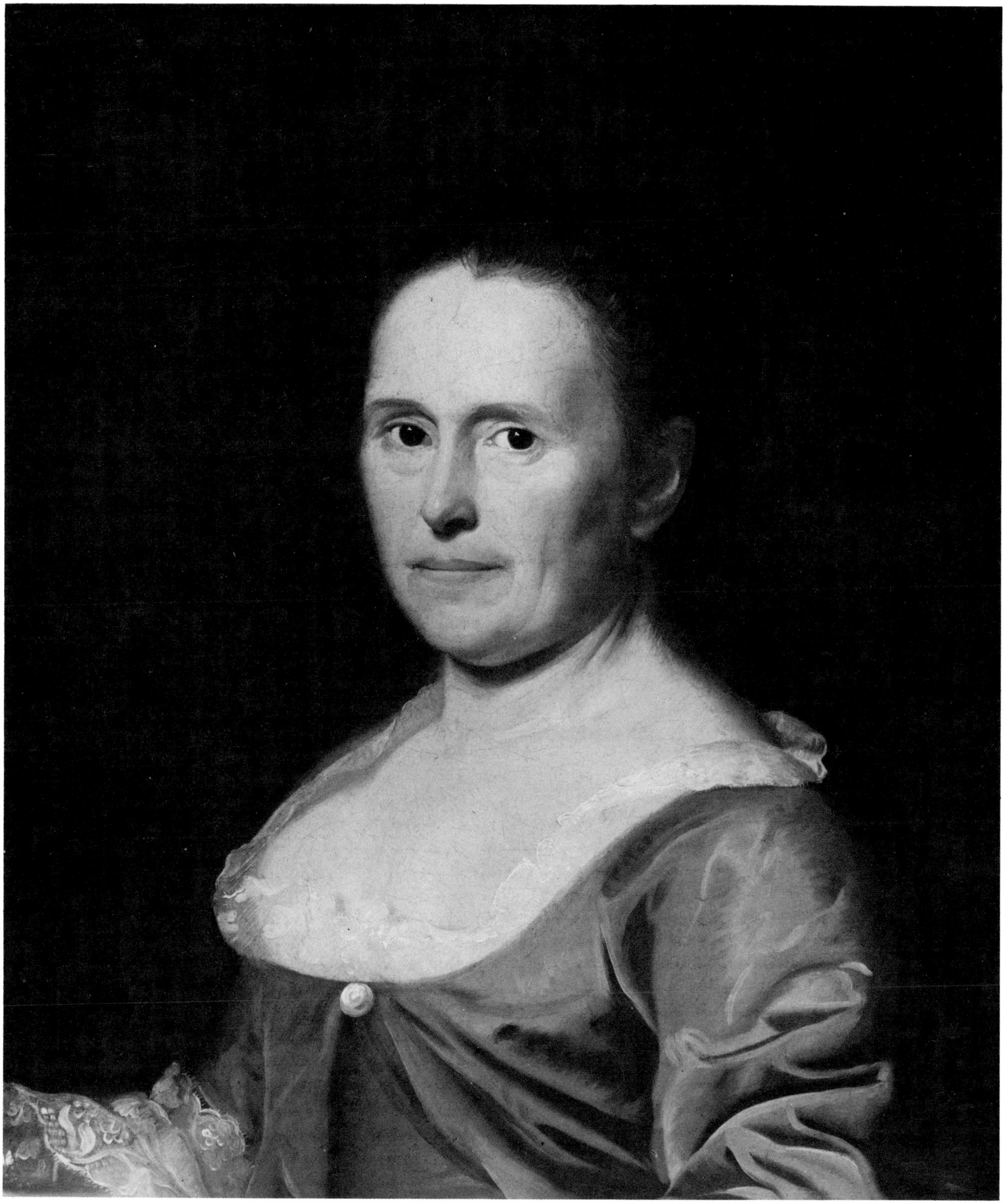

John Singleton Copley

Copley won his first success as a painter of elegance. The people of his time lived by a formal code of manners: their dress was stately and beautiful; their idea of portraiture, shared by artist and sitters alike, was formed by the works of English painters like Hudson and Highmore. But in the 1760's a new tone emerged in the English portraits shown in the print shops of Boston. In this New Wave men were posed with greater ease and naturalness while women's portraits became lighter, gayer, and showed touches of charming artifice. Copley responded in such a portrait as that of *Mrs. Daniel Sargent*.

Mary Turner of Salem, Massachusetts, married Daniel Sargent, son of a shipowner of Gloucester, in 1763. This is her portrait as a bride. One feels not only the young woman's pride of beauty but the pride of the young artist, who now at twenty-five found himself master of his art. Copley never painted better than in this portrait with the imperceptible modeling that creates her face and expression, the luminosity of her skin, the lustre of dark eyes and hair, the shimmer of satin and silver and organdy. The artifice of placing her beside a wall fountain, holding out a shell to catch the sparkling water, and contrasting her freshness against the massive, ancient stones behind, is highly imaginative. Copley for the first time had hit his stride.

Canvas: 50 x 40 inches. Signed at the lower left: *John Singleton Copley/Pinx 1763*

10 *Mrs. Daniel Sargent 1763*

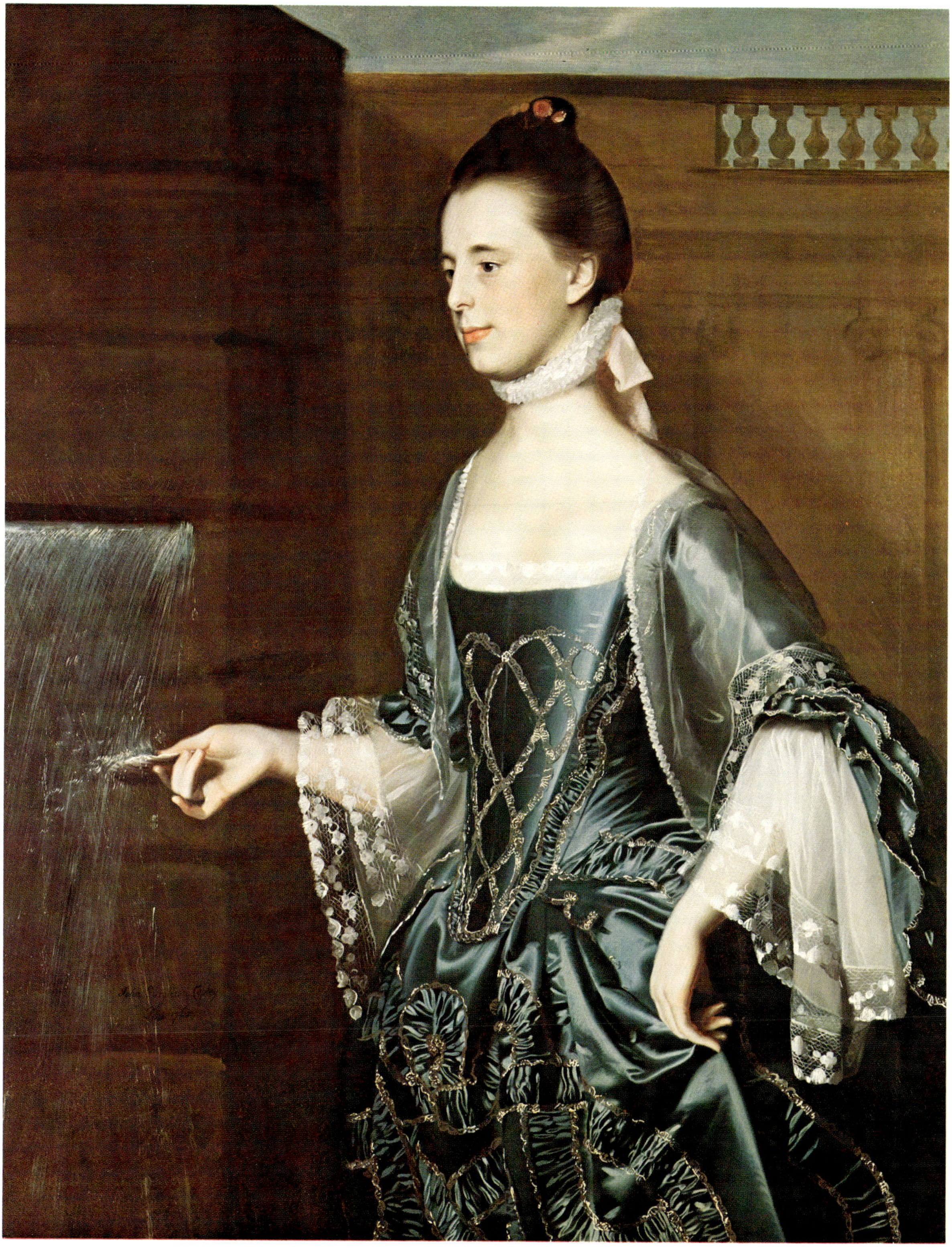

John Singleton Copley

This double portrait, one of the most interesting that Copley painted in America, represents William Vassal, who was nearing sixty, and his son Leonard, born in 1764, who was six or seven when Copley painted them together. Copley had painted a few portraits showing more than one figure, while still a beginner and content to show figures simply looking out of the canvas together. In the 1770's he returned to the double portrait with a mature artist's interest in personality, no longer satisfied with a purely formal relationship between two people. How should they relate to each other? One might look out at the observer, but what should the other do? Here he chose to paint the elderly father sitting relaxed in his chair, giving his attention to the observer but aware of the child who has come into the room, asking his father to explain something in his lesson. The two heads show Copley's grasp of character: the elder grave, worn and attentive; the boy's face, still touched with childish softness, puzzled and appealing.

John Adams later described William Vassal as "one of my old friends and clients, a mandamus counsellor against his will, a man of letters and virtues, without one vice that I ever knew or suspected, except garrulity." He was a man with whom Copley could sympathize, for like the artist, he had no interest in the darkening scene of Massachusetts politics except to stay out of it. A man made wealthy by his sugar plantation in Jamaica, owner of large properties in Massachusetts and Rhode Island, he lived in a house on Pemberton Hill commanding a splendid view over Boston Harbor, with terraced gardens descending to the road below. Neither a merchant nor office holder, neither Whig nor Tory, he was a man of leisure who wished no part in the quarrel with the mother country. But in time of revolution the neutral is often a victim. After the riots of 1774 in Boston, the Vassal family, attempting to take refuge on their Rhode Island county place, "were pelted by the mob in Bristol, to the endangering of their lives." They returned to Boston but as soon as possible after Lexington hired a ship and went first to Nantucket, then to England. Vassal spent his remaining years among a little colony of American exiles in Battersea Rise, a suburb of London (Sibley, 1937). The portrait was unknown until it appeared at a London auction in 1972.

Canvas: 50 x 40¾ inches.

11 *William Vassal and His Son Leonard ca. 1770–1772*

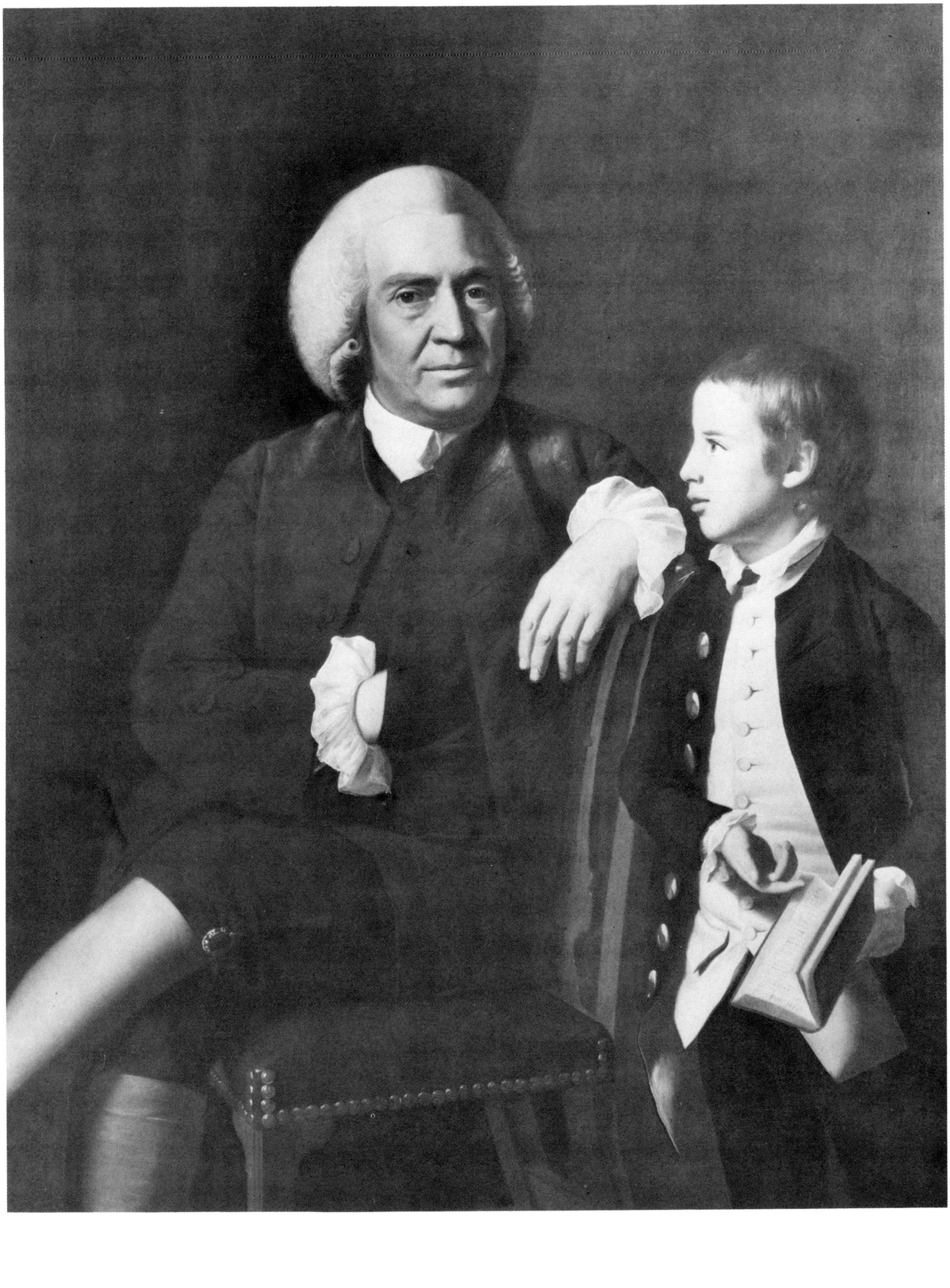

Charles Willson Peale 1741-1827

Peale, born on the Eastern Shore of Maryland, died at the age of eighty-six in Philadelphia. His life was long but he crowded into it enough activity as artist, craftsman, naturalist, soldier, inventor, politician and scientist to fill several long lives. At first self-taught in Annapolis, he studied with Benjamin West in London 1767-69, returned to Maryland 1769-75, and then moved to Philadelphia. An ardent Whig in politics, he was an officer of the Philadelphia militia in the campaigns of Trenton, Princeton and at Valley Forge. As the chief portrait painter in the revolutionary capital, he painted an invaluable record of the American leaders, both civil and military, and their allies. In the 1780's he began his collections of natural history that developed into the first American scientific museum. Housed for twenty-five years in the upper floors of Independence Hall, it served as our first quasi-national museum.

The portrait of Mordecai Gist, painted in the early 1770's, is an admirable example of Peale's Maryland style after his return from London. It shows Gist in his earlier career as a merchant and sea-captain, holding dividers, a chart and a copy of Euclid; a brig under sail, seen through the window, shows the practical use to which chart and geometry were put. In 1775 Gist was elected captain of the Baltimore Independent Company, one of the early military units organized as the war approached. In 1776 he was a major in Smallwood's First Maryland Brigade that fought gallantly at Long Island, the Brandywine and Germantown; he was a brigadier general of the Maryland Line in Greene's southern army, winning great distinction at Camden and Combahee. After the war he settled at Charleston, South Carolina.

When, before the battle of Germantown, some Maryland officers were quartered outside Philadelphia in a house where a family of refugees from the city were also living, a young Quaker girl in the house wrote of him in her diary: "He is very pretty; a charming person; his eyes are exceptional; and he so rolls them about that mine always fall under them." (Wister, 1885.) Tall, handsome, brave, single-hearted in the cause of the war, Gist was a born leader. *The Dictionary of American Biography* says of him, "It was certainly this type of American who won the Revolution."

Canvas: 30 x 25 inches.

12 *General Mordecai Gist ca. 1770-1772*

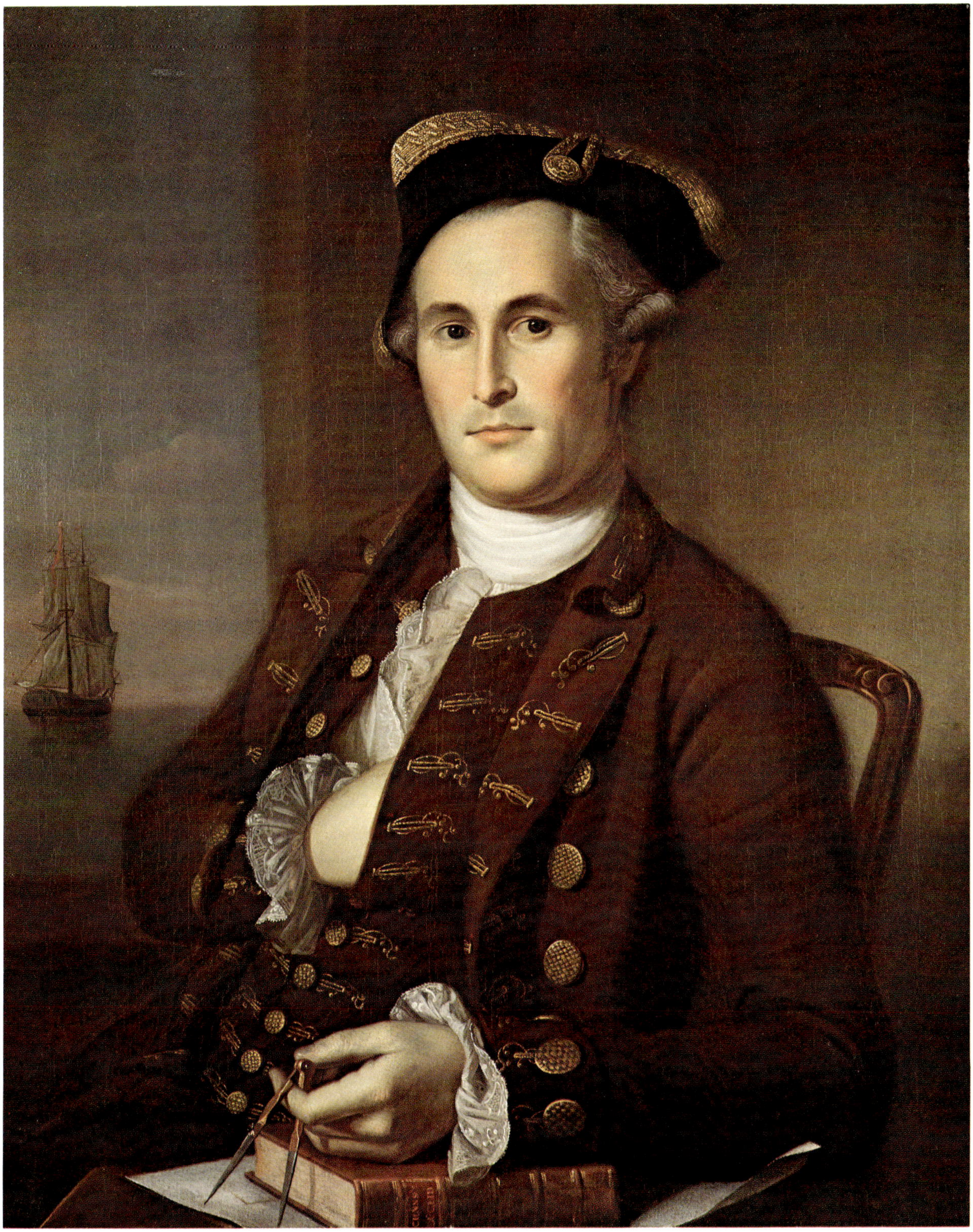

Charles Willson Peale

For twenty or so years, while he was absorbed in his museum project, Peale painted little, only now and then a portrait of a member of the family or a landscape on his farm, Belfield, in Germantown. The appointment of his son, Titian Ramsay Peale, as assistant naturalist of Mayor Stephen H. Long's exploring expedition to the Rocky Mountains was one of the things that brought him back to painting: the portraits of Long and his scientific staff, painted before their departure in 1819, are among his strongest works.

The portrait of Fitzgerald, a revolutionary soldier and old friend of the artist, was done about this time and shows the sober, solid painting and vigorous characterization which was typical of the artist's work in his final decade.

Canvas: 26½ x 22½ inches.

13 *Thomas Fitzgerald ca. 1816*

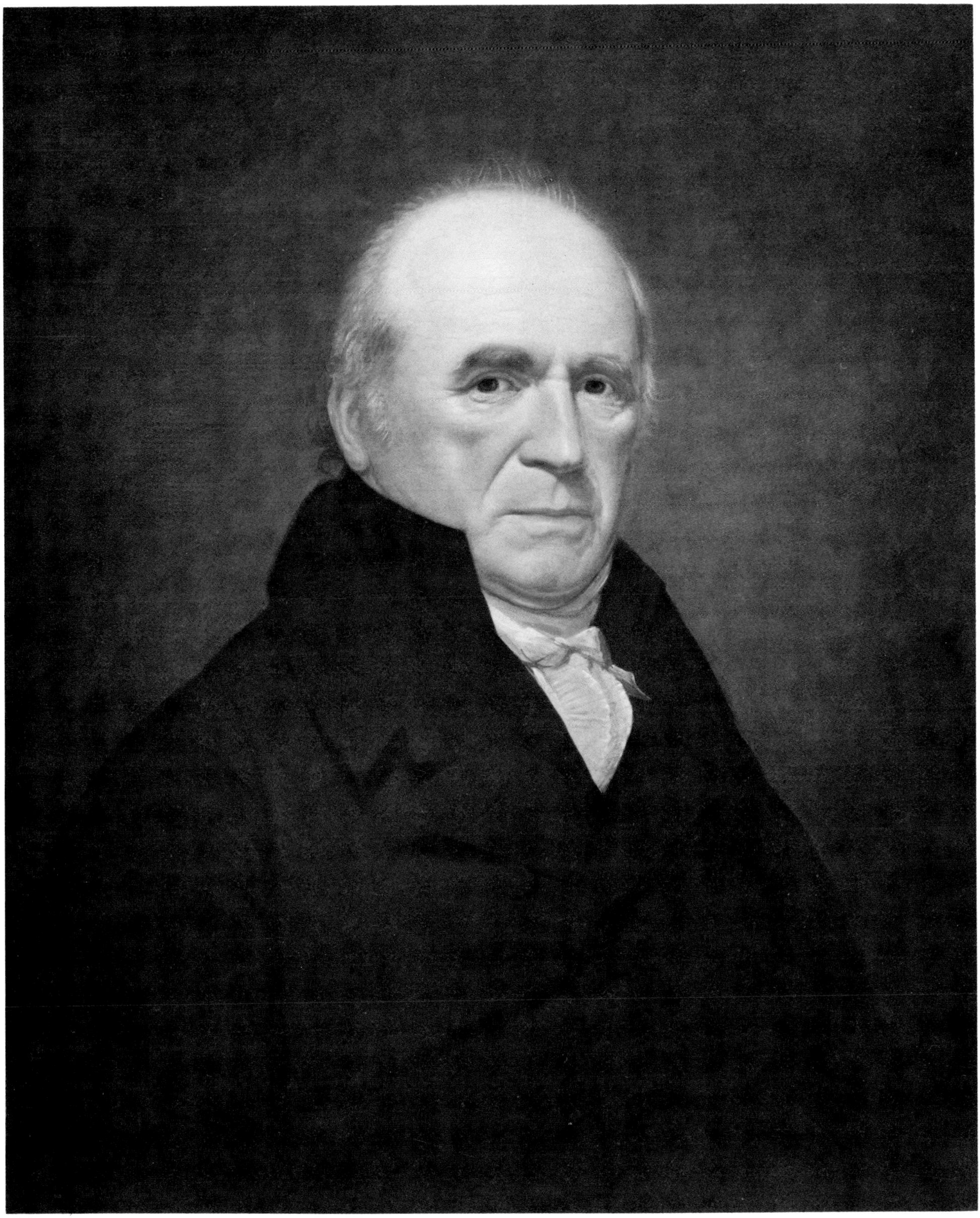

Charles Willson Peale

Peale painted this self-portrait in 1822 as a gift to his daughter Sophonisba, Mrs. Coleman Sellers; it was exhibited at the Pennsylvania Academy of the Fine Arts in that year. A note in the catalogue said, "Painted in the 81st year of his age without spectacles." It remained in the family until given in 1972 to the Museum of Northern Arizona, Flagstaff, to be sold for the benefit of its endowment. Peale, who struggled for half his life to establish his own museum on a sound financial basis, would have sympathized. His museum, after his death, could not maintain itself against the gaudy competition of showmen like P. T. Barnum and went out of existence; its collections were dispersed in the 1850's.

This portrait of the old artist-scientist has a sober power worthy of a Dutch seventeenth-century painter. Intelligence, searching powers of observation, and firm will are the traits that emerge most strongly; but Peale was also a creature of affection, sensibility and idealism. He was one of the remarkable men of his time. His life has been well told, with humor and insight, by his scholarly descendant, Charles Coleman Sellers (1969, No. 1), who is also author of the catalogue raisonné of Peale's work (Sellers, 1952; 1969, No. 2).

Canvas: 29½ x 24½ inches.

14 *Self-Portrait* 1822

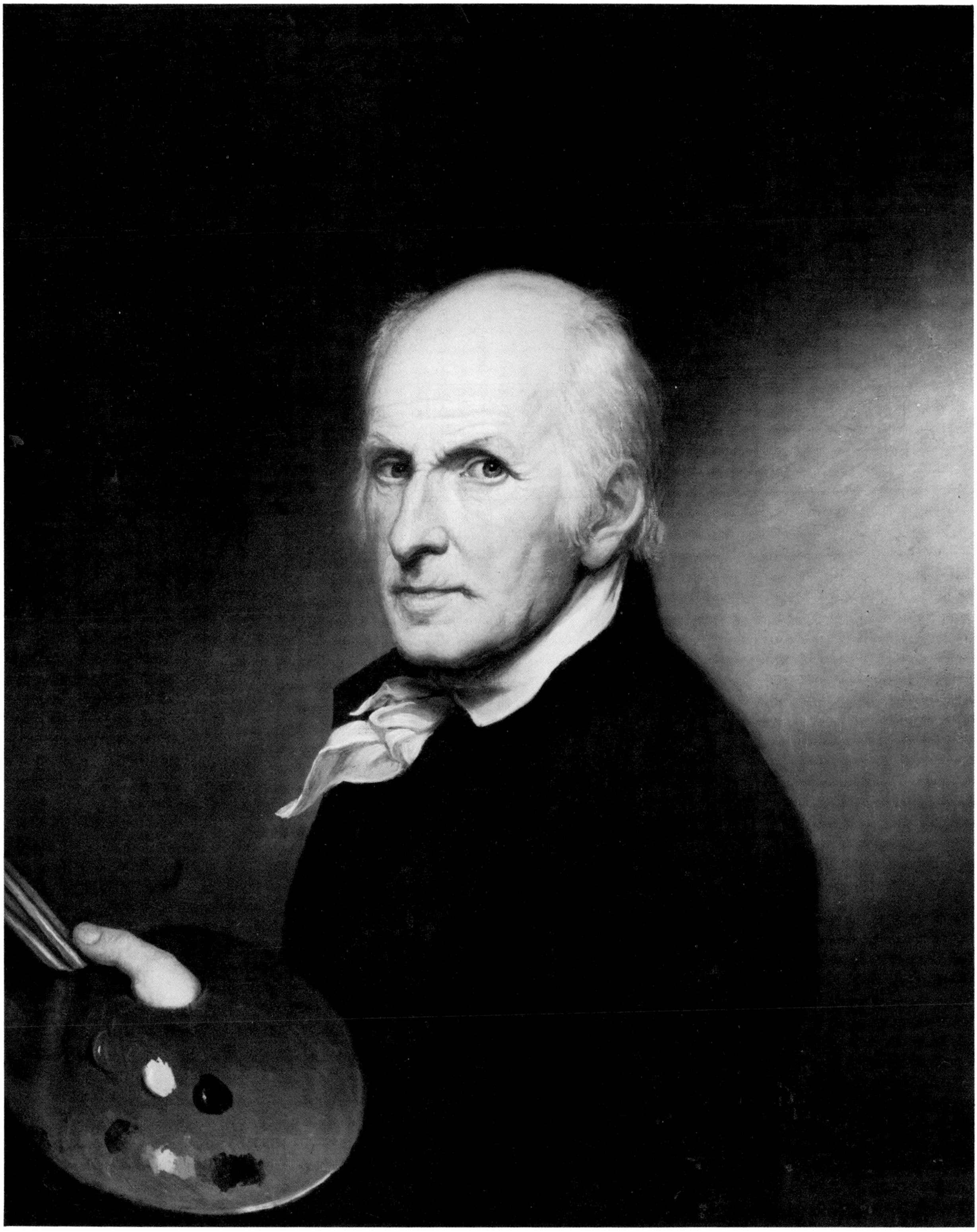

IV

The Transition to the New Republic

When our ancestors won political separation from Great Britain, they made no break with their own past or with their role in western culture. In this respect, our revolution differed from many that have taken place in our own time. After the war, Copley, Peale and West continued their careers as before. The new generation which came forward—the two Earls, Stuart, and Trumbull—had much the same interests as their predecessors. Painting in the new republic belongs to the period of neo-classicism in its clear, serene, objective spirit, uncomplicated by the archaeological "fancy dress" adopted by artists on the Continent.

One difference makes itself felt, however. As population began to spread away from the seaport cities, art went with it. Winthrop Chandler, an ingenious artisan and self-taught portrait painter, is the first of a new type of artist that sprang up in the back country as our people began their march into the interior.

Winthrop Chandler 1747-1790

Chandler was born at Woodstock in Connecticut and spent almost his entire career as a house decorator in or near his native village. Such a desire for portraits appeared in his lifetime that a skilled artisan in a country village could turn his hand to portrait painting as a profitable sideline. Chandler was one of the first of many such painters to appear in the back country of Connecticut and one of the most interesting. His portraits are executed in the firm, rather flat style of the artisan painter and exhibit both decorative invention and keen observation of human nature. This country minister and his wife, the one austere, the other taking a more gentle and humorous view of the world, show the strength of character for which New England was famous.

15. *Canvas:* 24¼ x 18¼ inches.

16. *Canvas:* 24¾ x 18¼ inches.

15 *The Reverend Mr. Quackenbush ca. 1780-1790*

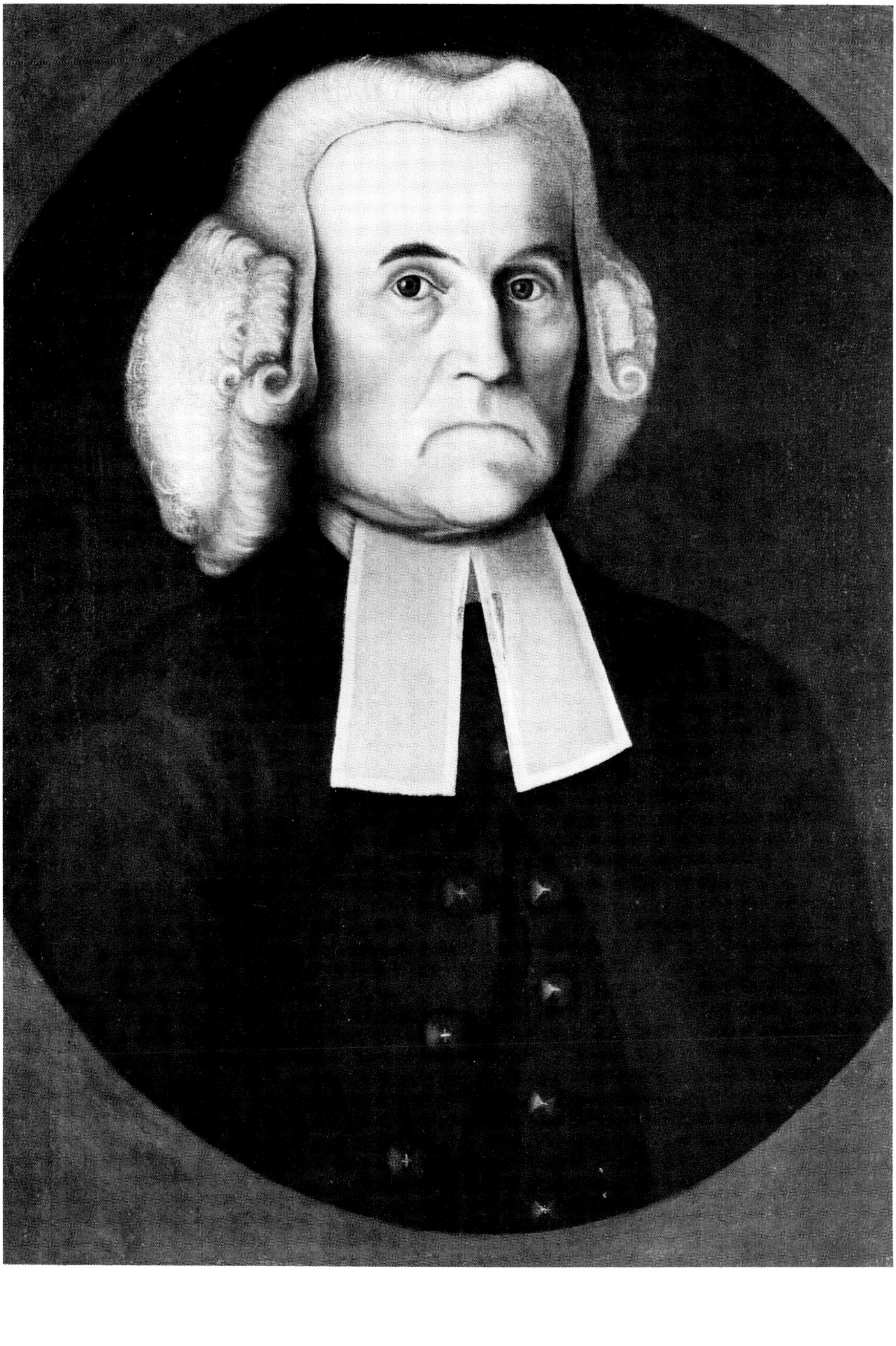

Winthrop Chandler

16 *Mrs. Quackenbush*

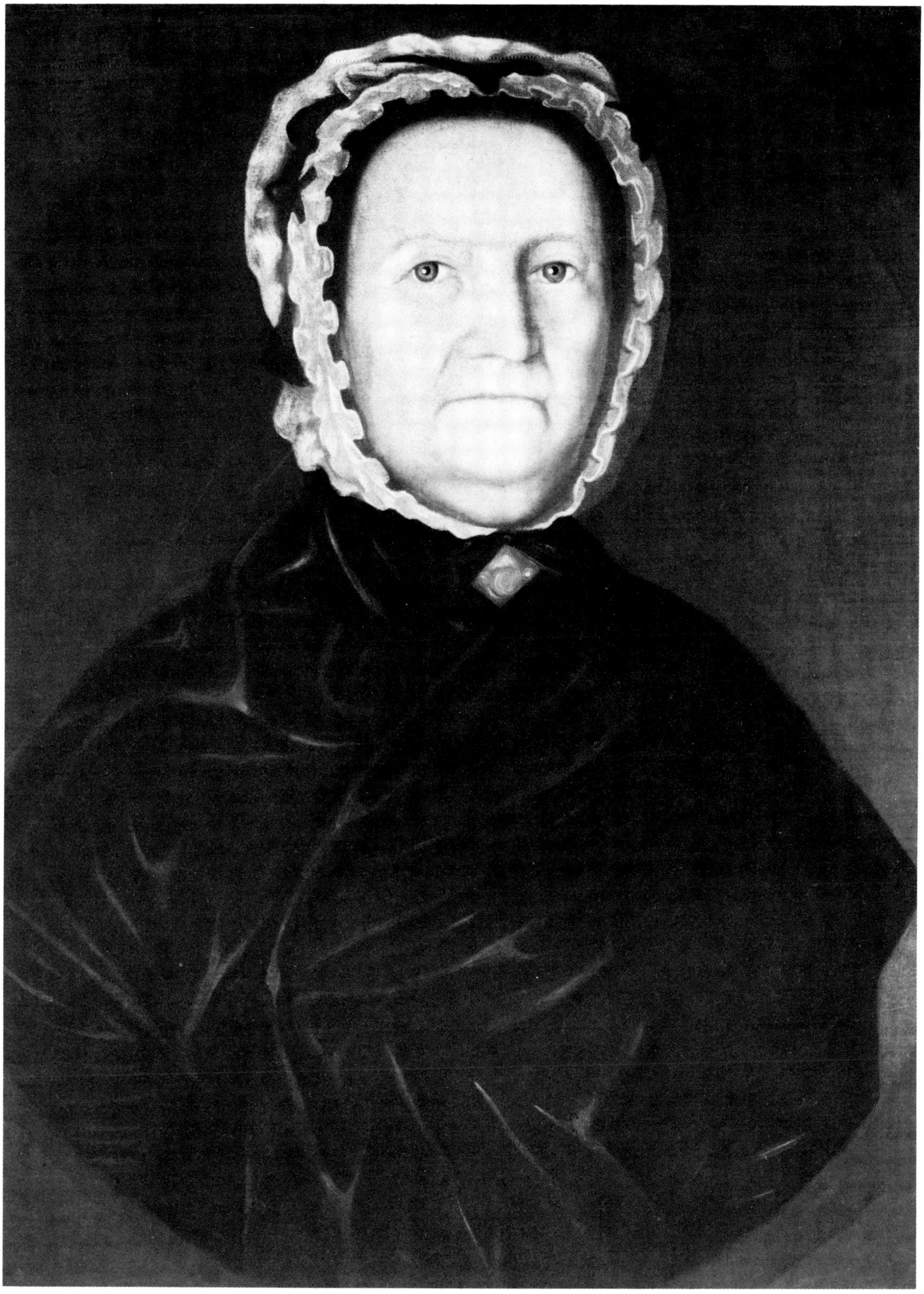

James Earl 1761-1796

Had James Earl enjoyed the normal span of life, Gilbert Stuart might have found him a dangerous rival. James, the younger brother of Ralph Earl, went to England after the war, studied in London, exhibited at the Royal Academy, and returned in 1794 with the urbane and pleasing style one sees here. He settled in Charleston, painted brilliantly for two years and died of fever. His impression upon his contemporaries is recorded in the notice of his death in *The South Carolina State Gazette and Timothy and Mason's Daily Advertiser,* August 20, 1796: "This gentleman has resided for nearly two years in this city, in which time he has exhibited so many specimens of his art as to enable us to speak with decision of his talents. To an uncommon facility in hitting of (f) the likeness, may be added a peculiarity in his execution of drapery, and, which has ever been esteemed in his art the NE PLUS ULTRA, of giving life to the eye, and expression to every feature." (Rutledge, 1949.) He died leaving a wife and children. His son Augustus also became an artist, led a wandering career over most of the world, and died while serving as a draughtsman on H.M.S. *Beagle* on which Charles Darwin was serving as a naturalist.

Canvas: 35 x 29 inches.

17   *Elizabeth Rodman Rogers*

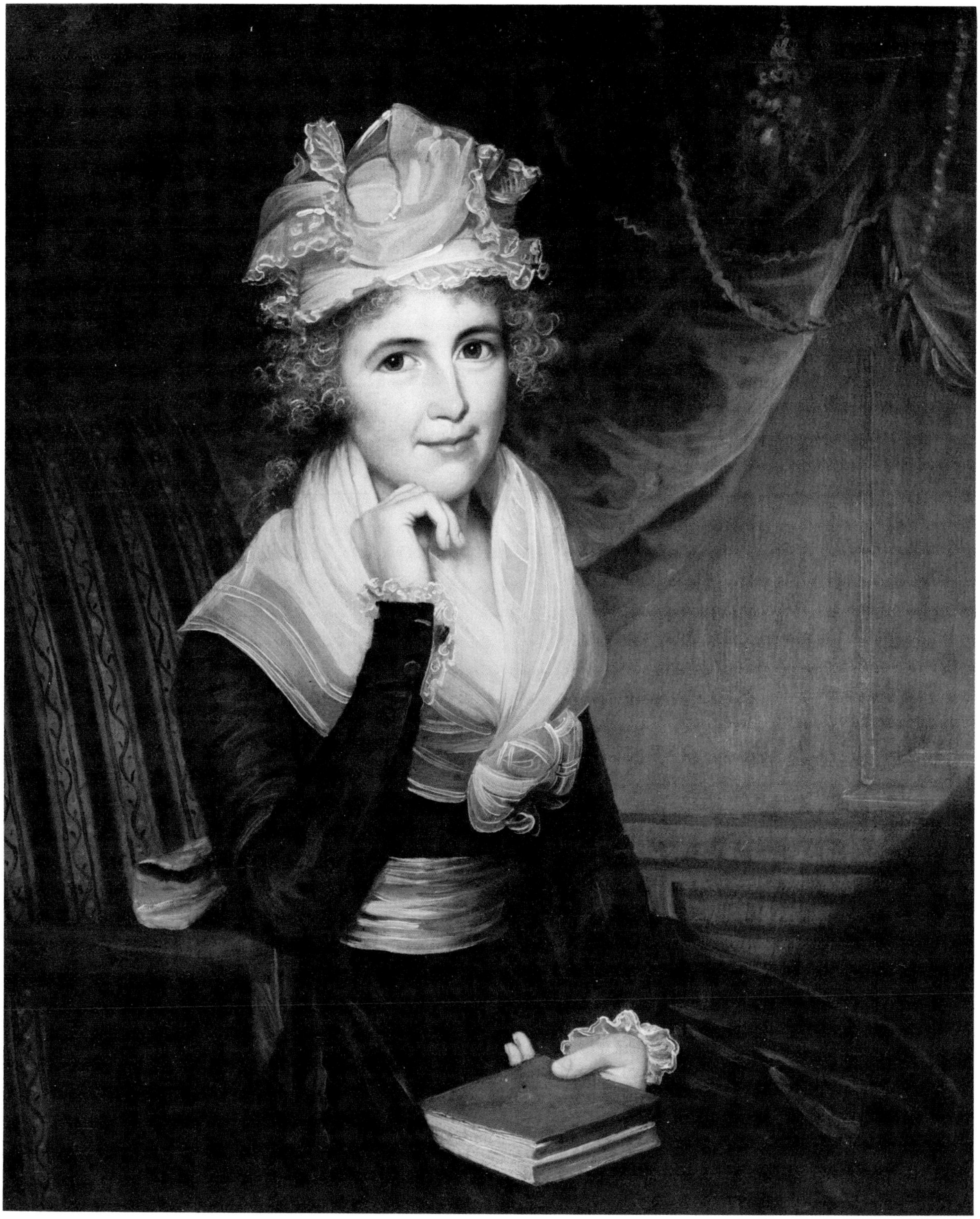

Ralph Earl 1751-1801

Ralph Earl was born at Shrewsbury in the hills of Worcester County, Massachusetts. He lived and painted for some years in England and worked also for a time in New York City. He is considered the chief of the artists painting in the back country of Connecticut after the Revolution, from 1788 until his death in 1801. His earlier works done in England or New York were the first to be collected fifty years ago.

Earl made his first appearance as an artist in 1775. He was then living in New Haven, Connecticut. After the battles of Lexington and Concord, an enterprising young engraver in New Haven named Amos Doolittle enlisted his help to prepare a series of engravings of the engagements. They went together to the scene of the fighting, where Earl made the drawings from which Doolittle produced the four engravings which are now so celebrated and so rare. But although Ralph Earl is associated, at least as an artist-illustrator, with the opening battles of the Revolution, and although his father and brother fought on the Whig side, he himself was a Loyalist (Laurence B. Goodrich, 1967; Quimby, 1968).

After some politically uncomfortable years in Connecticut, he was able to escape in 1778 to England. There he painted portraits with some success, married and exhibited at the Royal Academy. This portrait of a witty and worldly woman shows the skill and perception of character he attained during his stay there. On his return to America in May 1785 he settled in New York City. The Whig leaders of the town welcomed a portrait painter. He painted General von Steuben, General Clarkson, Mrs. Alexander Hamilton and others. Earl was improvident, however, drank too much, and was obliged to ask some sitters to come to him in debtors' prison, from which he was released by declaring bankruptcy (January 1788) and moving once again to Connecticut.

Canvas: 36½ x 28¼ inches. Signed at the center left, *R. Earl P^t 1784*.

18 *Portrait of a Lady* 1784

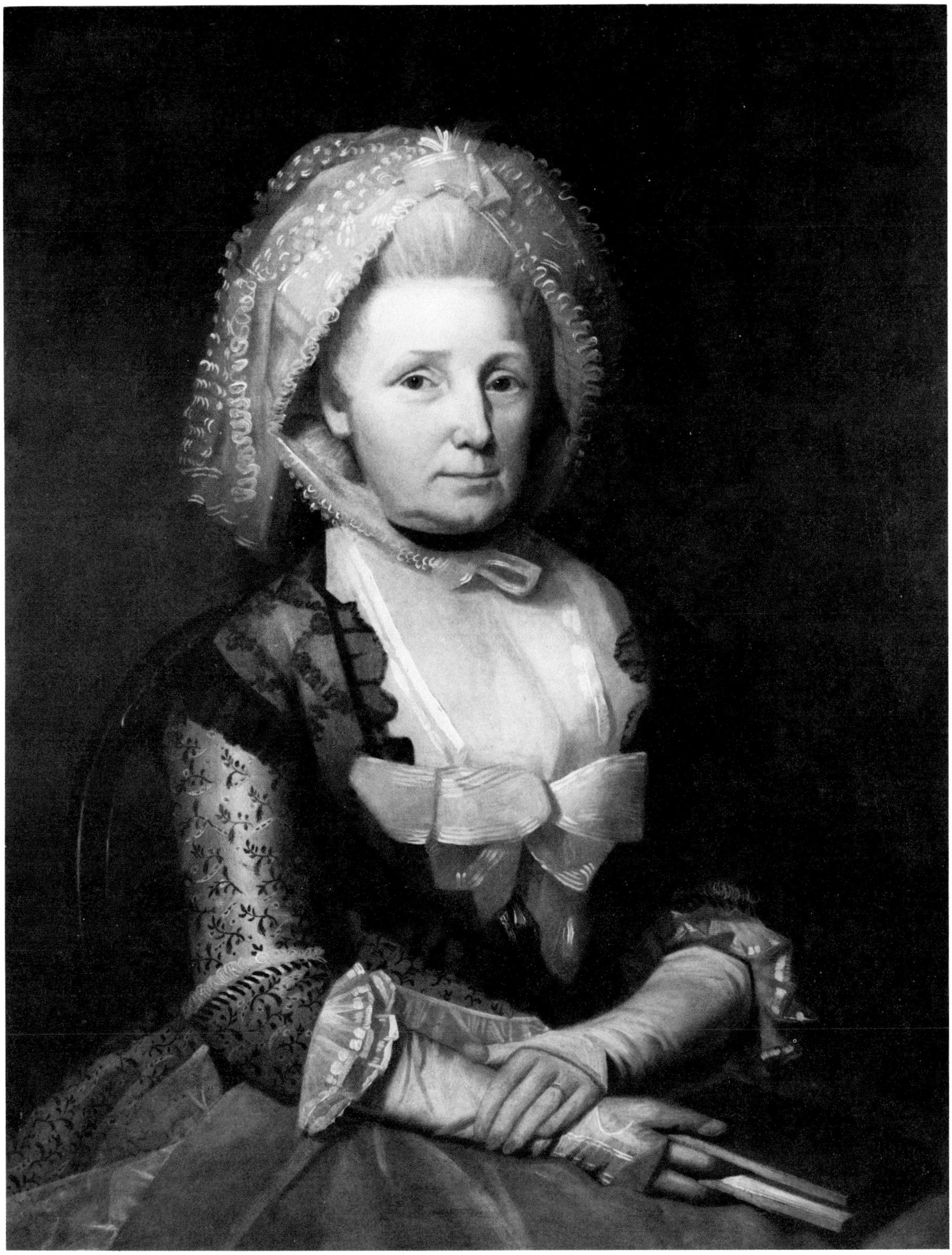

Ralph Earl

Earl had about ten years of good painting in Connecticut before intemperance caught up with him. He died of drink at Bolton in the hills east of Hartford in 1801. Connecticut in the 1790's was a state full of prosperous small towns but no large cities. Litchfield, with its formal white houses and wide streets, green and tree-shaded, still preserves its appearance of that decade; Earl painted some of his best portraits to hang in those houses. His patrons were prosperous, educated but rural people. Earl's style assumed a new character as he painted them. Shapes took on a bold, geometric simplification; color became bright, strong and rather flat. The appreciation of Earl's Connecticut portraits had to wait until modern painters had accustomed our eyes to flat patterns of color and deliberate simplifications of form. Today his late works, appealing to this vision, enjoy greater popularity than his earlier ones. Another revolution of taste may reverse the order.

   This shrewd, elderly country woman, seated beside a window, her spectacles on the table beside her and a piece of knitting in her hands, is an admirable example of Earl's later period. He liked to paint a kind of *portrait d'apparat*, showing a merchant at his desk in his country house, a lawyer among his books, a statesman and his wife seated in their living room. Through the window one sees the subject's home, white against the green background of river and low hills. *Mrs. Hubbell* shows how well he could observe the New England character. The broad pattern of golden brown, white, black and red is typical of his striking color. Every form is simplified, stylized, yet filled with nature and truth.

Canvas: 37¼ x 30 inches. Signed on the wall at the lower left, *R. Earl Pinxt/1795*.

19 *Mrs. David Hubbell* *1795*

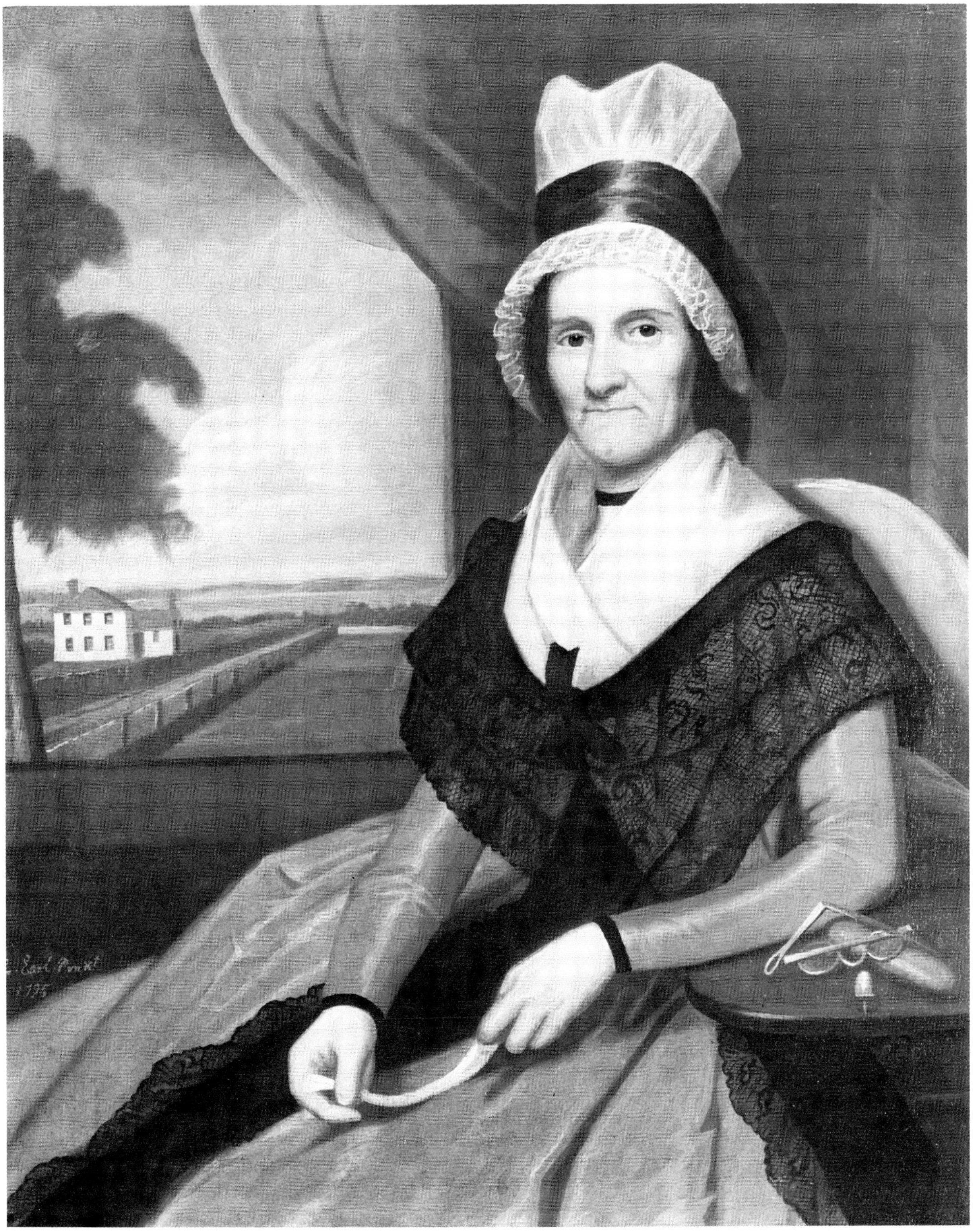
Earl Pinxt
1795

Gilbert Stuart   1755-1828

William Ellery Channing (1780-1842), Unitarian minister, author, preacher and mystic, exerted a profound influence upon his contemporaries in the fields of religion, literature and social ethics. He was a preacher of extraordinary powers whose sermons in the pulpit of his Federal Street church, Boston, famous for their "fervor, solemnity, and beauty," were a principal force in the separation of Unitarianism from New England Calvinism. His literary writings may be said to have opened the door for Emerson and the Transcendentalists. His essays in the *North American Review* and the *Christian Examiner* gave him a reputation both in England and at home. An observation from his essay on "Self Culture," as good today as it was then, states, "The great sources of wisdom are experience and observation, and these are denied to none. To open and fix our eyes upon what passes without and within us, is the most fruitful study. Books are chiefly useful, as they help us to interpret what we see and experience."

Small and frail in physique, Channing nonetheless had an extraordinary degree of magnetism. A famous portrait of Channing by his brother-in-law, Washington Allston, painted at about the same time as Allston's portrait of his mother (No. 22), is in the Museum of Fine Arts, Boston. It emphasizes the mystical and ethereal quality of the man. Stuart's likeness is later and more corporeal; yet one sees in it too the fragility as well as the magnetic quality of his personality.

Canvas: 30 x 25 inches.

20 *William Ellery Channing*

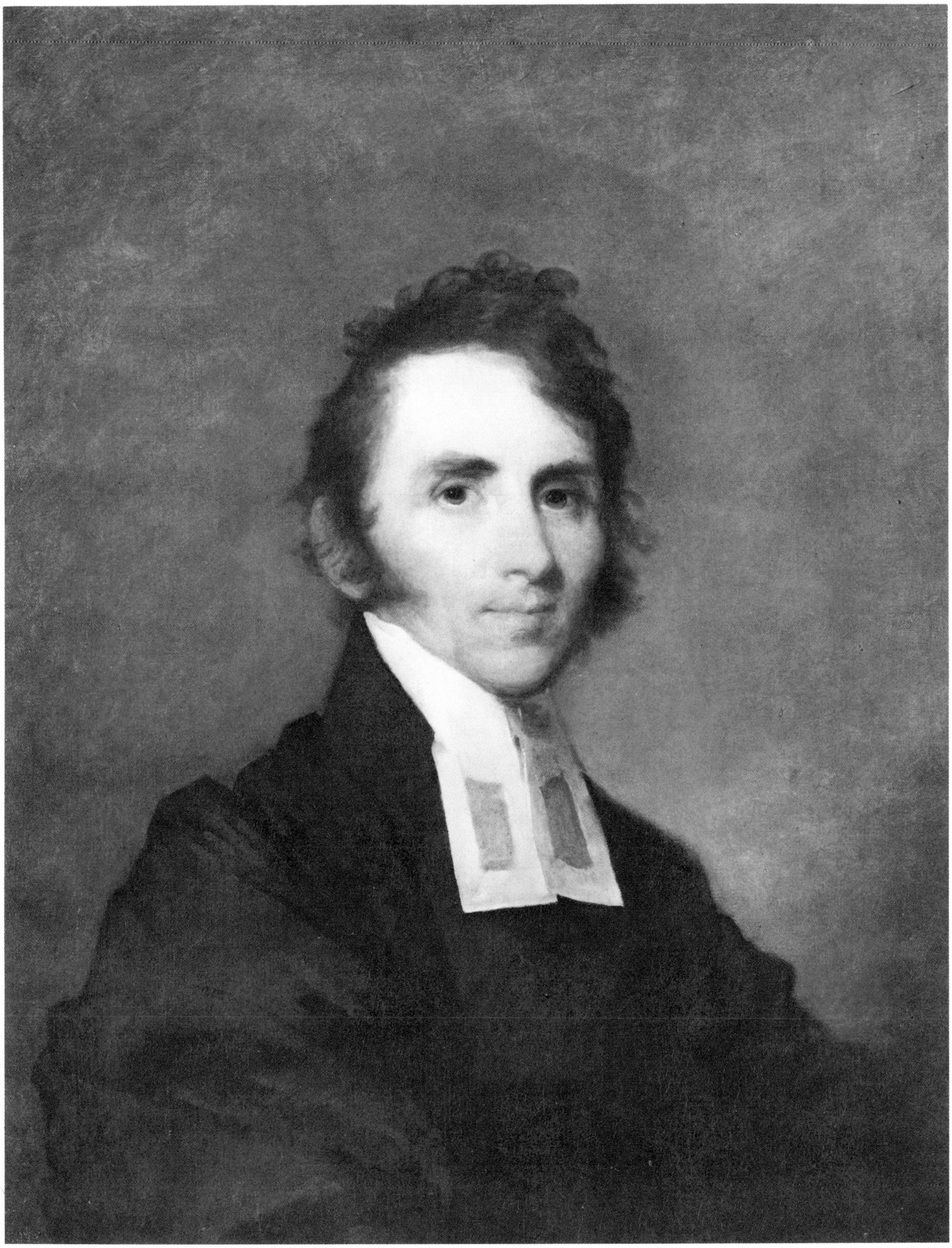

John Trumbull 1756-1843

The son of the wartime governor of Connecticut, Trumbull was self-taught as a painter. When the war came, he served as one of Washington's staff officers and as Adjutant under General Gates. After the peace he studied painting with West in London, there forming the desire to paint the history of the American struggle for independence. Returning to the United States in 1789 with his first two compositions, *The Battle of Bunker Hill* and *The Death of Montgomery before Quebec*, he painted from life many portraits of the men who were to appear in subsequent scenes of the series. In 1794 he returned to London as John Jay's secretary; he lived there until 1804 and again from 1808-1815. In 1815 he returned to secure from Congress the commission to decorate the rotunda of the Capitol with enlarged versions of four of his historical subjects. These are less successful artistically than the small original paintings in the Yale University Art Gallery.

His portrait of Philip Church is interesting for two reasons. Portraits of children are rare in our eighteenth-century art, and this little boy with his toys is a charming picture of childhood. The story of the portrait also throws light upon what a confused civil war our fight for independence was. Trumbull tells the story in his autobiography (Sizer, 1953).

While serving with Gates' army Trumbull made the acquaintance of an American officer named John Carter, who in 1777 married Angelica Schuyler, the eldest daughter of General Philip Schuyler. When Trumbull went to London after the war he found Carter living in great elegance there; his name now John Barker Church, Carter having been a *nom de guerre*. Church was now a member of Parliament and moving in a distinguished circle. Trumbull was often a guest at dinners in his home and had his financial backing during the years of struggle to establish himself as an artist. In gratitude Trumbull painted several portraits of Church's family, including two of his little son, Philip. This is one.

Canvas: 17¼ x 13¼ inches.

21 *Philip Church* 1784

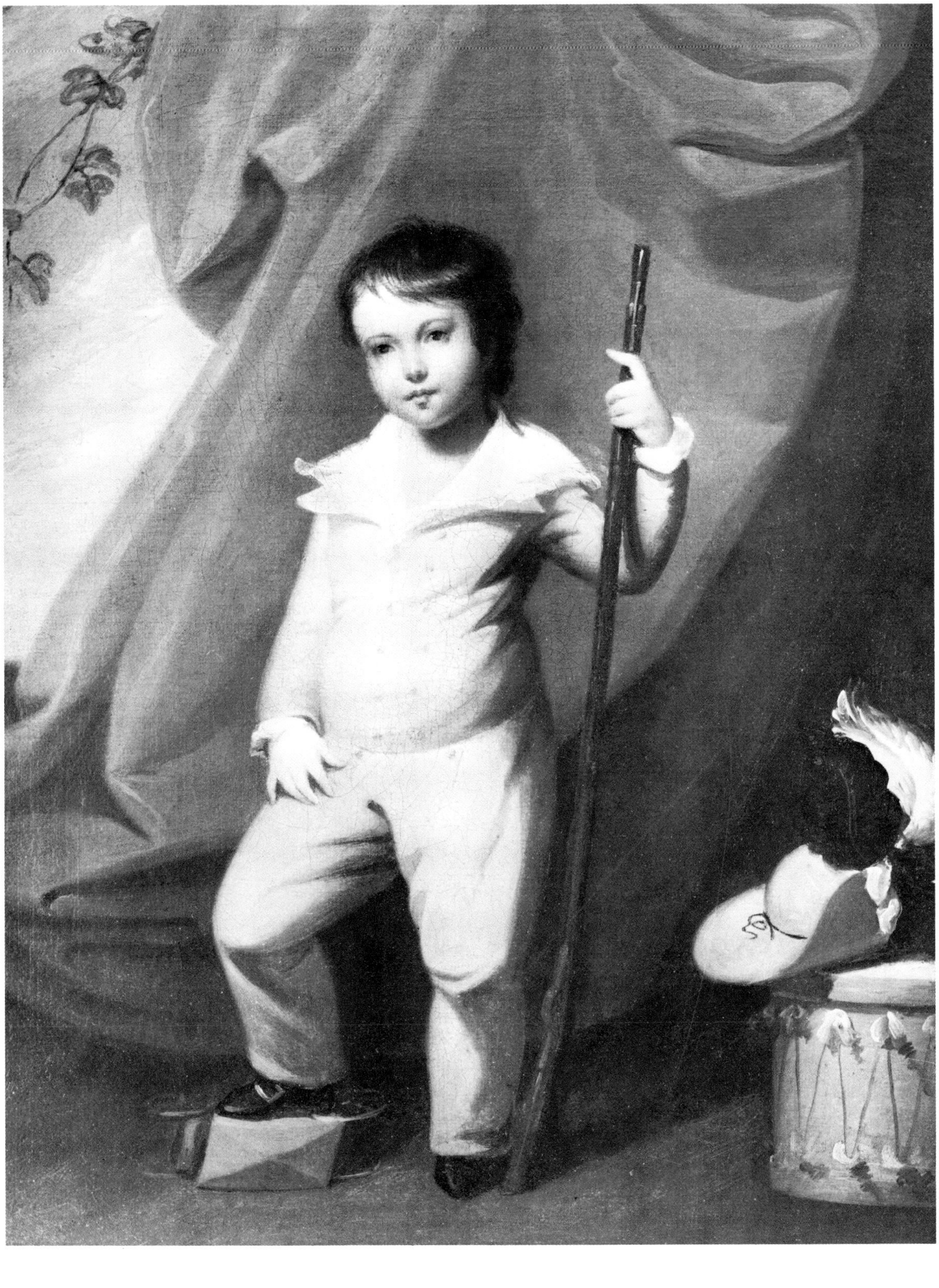

V

The Generation of 1800: The First Romantics

A notable widening of subject matter and change of mood appears in American painting after 1800. The artists of this generation were the first without memories of the world as it had been before the revolution. Portraits were still a major theme, but Allston in his rare portraits of his own family introduced a mood of deep introspection. Sully began a long career of romantic portraiture. Others turned to nature, to landscape painting, still life, the instinctive life of the animal world, to primitive man. It was the age of romanticism, when a similar turn of attention was felt throughout the western world. However, art on this side of the Atlantic had a distinctive flavor. Audubon discovered the passion of his life in the birds and animals of an unexplored continent; his art is filled with the excitement of discovery. Catlin found in the Indians of the great plains a vision of dignity and wild heroism that his European contemporaries saw in ancient Rome or the legends of the middle ages. It was an age of religious revivals. Edward Hicks, a pious artisan of the Philadelphia back country, typifies the spontaneous nature of many of these religious movements by the novelty and non-liturgical character of his religious images.

Washington Allston 1771-1843

This rather melancholy face is that of Lucy Ellery Channing of Newport, Rhode Island. She was a daughter of William Ellery, who signed the Declaration of Independence for Rhode Island, and she was the mother of Ann Channing, Allston's first wife, and William Ellery Channing, whose portrait by Gilbert Stuart is also in the Rockefeller collection.

Allston was a South Carolinian of good family who, like many southern boys, was sent to New England for his education. At school in Newport, and at Harvard College, he was a friend of William Ellery Channing. When the artist returned from Italy in 1808 he married Ann Channing and lived for three years at Boston before re-crossing the Atlantic. Although he was not temperamentally a portrait painter, Allston in those three years (1808-1811) painted a number of portraits of close friends and family that were of a new kind of American art. Stuart at this time was giving Boston clear, calm, decorative likenesses in his neo-classic manner. Allston, a brooding romantic spirit, made his portraits statements of mood, of shadow, of pensive solitude and reverie.

Mrs. Channing's portrait descended through the family of her daughter, Lucy Channing Russell. In the migratory American way, it hung in houses in Newport, Staten Island, Fishkill-on-Hudson, Boston, Santa Barbara, and North East Harbor before coming to its present owners.

Canvas: 26½ x 21¾ inches.

22 *Mrs. William Channing* *1811*

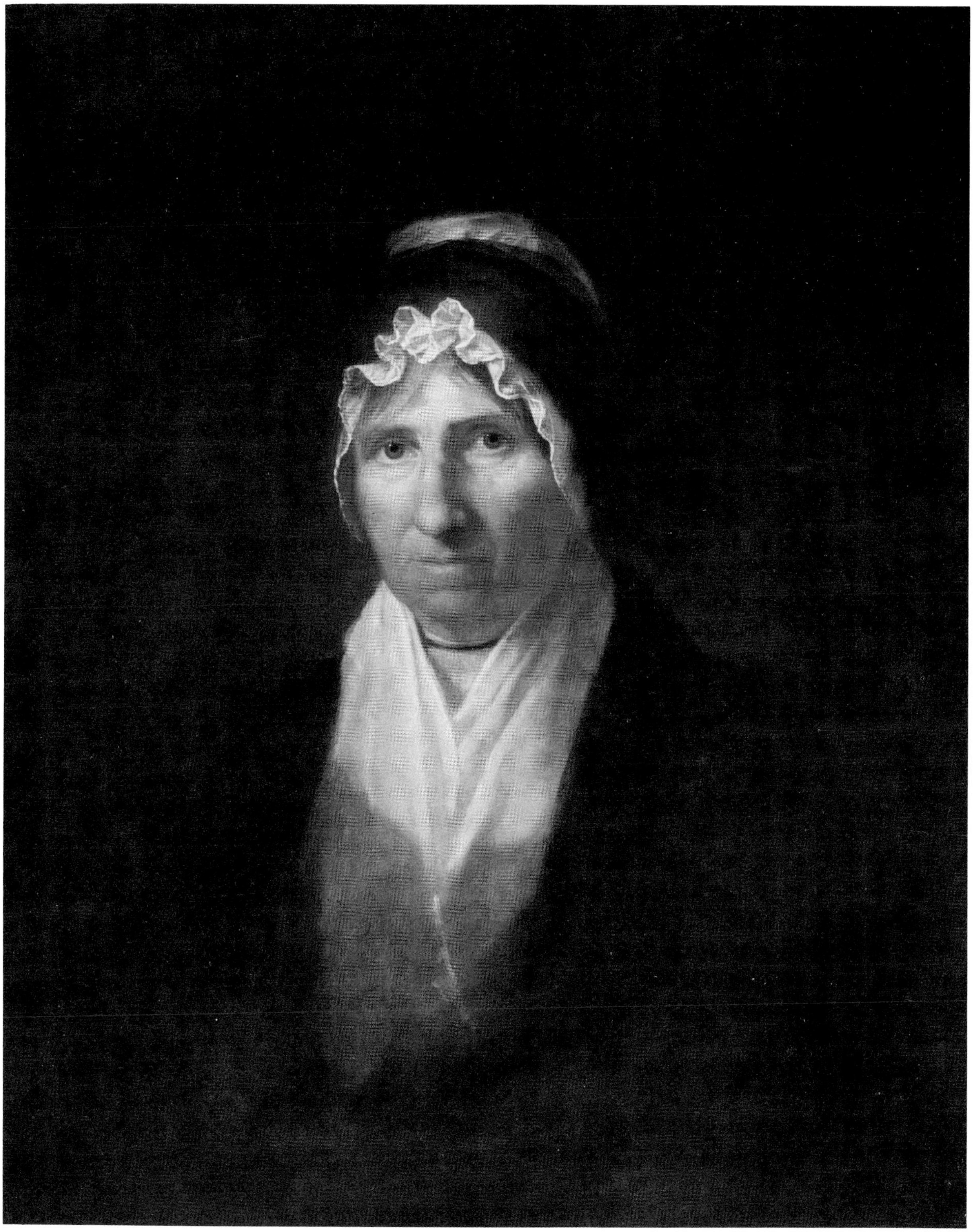

John James Audubon 1785-1851

In 1843 Audubon realized a long-held ambition to go west. The elephant folio of the *Birds of America* (1827-1838) was complete and the octavo edition (1840-44) was well under way. He turned next to his final great project, the *Quadrupeds of North America*. He had spent his early manhood on the Ohio and Mississippi rivers; he had traveled the eastern coast from Florida to Labrador; at last in 1843 he ascended the Missouri River to see the elk and buffalo, the bighorn and other animals of the high plains. On April 25, 1843, he left St. Louis on a small steamboat, the *Magnet*, belonging to the American Fur Company, and reached Fort Union at the mouth of the Yellowstone on June 12. His journal of that expedition, crowded with notes and vivid observations, was found in an old secretary (after having been lost for fifty years) and was published by one of his granddaughters in 1898 (Audubon, 1898). He completed the illustrations for the *Quadrupeds* between 1843 and 1846 (Herrick, 1938).

Over a long period of constant application Audubon had developed a style of drawing in pencil, pen and watercolor that not only describes a bird or animal with precision but gives a remarkable impression of the energy and wild spirit of the creature. That is the case with this Douglass squirrel, or chickaree, a western species corresponding to the red squirrel of the eastern forests. The drawing is a study for one of the squirrels in plate XLVIII, and as Herrick noted, the squirrel plates are equal to his finest earlier works.

The dramatic quality of Audubon's drawings has created a prejudice against him in certain scientific quarters. But when the first volume of the *Birds of America* appeared, the famous French naturalist, Baron Cuvier, wrote that Audubon's work was the most magnificent monument yet raised by art to science. Quoting this, Edward Dwight added, "And so it remains." (Dwight, 1963.)

Ink, pencil and watercolor: 9½ x 12½ *inches. Inscribed at the lower left,* Douglass' squirrel.

23 *Douglass (or Chickaree) Squirrel* 1843-1846

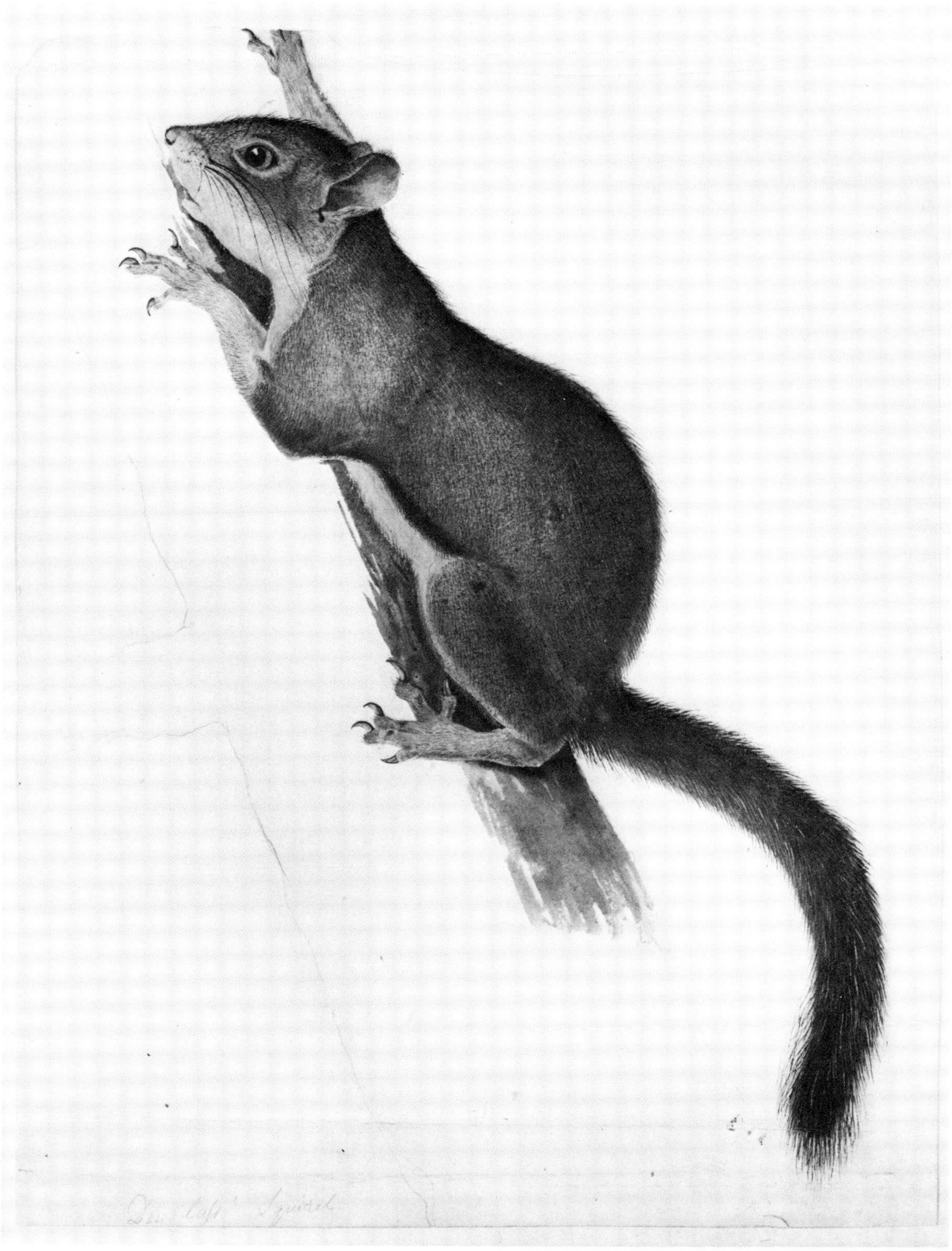

Thomas Birch 1779-1851

Landscape painting has a longer history in America than is commonly supposed. Lack of understanding of its history has had the result that landscapists working in oils, watercolor or engraving before 1825 have not received the attention to which their talents are entitled. William Dunlap, writing of Birch in his *History of the Arts of Design in the United States of America* (1834), speaks of him as "unrivalled in our country."

Thomas Birch was the son of William Russell Birch, a miniature painter and engraver who migrated to the United States in the early 1790's. Thomas began as an engraver helping in the production of the plates of his father's *Views of Philadelphia* (1800), the earliest and one of the most delightful sets of engraved views of American cities. He turned to painting in oil during the first decade of the new century; *The Narrows* is one of his earliest signed and dated works. The rich pastey touch, the strong contrasts of light and dark, the attention given to the foreground which strengthens the charm of air and light in the distance, are characteristic of his earliest pictures. The title is traditional but the scene is one other than The Narrows of New York Harbor.

Panel: 26¾ x 20 inches. Signed and dated at the lower right, *Birch 1812*.

24 *The Narrows* 1812

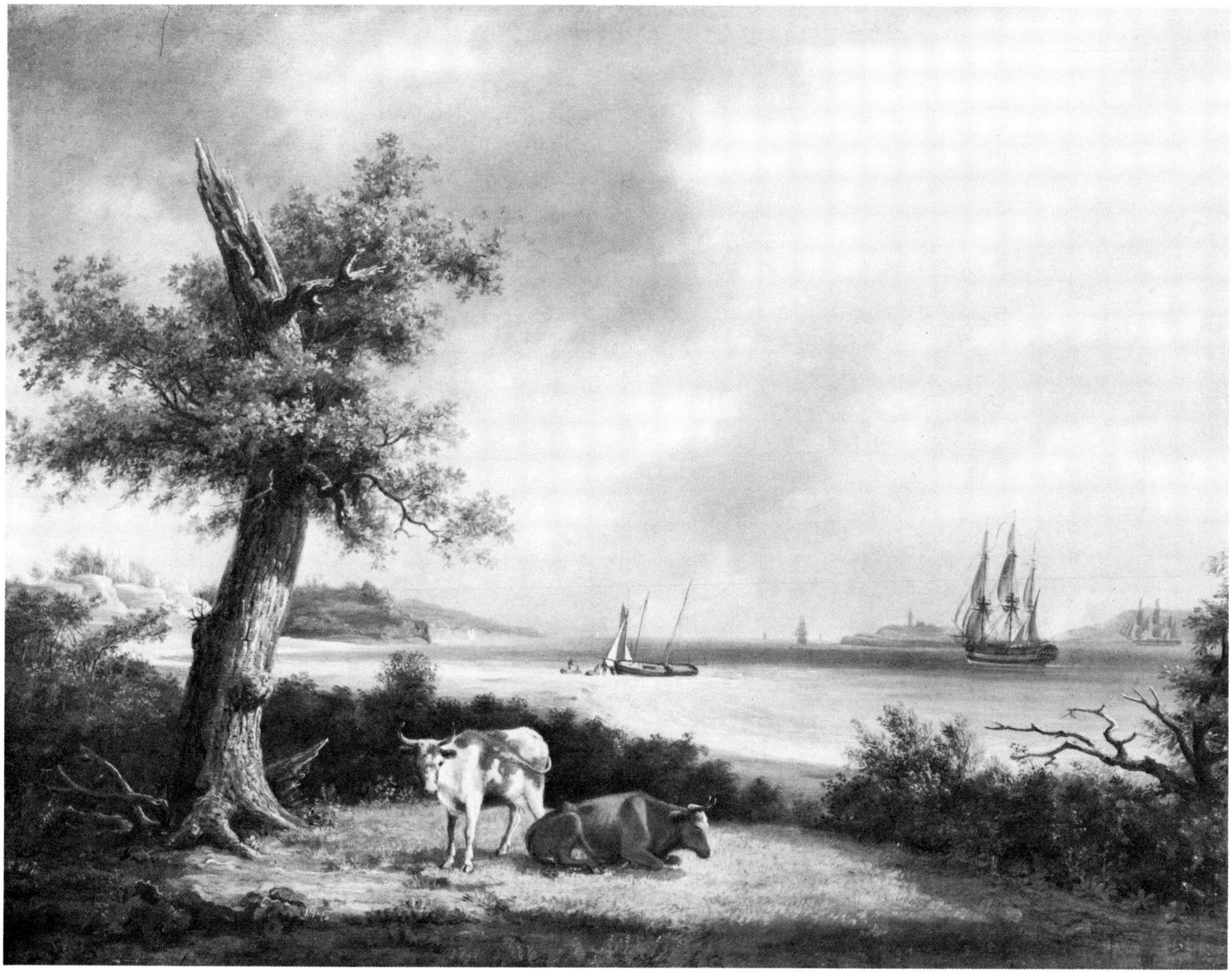

George Catlin 1796-1872

George Catlin, miniature painter, portraitist and ethnologist, was born at Wilkes-Barre, Pennsylvania in 1796. He first studied law but in 1820 set up as a miniature painter in Philadelphia. From 1825 to 1828 he worked in New York State, but he moved to Richmond, Virginia in 1830, and in that same year began eight years of travel and study among the Plains Indians. In 1839 he took his collection of Indian portraits and artifacts to Europe, where he lived the next thirty years, except for five years spent in South America from 1852 to 1857. His major collections were saved from being sold to pay his debts by the industrialist and collector, George Harrison of Philadelphia, who bought them and gave them to the Smithsonian Institution. Catlin returned at last to America in 1870 and died in 1872.

When Catlin went west in 1830 the frontier of settlement was at the edge of the eastern forest. Beyond, in the open grasslands, Indian tribes lived as they had done since the horse gave them mobility to range the plains and live upon the buffalo. In the 1820's, inspired by the sight of a delegation of Plains Indians in Philadelphia, Catlin formed the design to be the pictorial historian "ultimately, of every tribe of Indians on the Continent of North America, and of bringing home faithful portraits of their principal personages, and full notes of their character and history. I designed also, to procure their costumes, and a complete collection of their manufactures and weapons, and to perpetuate them in a *gallery unique*, for the use and instruction of future ages." (*Letters and Notes on the Manners, Customs, and Conditions of the North American Indians*... London, 1841). A design which today, if undertaken at all, would require a vast team of specialists, supported by a host of universities, museums, foundations and federal grants, was undertaken then by one man with no money, little training, and limited skills. The effort took his whole life and strength and brought tragedy to Catlin and his family. The wonder is that he accomplished as much as he did. He was a self-taught ethnologist, and as an artist, his natural talent was for miniature painting. In work on a larger scale one is aware of his lack of training. Yet a passion for his goal coupled with great opportunities enabled him to produce memorable work.

At various times Catlin made duplicates in oil or watercolor of his early sketches. This is one of a series of oils executed in the year before his death. The enthusiasm of his youth still burned in the indomitable old man and this painting of the drama of a prairie fire is Catlin at his best.

Oil on board: 18 x 24-5/16 *inches (sight). Signed at the lower left:* G. Catlin 1871

25 *Fire in a Missouri Meadow, and a Party of Sioux Indians Escaping From It; Upper Missouri* 1871

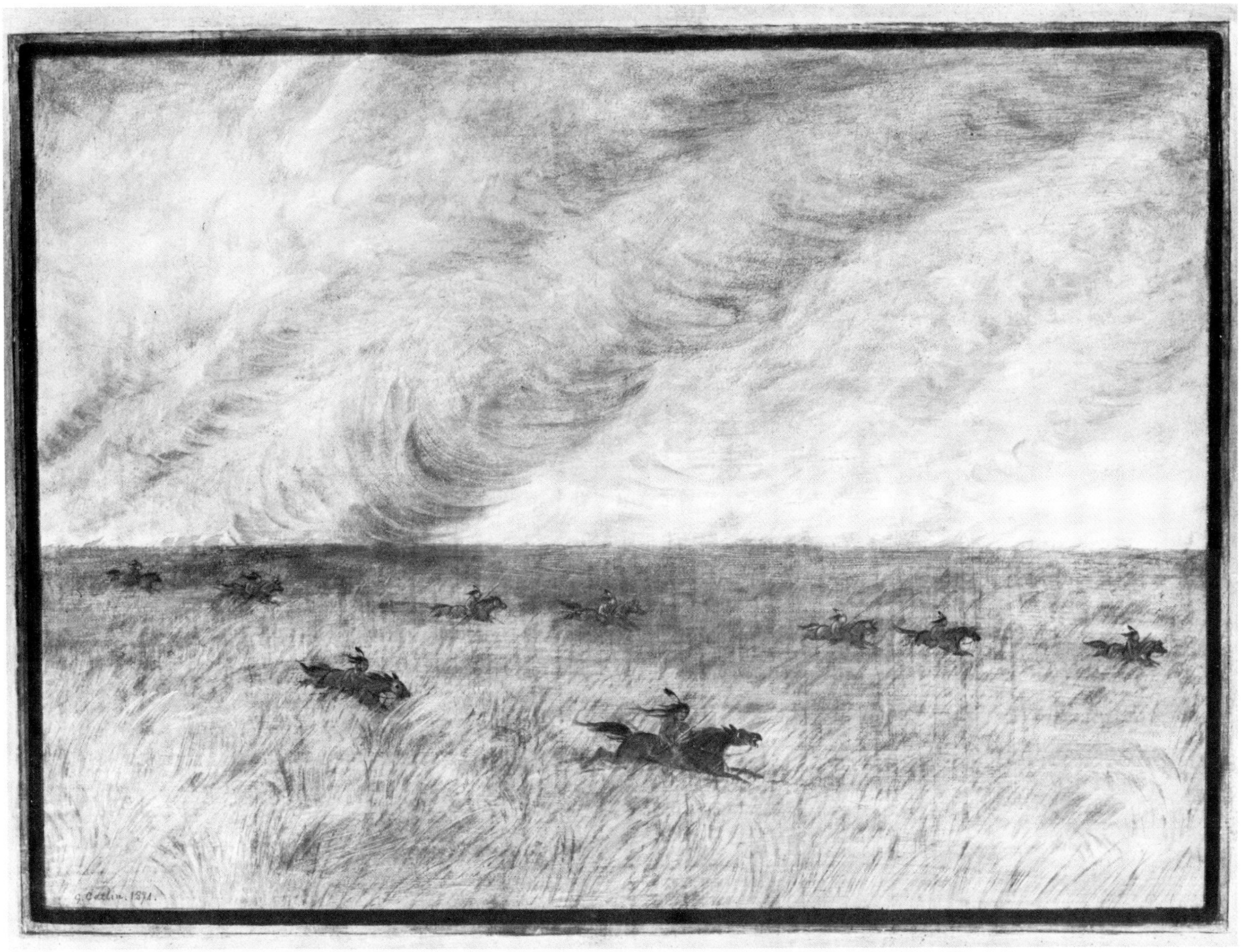

Edward Hicks 1780-1849

Edward Hicks, perhaps the best known of all the artisan painters (known popularly as "folk artists"), spent his life as a coach, sign and ornamental painter in Newtown, Bucks County, Pennsylvania, an old Quaker settlement. He was a cousin of Elias Hicks whose preaching of a return to the primitive simplicities of Quakerism split the Society of Friends into Orthodox and Hicksite branches. Edward Hicks was also an active preacher among the Quakers. About 1820 he began to illustrate his faith by paintings which he gave away to friends and benefactors or in payment of debts (Ford, 1952). One of his favorite subjects was the *Peaceable Kingdom*, inspired by the verses of Isaiah (XI, 6) that gave voice to his gospel of peace and brotherly love: "The wolf also shall dwell with the lamb, and the leopard shall lie down with the kid; and the calf and the young lion and the fatling together; and a little child shall lead them. And the cow and the bear shall feed; their young ones shall lie down together; and the lion shall eat straw like the ox." He is supposed to have painted from eighty to a hundred of these, of which at least forty exist today. Details of their composition vary greatly although all are akin; Penn's treaty with the Indians is often inserted as a second theme.

This *Peaceable Kingdom* is especially rich in imagery. The leopard, the lion, the bull—animals which fascinated Hicks—are particularly spirited and expressive; and the haunting eloquence of the ancient prophecy, filtering through the simple heart of a rustic painter, seems touching indeed.

Canvas: 25⅛ x 28¾ inches.

26 *The Peaceable Kingdom*

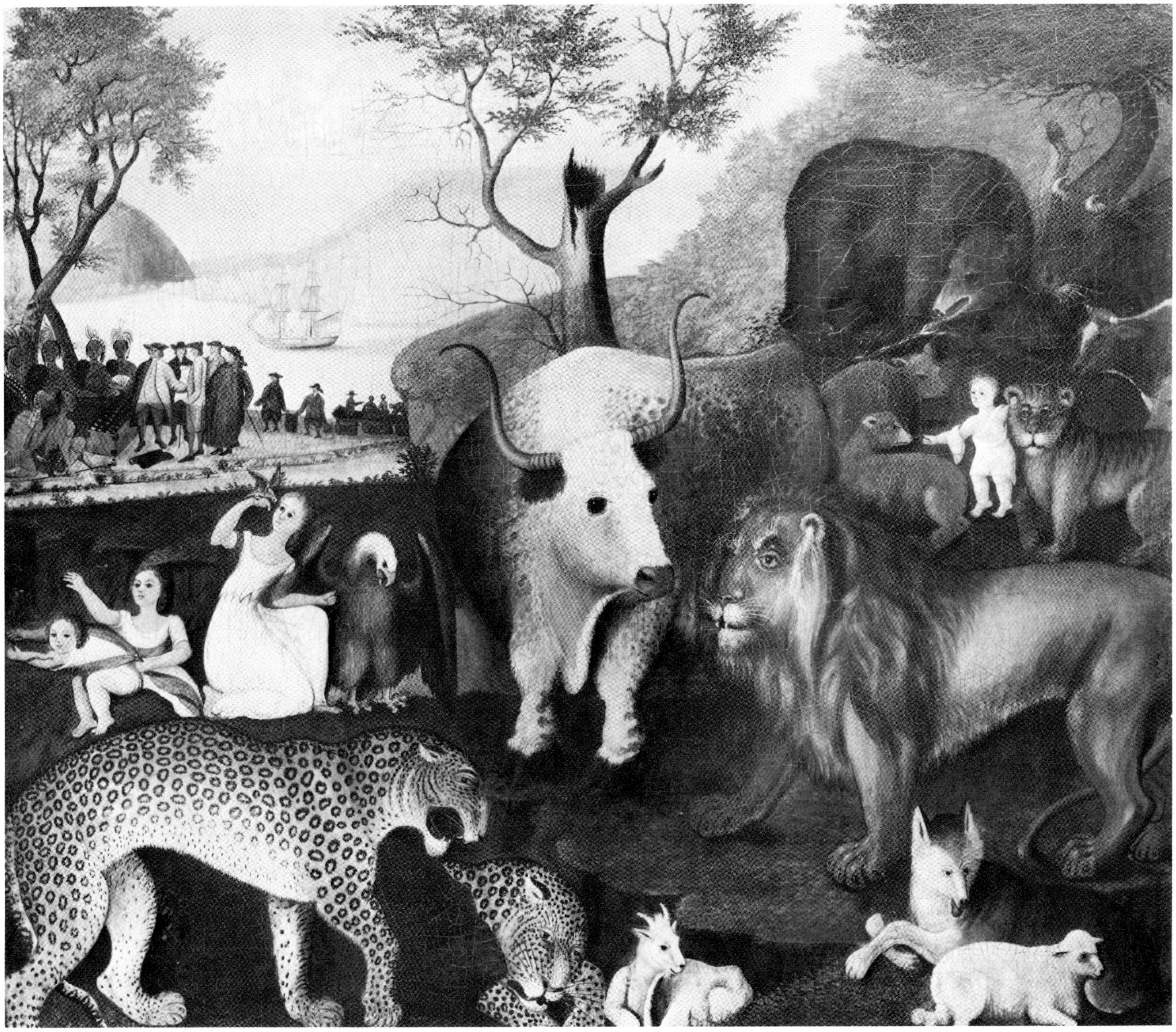

Raphaelle Peale 1774-1825

Raphaelle Peale, the eldest son of Charles Willson Peale to survive infancy, was an easy-going, warm-hearted man whom success and happiness eluded. As Charles Coleman Sellers said (1947), he "loved wit and laughter all his life, smothered his sorrows in the bowl... never made a living by his brush, and died a drunkard in early middle age." His portraits are strong and interesting to our eyes but they failed to please his subjects. His powers of observation and the poetry in his heart found an outlet in still-life paintings, of which he was a pioneer in America. The freshness and delight of this picture speak for themselves. Exhibited at the Pennsylvania Academy of the Fine Arts in 1814, it struck a new note in American painting and marked the beginning of a school of still life in Philadelphia that continued through the century, to Harnett and Peto at its close.

Panel: 7¼ x 10¼ inches.

27 *Blackberries ca. 1813*

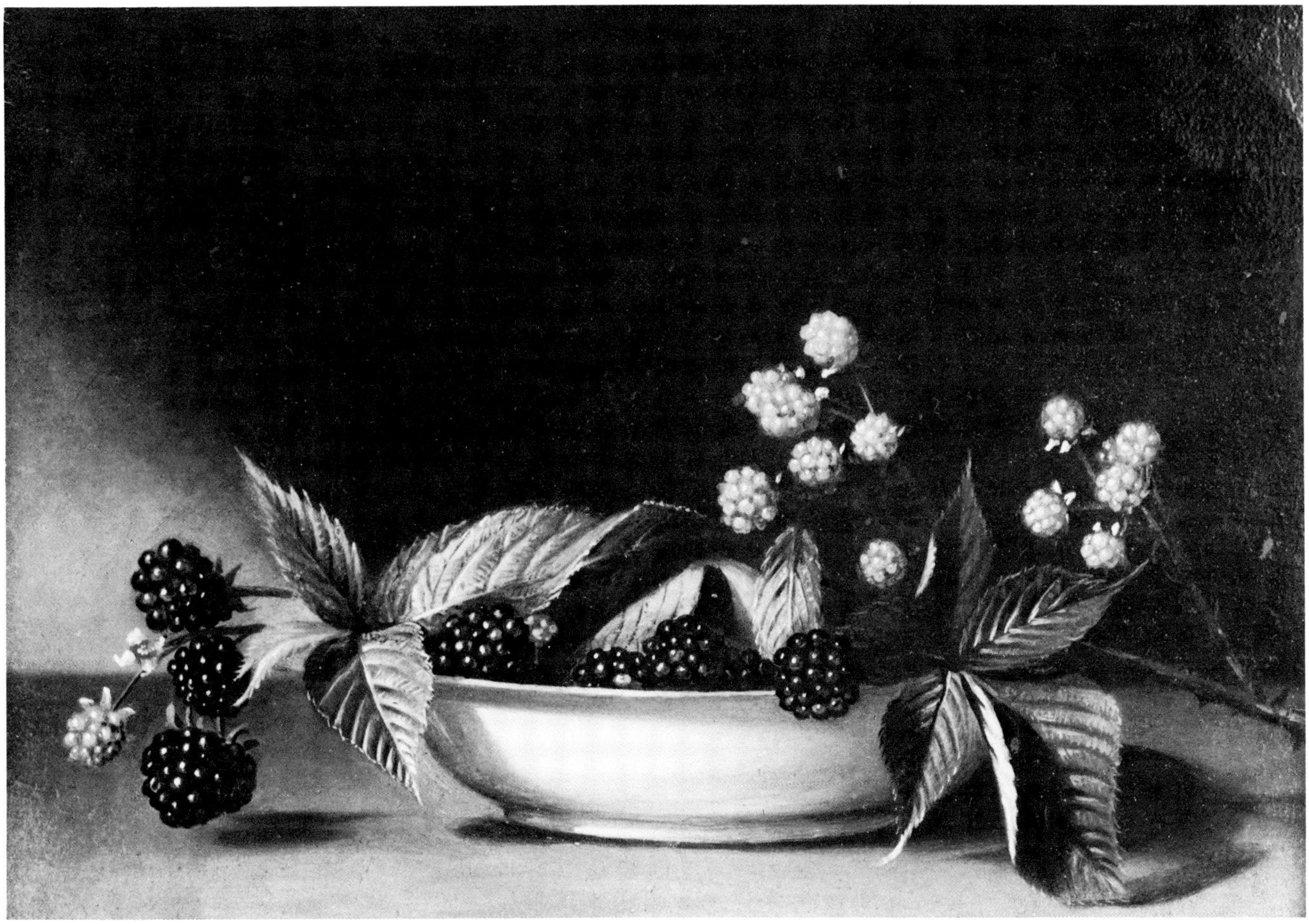

Thomas Sully   1783-1872

Charles Carroll of Carrollton was eighty-nine years old when Sully made this sketch, from which he afterward painted a full-length portrait for the Marquis of Wellesley and a seated full-length portrait for the State of Maryland.

Carroll was born in 1737. One of the Catholic Carrolls of Maryland, he was educated at Jesuit schools in France and studied civil and common law in France and England, living abroad from 1748 to 1765. He served in the Continental Congress during the war for independence, signed the Declaration of Independence, served in the Maryland Senate from 1777 to 1801, and was the first Senator from Maryland in the new federal government, 1789-1792. A Federalist in politics, he retired from public life in 1801.

Carroll was a man of great wealth, owning some 90,000 acres of land and, like Washington, was interested in national improvements such as the Potomac Company and its successor, the Chesapeake and Ohio Canal. He was an organizer and director of the Baltimore and Ohio Railroad, for which he broke ground on July 4, 1826.

He lived to be the last surviving Signer of the Declaration. Sully's study of the benign old face and long white hair suggests the old-fashioned courteous manners that made him a symbol to the new American nation of the dignity of its founders and of its past. The portrait was in family possession until offered to its present owners.

Canvas: 19⅛ x 15⅛ inches.

28   *Charles Carroll of Carrollton 1826*

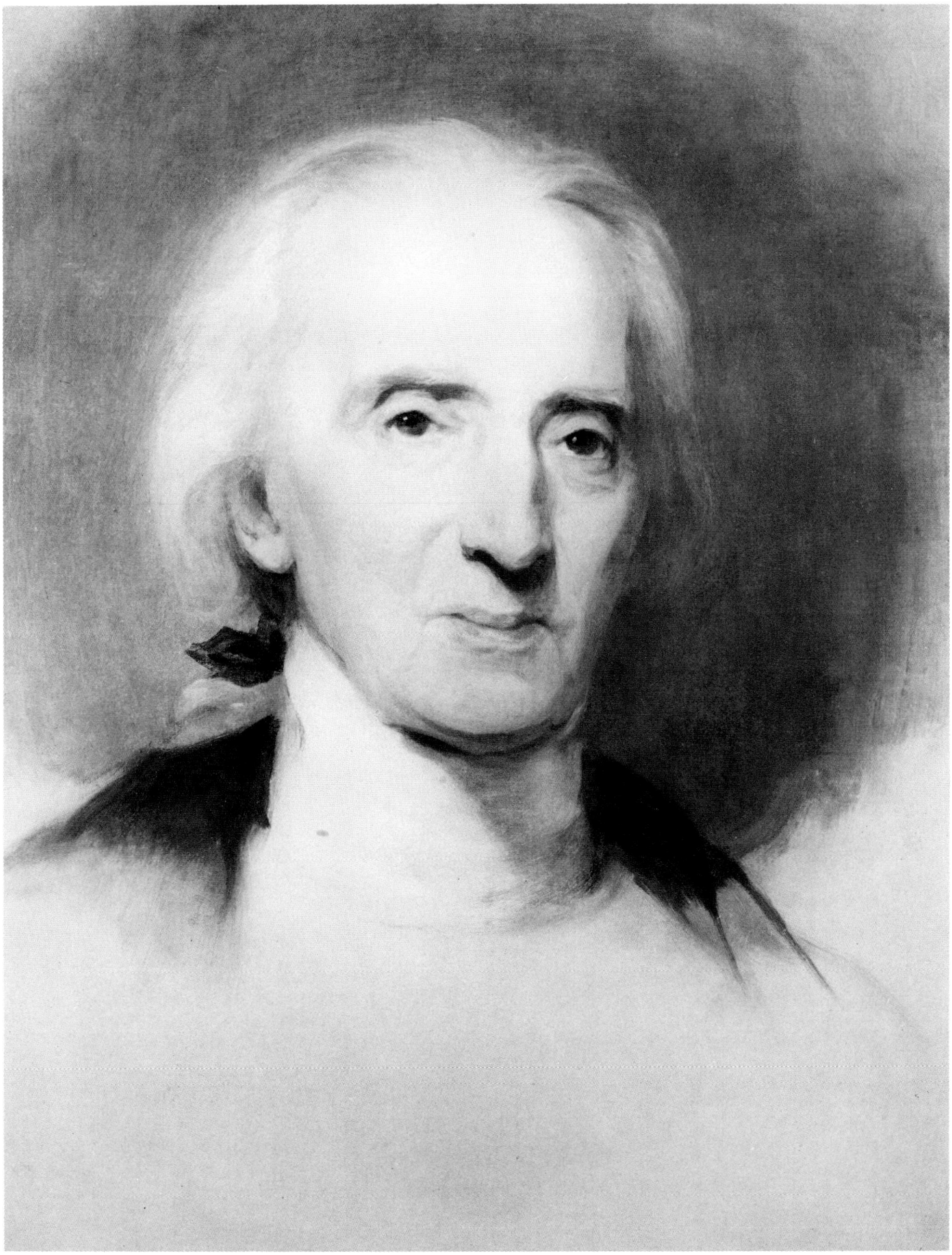

Thomas Sully

Alfred Sully, son of the artist, graduated from West Point in 1841. This portrait of him in the uniform of a West Point cadet was painted for his mother in July of 1839. It often happens that an artist is at his best when painting his own family, and this is a remarkably attractive and forceful example of the father's work.

Alfred Sully was assigned on graduation to the Second Infantry, then engaged in the Seminole War. He took part in the campaign against the Rogue River Indians in 1853 and the campaign against the Cheyennes in 1860. During the Civil War he fought at Fair Oaks, Malvern Hill and Chancellorsville. At the close of the war he was brevetted Major-General of Volunteers and Brigadier-General in the regular army. During a tour of duty in California in 1850 he married Manuella Zimeno of Monterey, California; she died at age seventeen, leaving an infant son, who died one month later (Sully, 1974). In 1864, he married Henrietta Sophia Webster, of England.

This painting came from the Sully family to the present owners.

Canvas: 24 x 20 inches.

29 *Alfred Sully 1839*

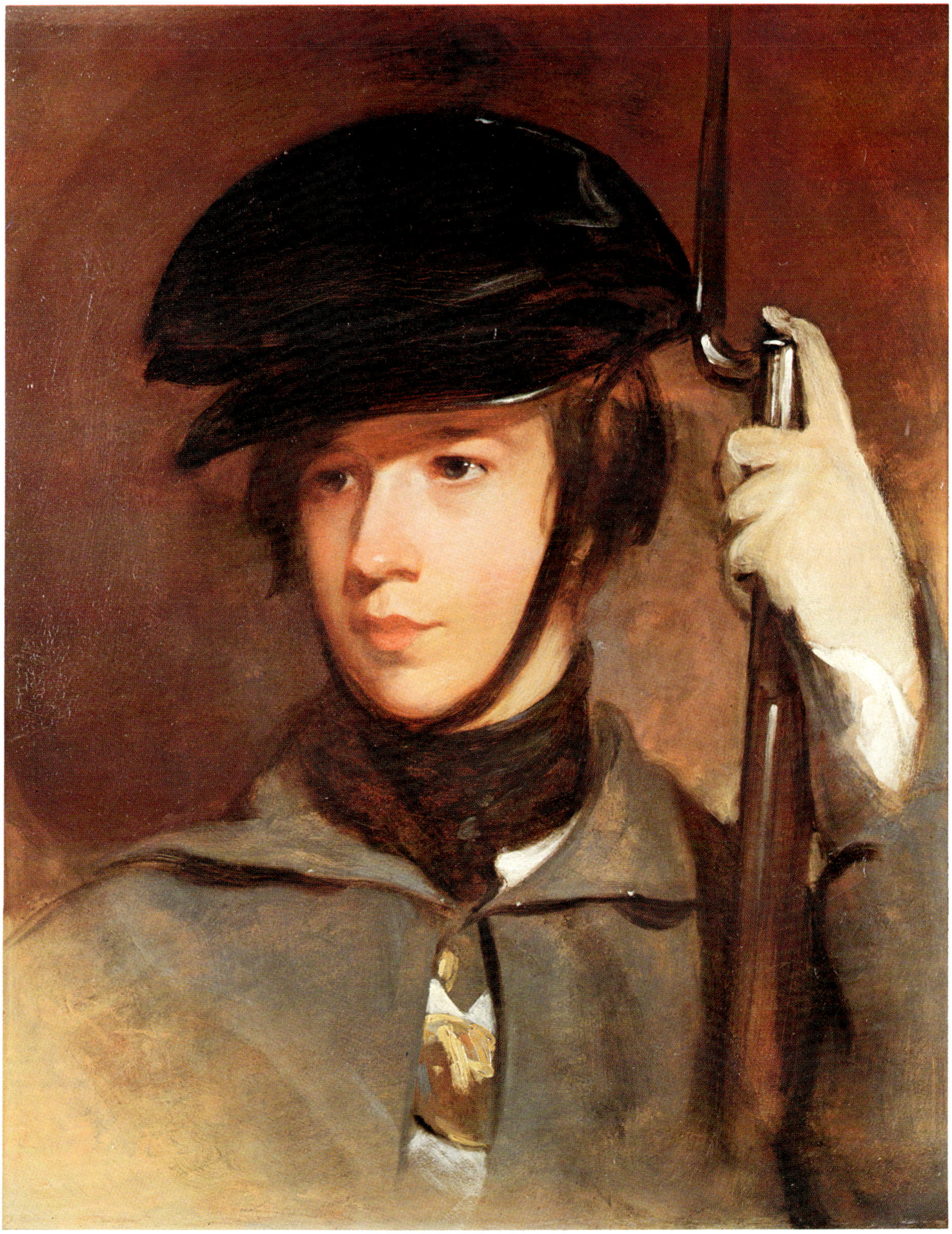

VI

The Generation of 1825: Landscape, Portrait and Genre

An insatiable hunger for pictures and every kind of visual expression is characteristic of this period. Mrs. Anna Jameson, an intelligent writer and art critic traveling through the country, observed with surprise, "The country seemed to swarm with painters." Artists took large paintings and panoramas from town to town, charging admission. Peddlers sold plaster statuettes from house to house. Illustrated books and magazines, prints and engravings, proliferated.

The American people were in the midst of a national experience of unprecedented character. In 1800 they had only begun to cross the Appalachians. In 1850 Sacramento became the capital of the first state on the shore of the Pacific Ocean. In fifty years they crossed an enormous continent, exploring new regions and climates, founding states and cities, inventing new ways of life. It seemed that anything which enabled them to see themselves as a nation or as individuals met with an eager welcome.

George Caleb Bingham 1811-1879

The march of the American people across the continent in the nineteenth century was painted by many artists, but by none more eloquently than Bingham.

He was born in Virginia, not far from Charlottesville. When he was eight, his family crossed the mountains and moved to the farthest edge of settlement, at Franklin on the Missouri River. The town has since vanished, replaced by Booneville, Missouri, across the river on the south bank.

The rivers Ohio, Mississippi and Missouri were then the highroads of the continent; St. Louis was the crossroads. Past Franklin up the Missouri went the fur traders and mountain men, the raftsmen and keelboatmen, the steamboats pushing upstream on their 1,000 mile voyage to fur trading posts in Indian country. In 1821 the first expedition overland to Santa Fe set out from Franklin. Kit Carson grew up there. Later, the overland trails to Oregon and California took off from a little farther upstream. The life of the great rivers was Bingham's own life; he grew up with it, as Mark Twain did.

All indications are that Bingham began as a self-taught artist. His early paintings in the 1830's are in the hard, earnest style of the untrained, back-country painter. In 1838 he went to Philadelphia to study at the Pennsylvania Academy. There, seeing the accomplished coloristic art of Thomas Sully and (by internal evidence) some of the Rubens in the collection of Joseph Bonaparte, exiled king of Spain, he began to develop his own style of fresh, pure color, luminous shadows and atmosphere. Drawing from casts of antique sculpture, he taught himself to see the human figure in a large, simple but expressive way. Several years painting portraits in Washington enlarged his experience. Returning to St. Louis in 1844, he saw the picturesque possibilities of the river life and set out to paint it.

In 1845 he sent two paintings to be exhibited at the American Art Union in New York. One was *Fur Traders Descending the Missouri* (now in The Metropolitan Museum of Art); the other, *The Concealed Enemy*, showed an Indian lurking in ambush (Peabody Museum, Harvard University). They were well received. The next year, 1846, he sent this picture, *Boatmen on the Missouri*.

The subject, three men in a boat drifting in the current, waiting to sell their load of wood to an approaching steamboat, was as ordinary an episode on the river as is today the sight of a filling station attendant filling a motorist's tank with gasoline. Bingham's imagination, his strangely beautiful, luminous color, his largeness of drawing, give these outrageous characters a grand poetry, making them part of the epic of America.

Canvas: 25 x 30 inches. Both this and No. 31 are newly rediscovered pictures. No. 30 was exhibited at the American Art Union, 1846, and awarded by lottery to J. R. Macmurdo of New Orleans. It remained in private hands in New Orleans until inherited by George Bergin of La Jolla, California. While the original was out of sight, the composition was known from a nineteenth-century copy in the Winterthur Museum. In 1966 the picture was shown to Alfred Frankenstein, who, recognizing it as the original, published it in the *San Francisco Chronicle*, June 6, 1966. It was then sold to its present owner. When John Francis McDermott published his excellent *George Caleb Bingham, River Portraitist* (1950), he knew only the copy at Winterthur; E. Maurice Bloch was able to include the original in the exhibition of Bingham held by the National Collection of Fine Arts, Washington, 1968, No. 14.

30 *Boatmen on the Missouri 1846*

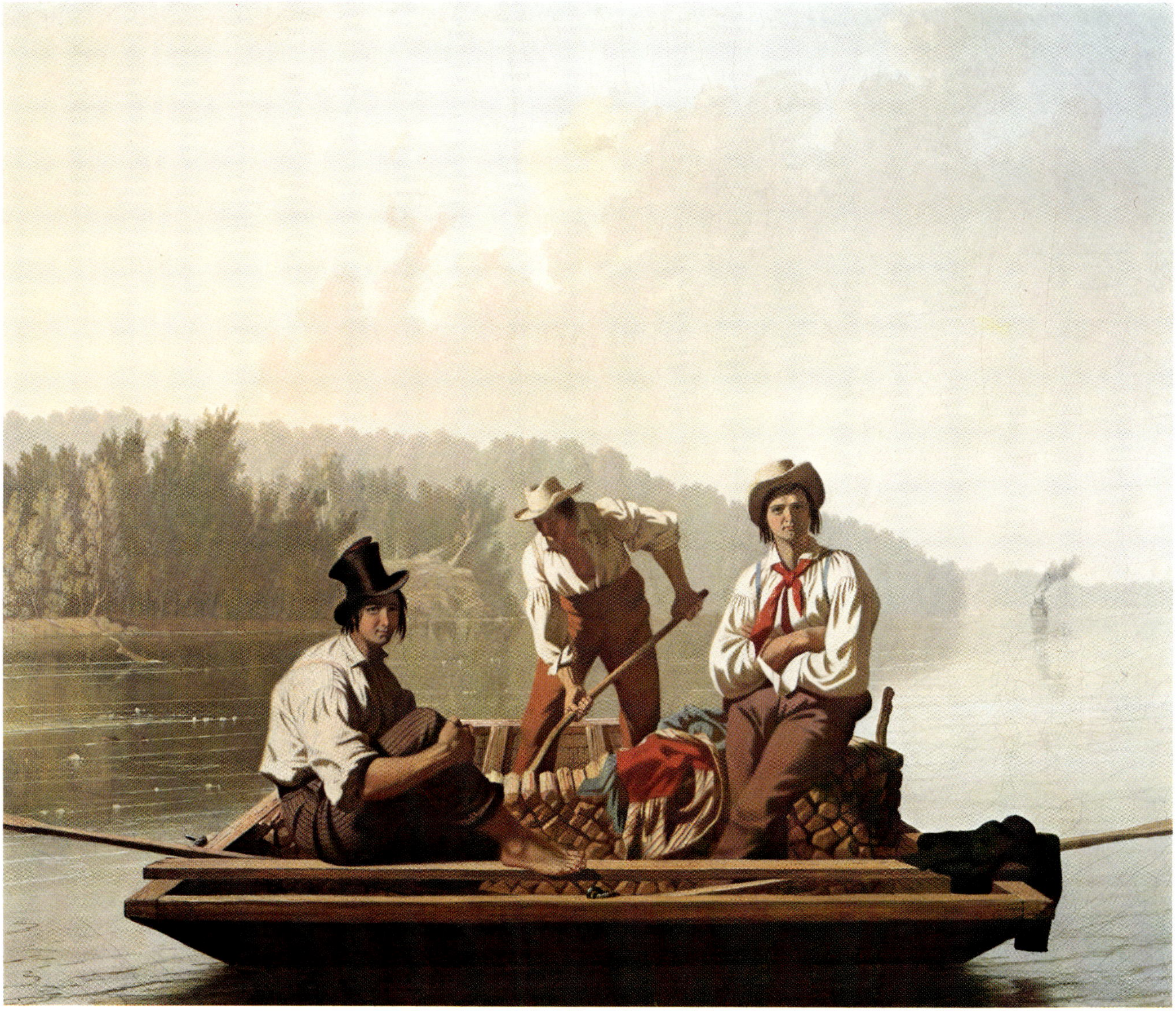

George Caleb Bingham

Politics was Bingham's second great theme, drawn again from his own experience. During the long years of private searching of conscience and public debate preceding the Civil War, of which the Lincoln-Douglas debates were the archetypal example, Missouri was a divided state. The Missouri Compromise of 1820 which drew a line westward to separate slave and free territory, the renewal of the compromise after the Mexican war, and the breaking of the compromise in 1854 were milestones on the road to war. Bingham was an ardent Whig and Union man, in and out of politics all his life, attending Whig conventions, painting banners for election parades, serving in the legislature. He had run for the legislature before he painted his first political subject, *The Stump Orator* (1848), now lost.

Country Politicians, his second, was painted during the bitter crisis over the admission to the Union of the territories won from Mexico, yet its tone is good-humored and easy. Here are four men within a country tavern. One is an enthusiastic debater, on fire to convince an elderly farmer; a third is the fat, jolly landlord, enjoying the argument; the fourth is a tavern loafer. Bingham made careful drawings from life for each. An artist's ability to draw his characters together into a psychological unity, a moment of life shared together, is the mark of a good genre painter: Bingham was a good one. The idler studying the poster of MARIES CIRCUS is a foil to the absorption of the other three in the argument. The canvas is one of the first in which Bingham shows the strong red-blue-yellow-white color chord set against a luminous atmosphere which marks his mature style.

Country Politicians went to the American Art Union in 1849 and was awarded to John Boyd of Winsted, Connecticut. It remained in the possession of that family until 1971, when it went to the Rockefeller collection. It was published by E. Maurice Bloch in the *American Art Review* in 1973.

Canvas: 20 x 24 inches. Signed at the lower left: *G. C. Bingham/1849*

31 *Country Politicians* 1849

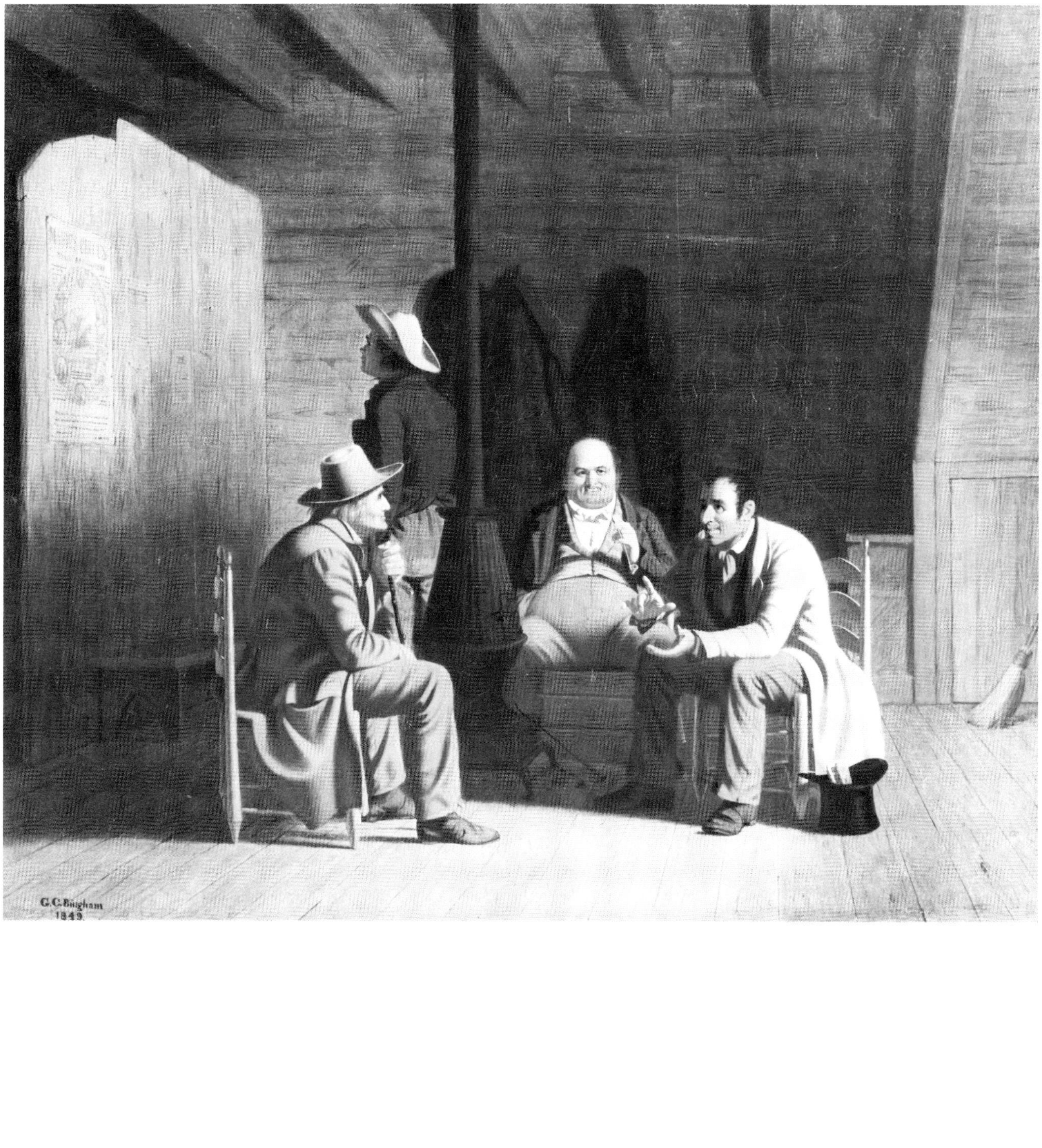
G.C.Bingham
1849.

David G. Blythe 1815-1865

The humor of the frontier with its rough jocosity and often grotesque exaggerations is prominent in our literature, but Blythe is almost its only representative in painting. The son of Scotch-Irish immigrants, he grew up on a farm in East Liverpool, Ohio, on the Ohio River. The frontier and the river were the world of his boyhood. The spirit of adventure led him at seventeen to enlist for a three-year hitch in the navy, which took him to the Caribbean. Returning afterward to East Liverpool, he became a self-taught portrait painter in the river towns of Ohio and Indiana. He also tried unsuccessfully to make money by painting a panorama (Miller, 1950). Finally settling at Pittsburgh in 1856, he devoted the last nine years of his life to painting humorous and satiric genre. No one knows what supported him or how he lived. Like his contemporary in Pittsburgh, Stephen Foster, he died penniless.

Pittsburgh, the heart and head of a great river traffic and just becoming a city of iron furnaces and foundries, was a boisterous, hard-bitten, democratic place that offered Blythe plenty of material for his satire and his sense of the ludicrous. The law courts were one of his themes: he had no more respect for judges, lawyers or constables than for the bedraggled troop of brawlers being ushered here into a night court. A characteristic of Blythe was to hide bits of symbolic comment in shadowy corners of his picture or on half-seen posters and fragments of torn newspaper.

Canvas: 20¼ x 24½ inches. Signed at the lower right, *Blythe*.

32 *Justice*

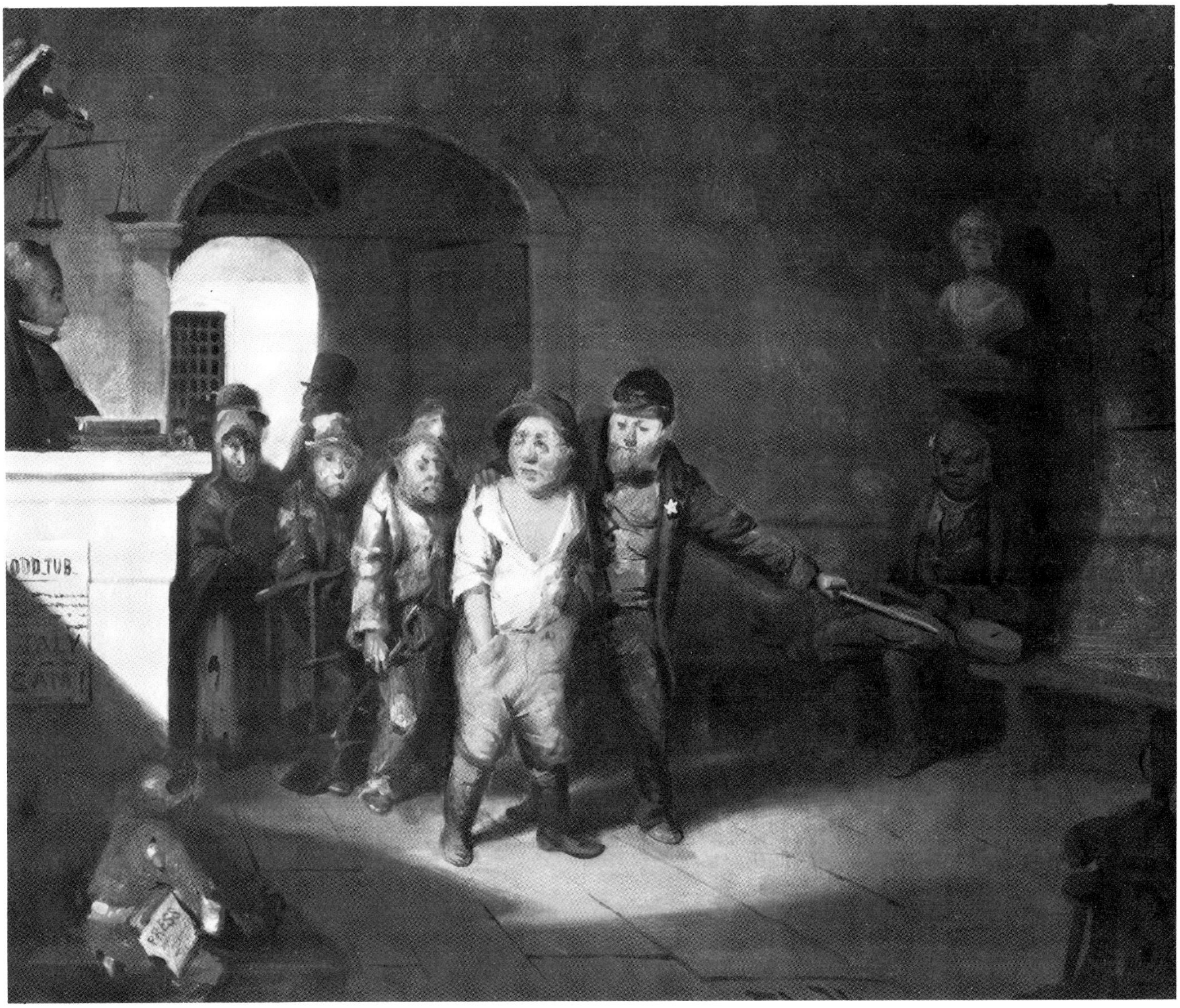
PRESS

Thomas Cole 1801-1848

There are few if any other instances in American art of such instantaneous acceptance and fame as greeted the first pictures by Thomas Cole. He arrived from Philadelphia in New York City quite unknown in April, 1825. That summer he made a sketching trip up the Hudson. Three paintings from these sketches shown in a shop window that autumn were immediately bought by three older artists, Col. Trumbull, William Dunlap and Asher B. Durand, who became his sponsors in New York. There were soon other friends, the poet Bryant and the novelist Cooper, whose most popular novel, *The Last of the Mohicans,* was published in 1826. In this gifted and influential circle Cole was accepted as the leading landscape painter of his generation.

Such immediate success shows that his work gave expression to a sentiment already strong and widespread but hitherto lacking a voice. That sentiment was a feeling for the beauty of the vast, wild, untamed continent so unlike the inhabited landscape of the Old World. Cole painted the wilderness in two moods, one dramatic, the other a gentler mood of solitude and peace. *Sunrise in the Catskills* (1826) is an admirable example of the wild dramatic mood; *View near Catskill Village* (1827), likewise done from a sketch of 1825, of the contemplative. *The Sunrise* was bought by Robert Gilmor of Baltimore, a great collector whose correspondence with Cole has been published by Howard S. Merritt in the Baltimore Museum *Annual* (Merritt, 1967). The *Sunrise* has no human figures. Gilmor suggested that "an Indian hunter judiciously introduced" might assist the idea of solitude, a suggestion Cole adopted thereafter. The *View near Catskill* (1827) is the first appearance of one of Cole's favorite subjects and, after he moved his home to Catskill, the scene of his favorite evening walk. He drew it first in 1825 and returned to it in drawings and paintings for twenty years after.

33. *Sunrise in the Catskills.* Canvas: 25 x 35¼ inches. Signed at lower center: *T. Cole/1826.*

34. *View near Catskill.* Panel: 24½ x 35 inches. Signed at lower left: *T. Cole 1827.*

33 *Sunrise in the Catskills 1826*

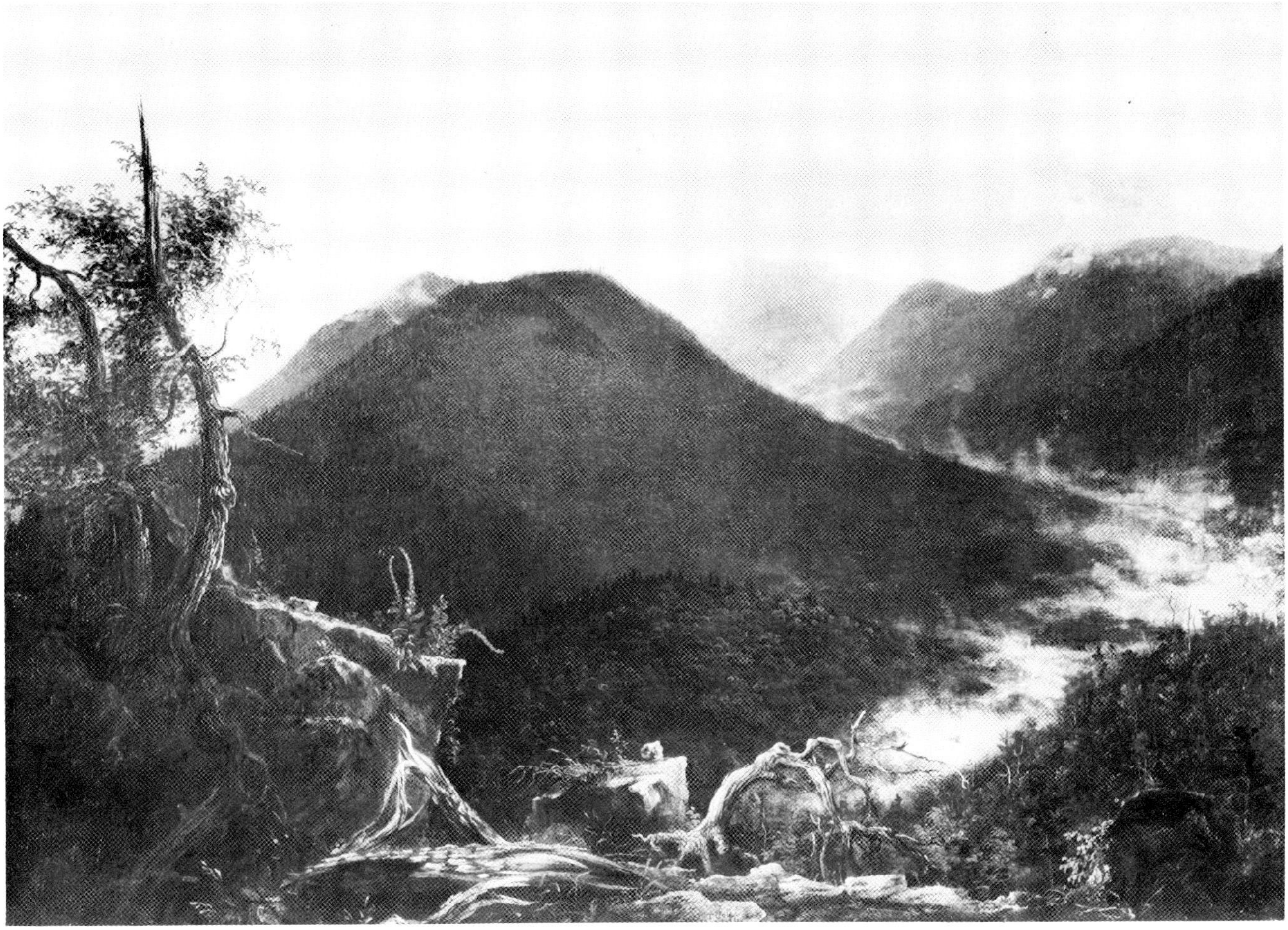

Thomas Cole

34 *View Near Catskill* 1827

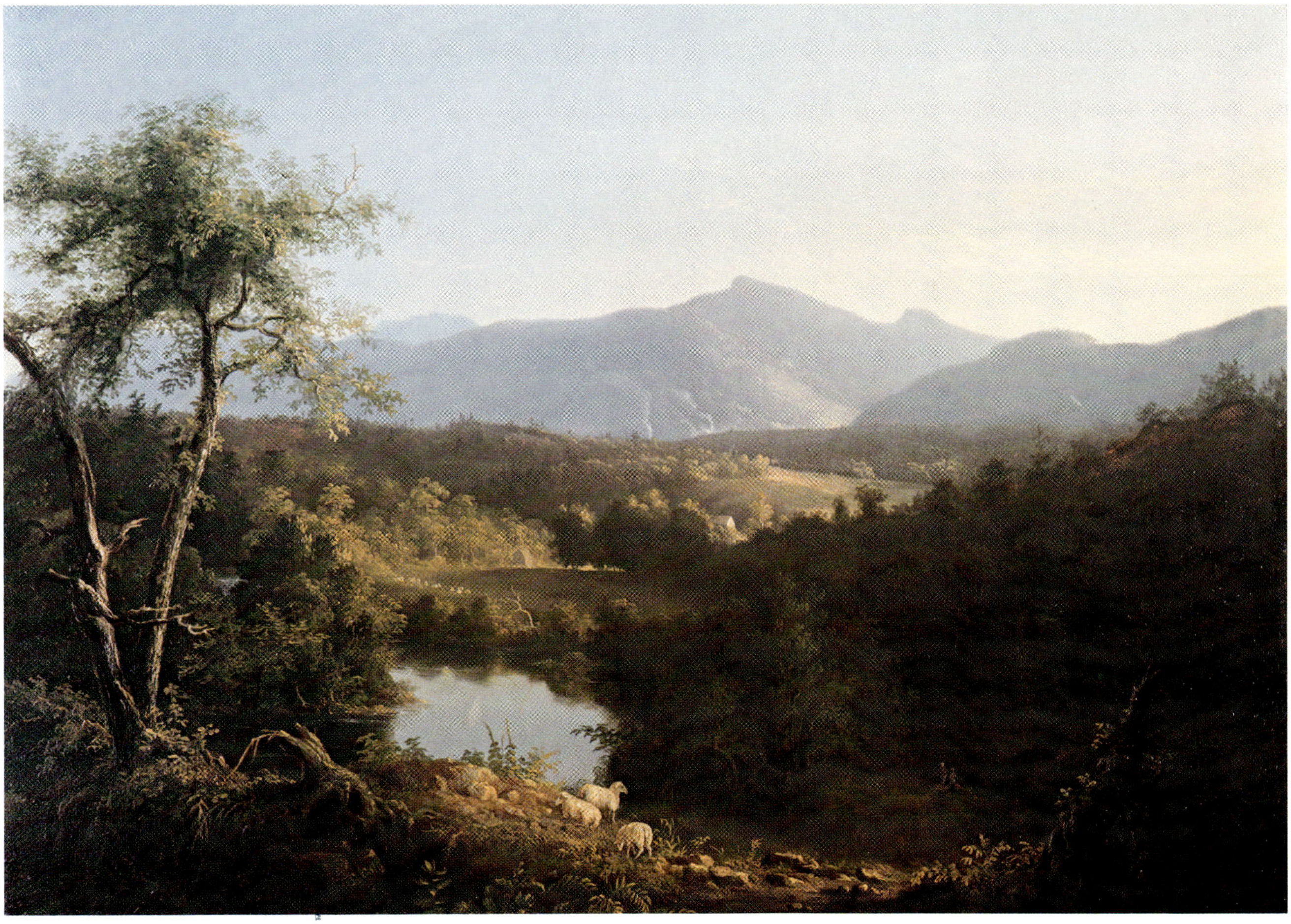

Asher B. Durand 1796-1886

Durand was the son of a farmer, watchmaker and silversmith in New Jersey. In 1812 he was apprenticed to an engraver, Peter Maverick, in Newark. At the end of five years' apprenticeship, he became Maverick's partner and moved to New York to open an office of the firm there. The partnership broke up, so William Dunlap says (Dunlap, 1834), because John Trumbull, aware of Durand's professional superiority, gave the engraving of his *Declaration of Independence* (1820-23) to Durand alone, to the exclusion of Maverick. It was a sign that Durand was recognized as the best engraver in New York City. His son (Durand, 1894) says that he engraved about seventy-five portraits. He also did illustrations for *Annuals* such as *The Atlantic Souvenir, The Gift, The Talisman, The Token* and produced miscellaneous work such as bank notes, business cards, lottery tickets, diplomas, ball tickets, and portraits of horses. In 1830 he projected a serial publication called *The American Landscape,* engraved after pictures by native artists, with text written by the poet Bryant. He engraved the first six plates but found they did not sell, aquatint having by this time become the more popular medium for landscapes. In the meantime he had begun to paint in oils. His friend Luman Reed in 1835 commissioned portraits in oil of the seven presidents of the United States from Washington to Jackson. Durand was to paint two sets, one for Reed himself (now in The New York Historical Society) and the other which Reed gave to the United States Naval Lyceum in the Brooklyn navy yard (now in the U.S. Naval Academy Museum, Annapolis). Andrew Jackson and John Quincy Adams were painted from life, the others copied from Stuart's portraits.

Luman Reed's encouragement and support played a large part in Durand's change of medium from engraving to painting in mid-career. Reed was a successful business man who, beginning to visit the exhibitions of the National Academy of Design, made friends among the artists and bought their pictures. The third story of his house was made into a picture gallery, and to Durand, Cole, Mount and many others he was a kind and generous friend. Durand painted several portraits of him, one of which, painted in 1835, exists in three versions. This painting shows him somewhat younger, by five years or so. The face is firm, decisive, intelligent, alert, yet remarkably kind. One can understand why the artists of that generation in New York looked upon Luman Reed as their best friend.

Canvas: 30¼ x 25¼ inches.

35 *Luman Reed*

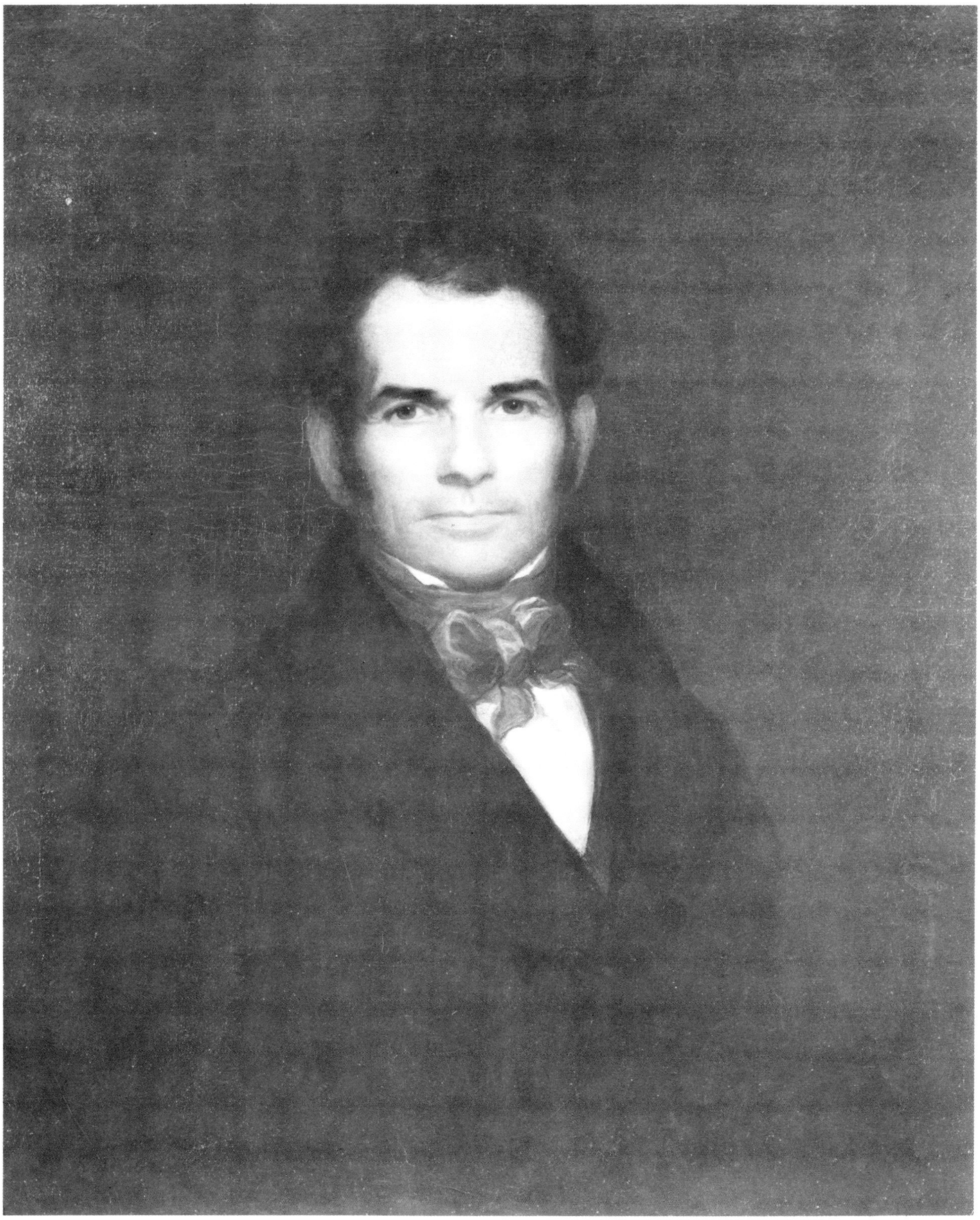

Asher B. Durand

William Dunlap, who knew Durand well, wrote of him (Dunlap, 1834), "This gentleman, although our first engraver, by universal acclamation, has passed so far on the journey through life with so few of those struggles or vicissitudes which give pungency to the tale of the biographer, that I have little more to say of him, than that he is one of the most amiable men I have known as well as one of the best artists." That is not the impression of a modern student of Durand, who thinks him a grave person and tinged by melancholy (Lawall, 1971). Be that as it may, in the landscapes to which Durand devoted himself from 1838 onward, amiability and calm seem the spirit of his art. The words tranquil, luminous, serene, come easily to mind as one looks at a picture such as this. It is a more complex composition than is common in his work. The great groups of trees on the right contrast with the open view on the left over water and hills to the spacious sky. Between the trees appear two smaller vistas, one directed again to the sky, the other losing itself in the woodland. These varied paths along which the imagination leads one into the picture, the majestic trees that Durand loved to paint, the changing forms of earth, water and sky all within a fine aerial unity, these show Durand's calm poetry at its best.

He was one of the pioneers of American landscape. What that meant one may learn from the words of an artist of the following generation. When Whittredge returned in 1859 from ten years abroad in Germany and Italy, he landed at New York knowing no one in the city. He went to the Historical Society, which then offered the only public exhibition of American art. He wrote afterward, "I may have been a little nervous, I cannot say, but when I looked at Durand's truly American landscape, so delicate and refined, such a faithful if in some parts sombre delineation of our own hills and valleys, I confess that tears came to my eyes." (Baur, 1942)

Canvas: 32¼ x 48¼ inches. Signed at the lower right, *A. B. Durand 1858*.

36 *A River Landscape 1858*

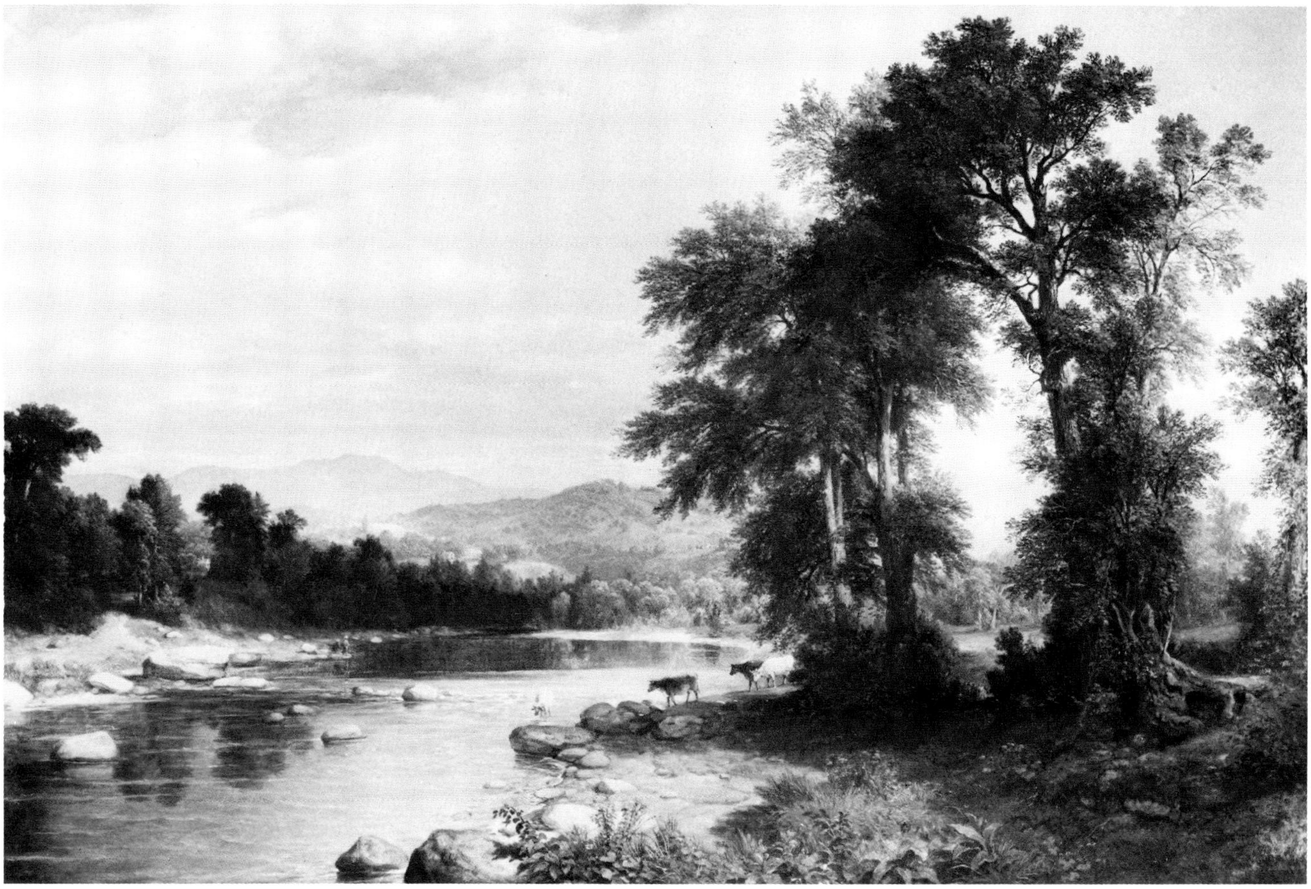

William Sidney Mount 1807-1868

We think of Mount as a genial genre painter, but he was also a sensitive landscapist and, perforce, a portrait painter. Late in life he remarked that if he had had to depend on genre painting for support, he would have been in the almshouse (1944, Cowdrey & Williams).

In 1845 Mount painted one of his most delightful works, *Eel Spearing at Setauket* (New York State Historical Association, Cooperstown), for a distinguished New York lawyer, George Washington Strong. These are two studies of the shore at Setauket for the landscape background in *Eel Spearing*. St. George's Manor had been built by the father of George Washington Strong, Judge Selah Strong, who had been a member of the Continental Congress and a captain in the Continental army. In 1845 it was the home of another son, Selah B. Strong. The second sketch shows a further stretch of the shore and a nearby farmhouse.

The two pictures show Mount's gifts as a landscape painter; the clear, soft light, the pale, golden color, the atmosphere of calm are most characteristic. They hung in St. George's Manor until offered to Mr. Rockefeller.

37. *St. George's Manor.* Oil on panel: 6¾ x 10 inches. Inscribed in ink on the reverse, "A sketch of the residence of the Hon. Selah B. Strong, L. I. 1845." There is also a slight sketch in oil on the reverse, inscribed, "View from Catskill, from the North River."

38. *Farmhouse.* Panel: 6½ x 8¾ inches. Inscribed on the reverse, "This sketch was taken during very dry weather."

37 *St. George's Manor at Setauket* 1845

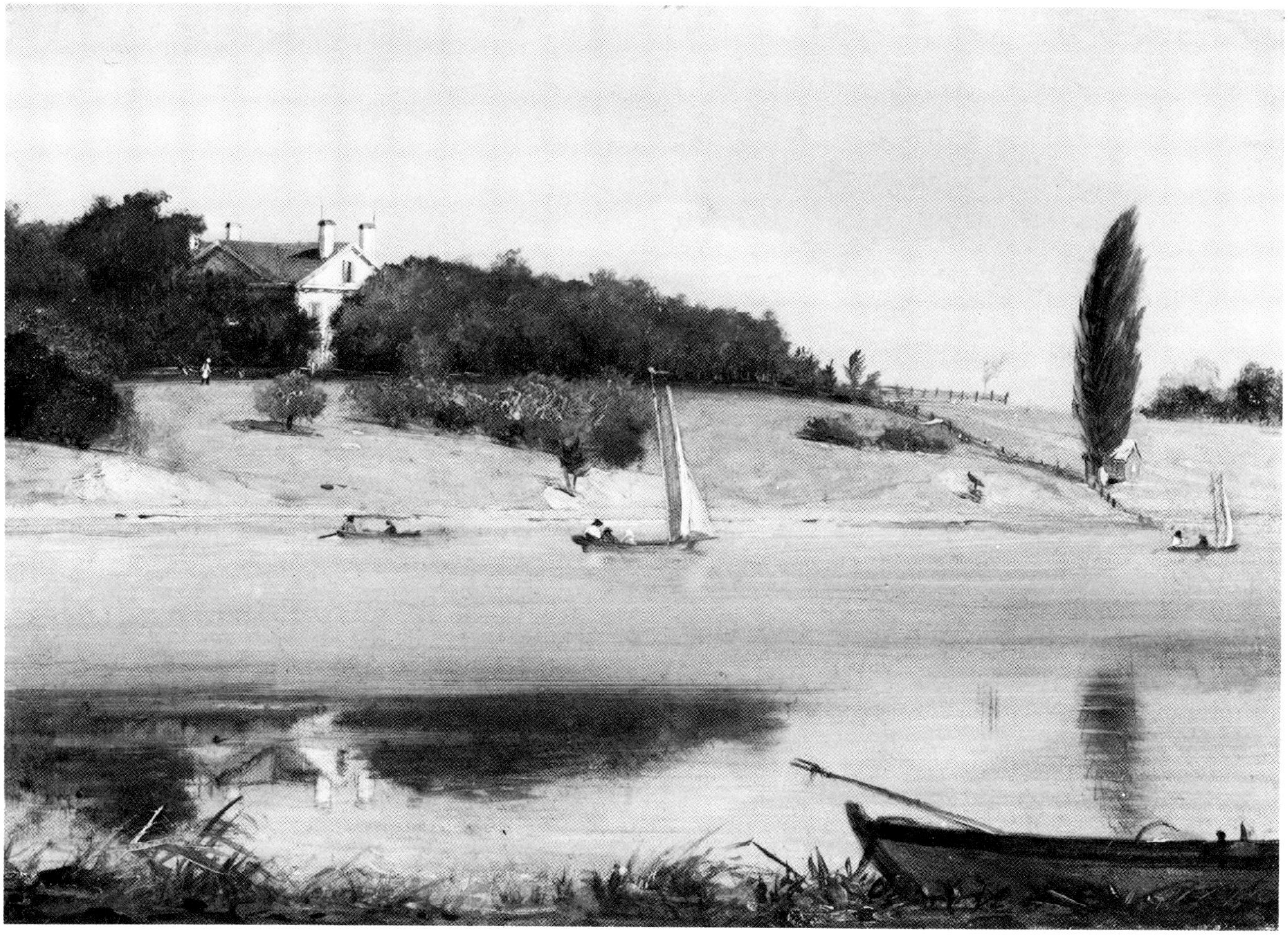

William Sidney Mount

38 *Farmhouse at St. George's* 1845

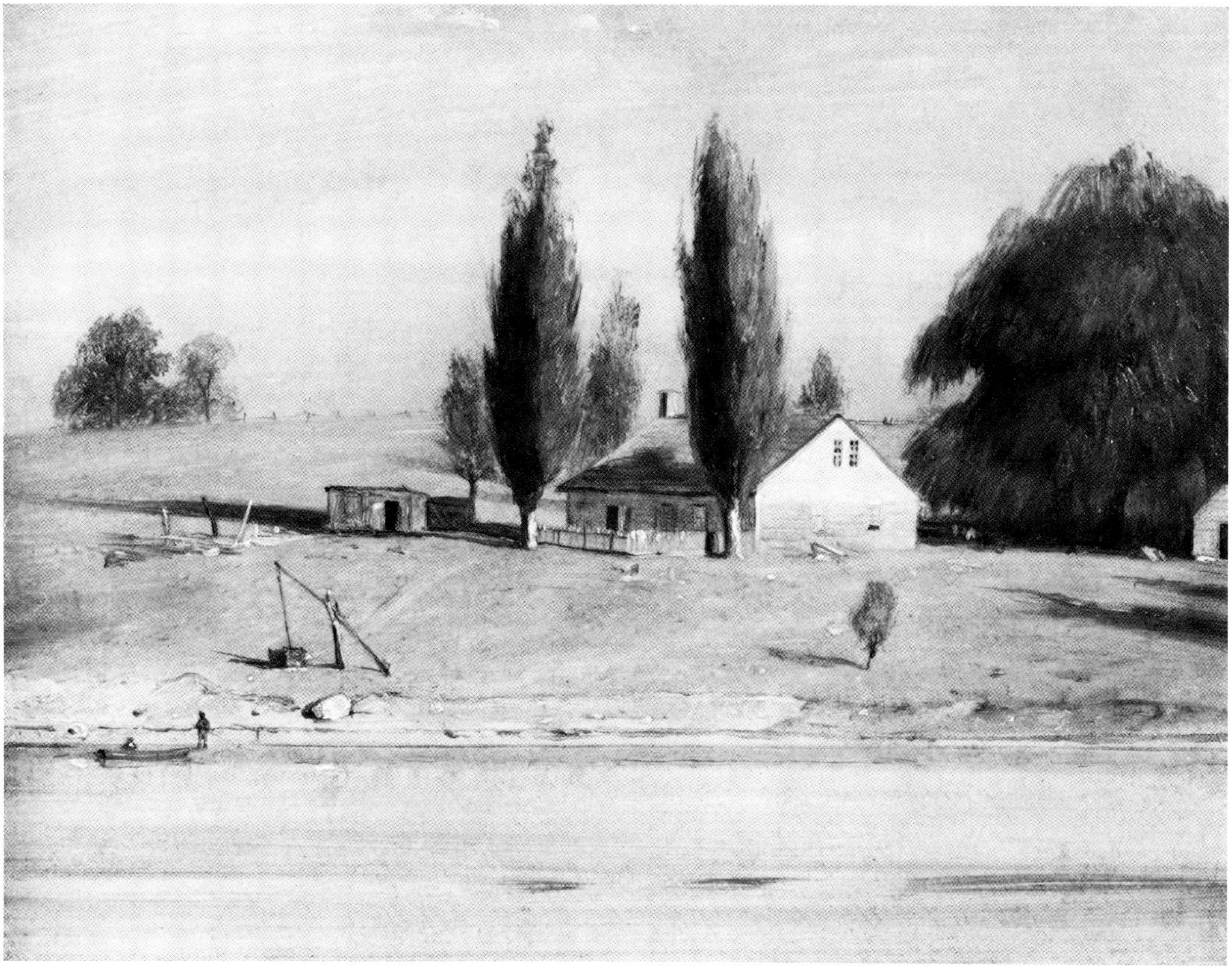

William Sidney Mount

This portrait of a shrewd, humorous and kindly man who seems to have stepped out of one of Mount's best genre paintings is another indication that an artist is often at his best when painting his own family. Mount's mother was a Hawkins. After the death of her husband, Thomas S. Mount of Setauket, she and her young children moved back to her father's home at Stoney Brook, Long Island. The Hawkins family among whom the artist thus grew up was an interesting and gifted one. One of his uncles, a New York businessman, Micah Hawkins, wrote the first successful comic opera, *The Saw Mill, or A Yankey Trick,* which was produced at Wallack's Chatham Garden Theatre, New York City, in 1824. The lively personality of Daniel Hawkins, a sea captain of Stoney Brook, speaks for itself in this portrait.

Canvas: 8½ x 6½ inches. Inscribed on the back, *Sketch of Captain Daniel S. Hawkins, by Wm. S. Mount, March 12, 1850, taken at 50 years of age;* but Mount's own list gives the date as 1849.

39 *Captain Daniel S. Hawkins 1849*

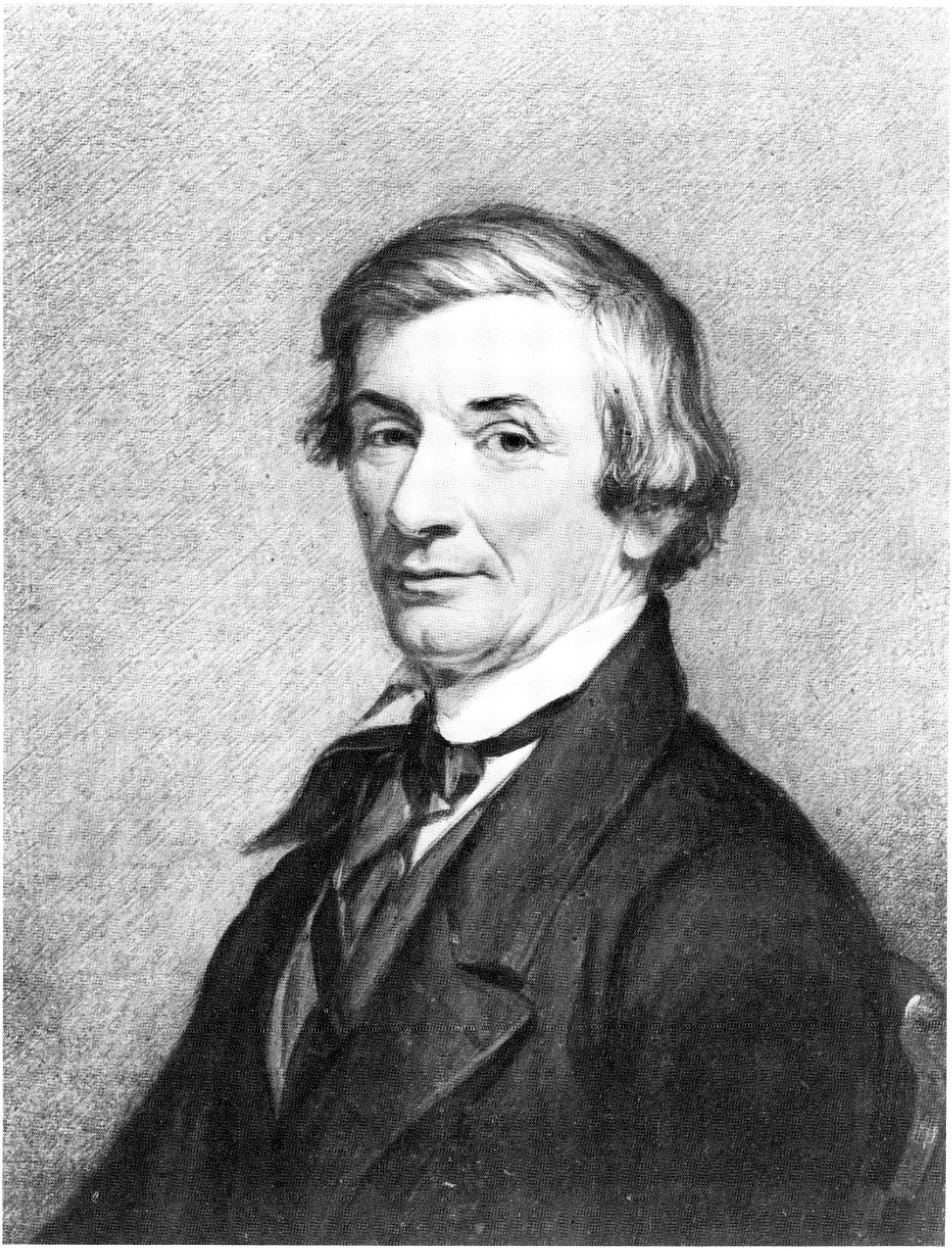

VII

The Flowering of the Nineteenth Century: Before the Civil War

A few concrete illustrations may show best what happened to life and attitudes in this period of our country's development. The first stagecoach line over the mountains from Philadelphia to Pittsburgh in 1800 promised to deliver its passengers at their destination in seven days. When Audubon took his bride by bateau down the wild Ohio to Louisville in 1807, they traveled about 20 miles a day if all went well. Wagon trains crossing the plains moved at about the same speed. Then, suddenly, the steamship and the railroad made the whole world seem accessible. It is difficult for us to imagine the enlargement of the horizon and the excitement these inventions brought with them. Travel became a poem and a passion. The artists of this generation could not sit still in a studio. They were constantly on the move; and an enthusiastic public eagerly drank in pictures of a widening world.

Yet there are always some whose world is within the mind; who travel by introspection or in memories of the great past that is history. So there were also artists like William Page and William Rimmer.

Albert Bierstadt 1830-1902

Bierstadt was brought to this country as a child of two from Solingen, near Dusseldorf in Germany, and grew up in New Bedford, Massachusetts. At twenty-three he went back to Dusseldorf to study painting. There he worked in winters in the studio of a fellow American, Worthington Whittredge, and in summers made long sketching tours through the countryside. In these studies of landscape in Germany and in a final year spent with Whittredge and Sanford Gifford in Italy, his future course was set (Hendricks, 1972). He returned to New Bedford in 1857.

The following year Bierstadt was allowed to accompany an exploring expedition commanded by General F. W. Lander, sent to find a wagon route through the Rocky Mountains to the Pacific Ocean. The expedition followed the Platte and the Sweetwater to the South Pass, which they reached on June 24, 1859. There Bierstadt and an artist companion left the expedition to spend the summer sketching among the Wind River Mountains and to work their way by slow stages through Wyoming and Kansas back to New York. This was the great experience of his life. It opened the way to a career devoted to the grandeur of the American continent. A second journey west in 1863 took him to California and Oregon. An account of this expedition by his traveling companion, a journalist named Fitzhugh Ludlow, appeared in the *Atlantic Monthly* the following year and was enlarged into a book, *The Heart of the Continent* (1870).

The sixties and seventies were the decades of his great artistic and popular success; in the eighties the growing influence of French painting and a new generation of artists trained in Paris thrust him aside. His work has two aspects—sketches from nature, sharply observed and brilliantly executed; and large pictures composed in the studio, freely adapted from the sketches. The latter, in his best years, were evocations of the excitement of discovery and were true to that initial feeling; however, they later grew increasingly theatrical. His reputation today rests on his sketches and the early paintings.

Sunshine and Shadow, painted from a sketch made in 1855 of a church at Kassel, was shown at the National Academy of Design in 1862 and brought Bierstadt his first considerable critical success (Henricks, 1972). It is the eloquent response of a young American (by education if not by birth) to the Old World and the poetry of time past. Artistically it shows his mastery of light and chiaroscuro and the sureness of his harmonies of tone.

Canvas: 41½ x 35½ inches. Signed and dated at lower right, *A. Bierstadt 1862.*

40 *Sunshine and Shadow 1862*

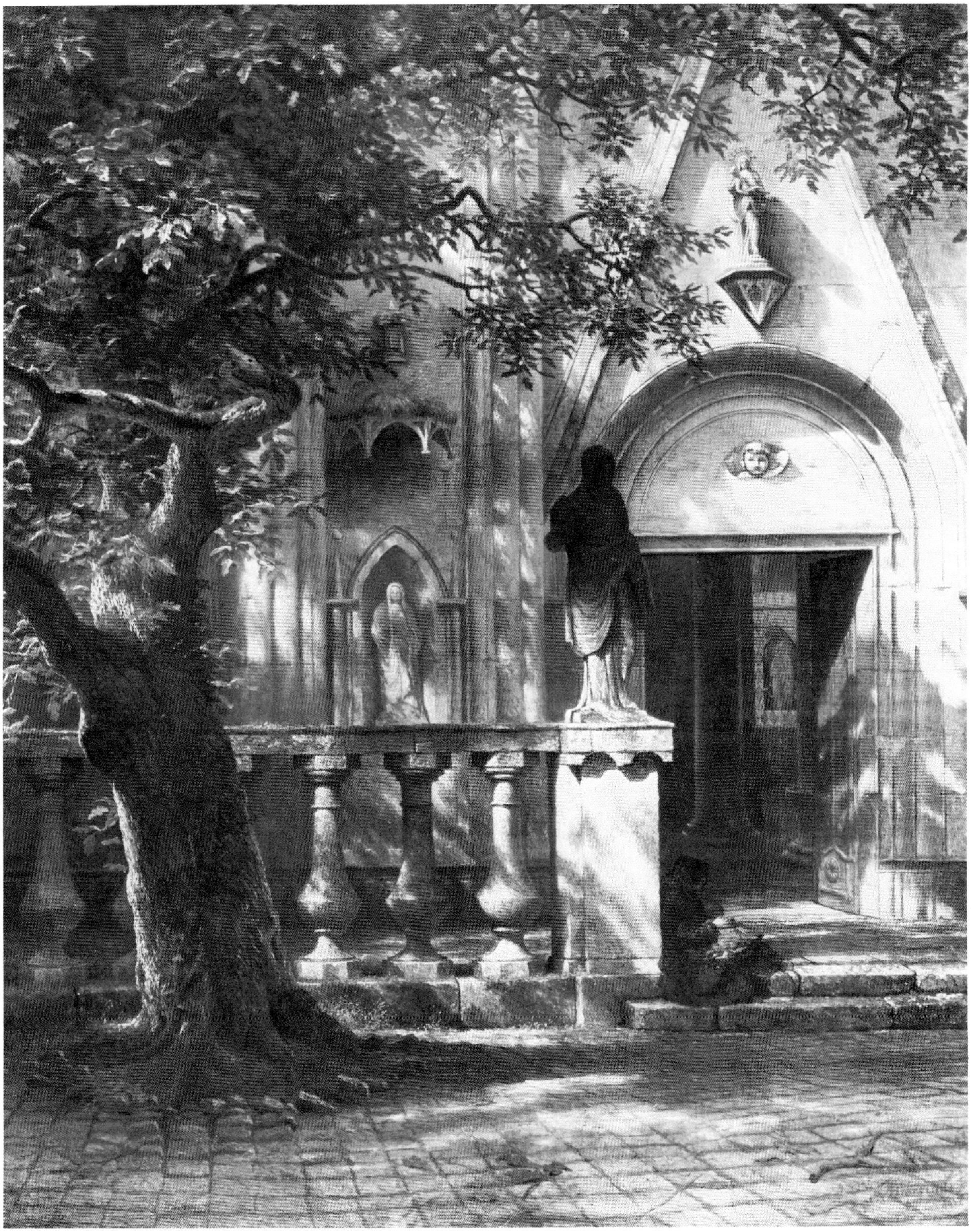

Albert Bierstadt

This delightful little picture in his best early style was painted during the few months spent in New Bedford, between his return from Europe in August 1857 and his departure with General Lander's expedition the following year.

Panel: 5½ x 9¼ inches. Signed at lower left, *A B 1858*.

41   *River Scene 1858*

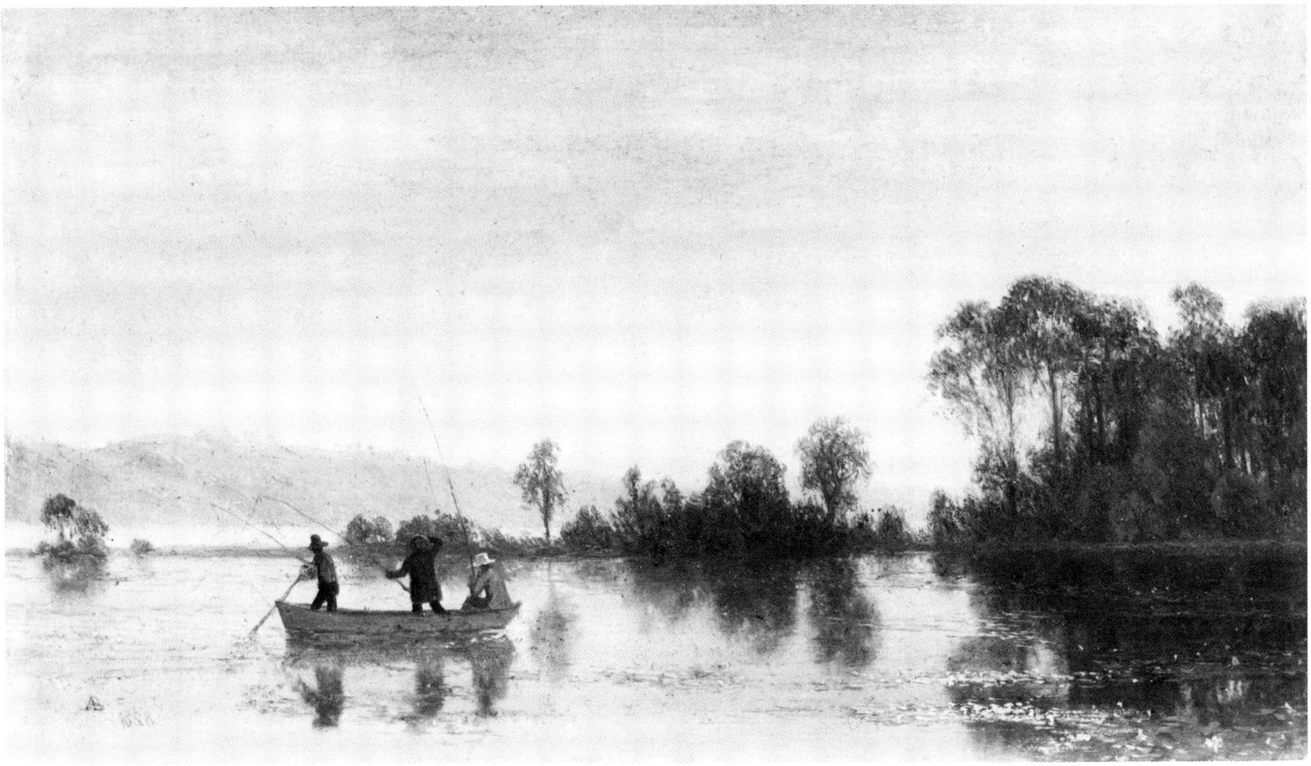

Albert Bierstadt

Bierstadt first visited the Yosemite in 1863. In subsequent years he painted many pictures of it from his sketches. They are evocations of its awe-inspiring grandeur, the power of its storms and cold, the poetry of its solitudes. There is a fine artistic imagination at work here on the theme of the grandeur of this continent.

Canvas: 26 x 36 inches, sight. Signed at lower left, *A. Bierstadt.*

42 *Winter—Yosemite*

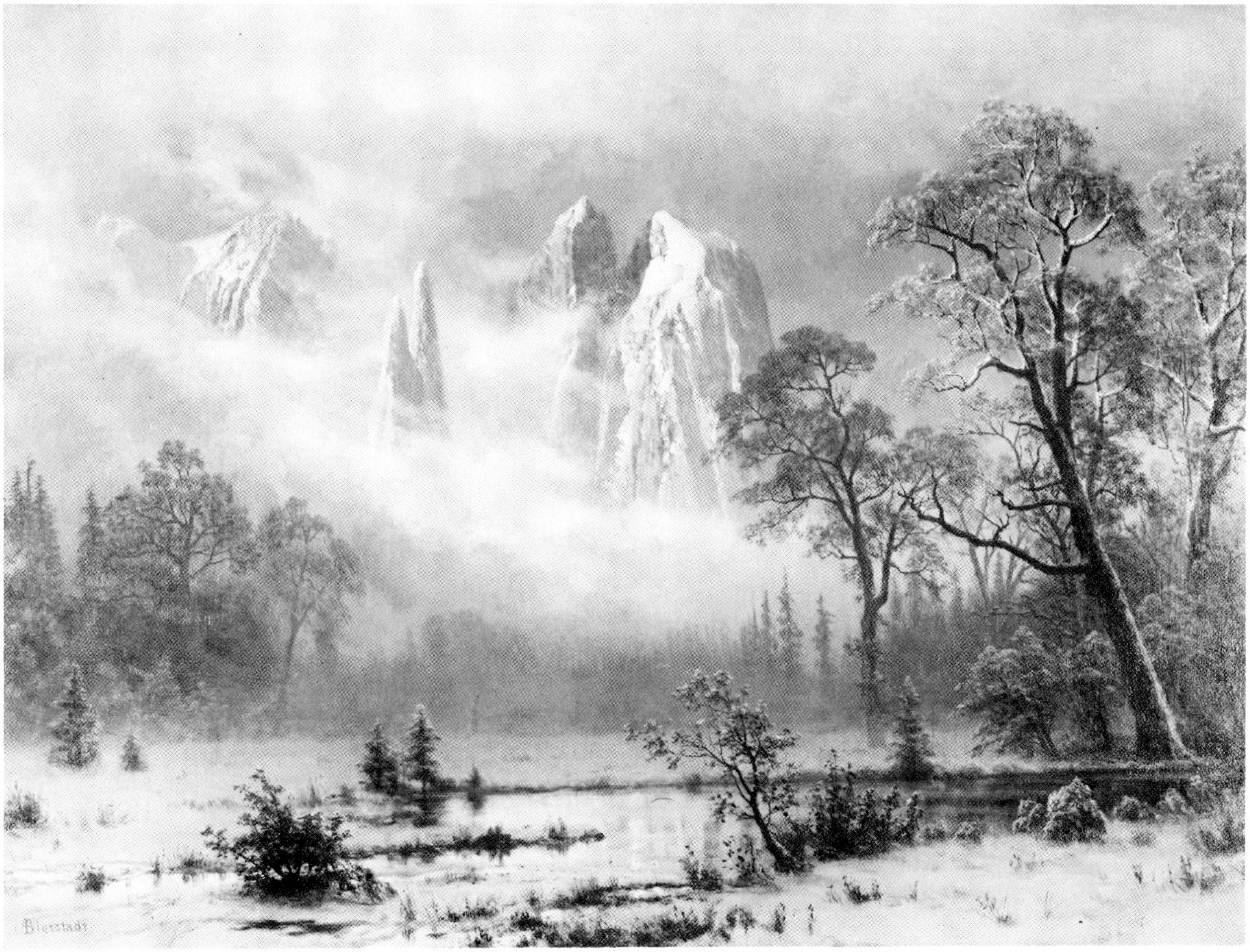
Bierstadt

Albert Bierstadt

The artist and his wife visited Niagara in 1869. This study speaks for itself of his ability to put on canvas, with the greatest directness, an image of movement and vast power.

Canvas: 14¼ x 19¼ inches. Signed at lower right, *A. Bierstadt.*

43   *Niagara Falls 1869*

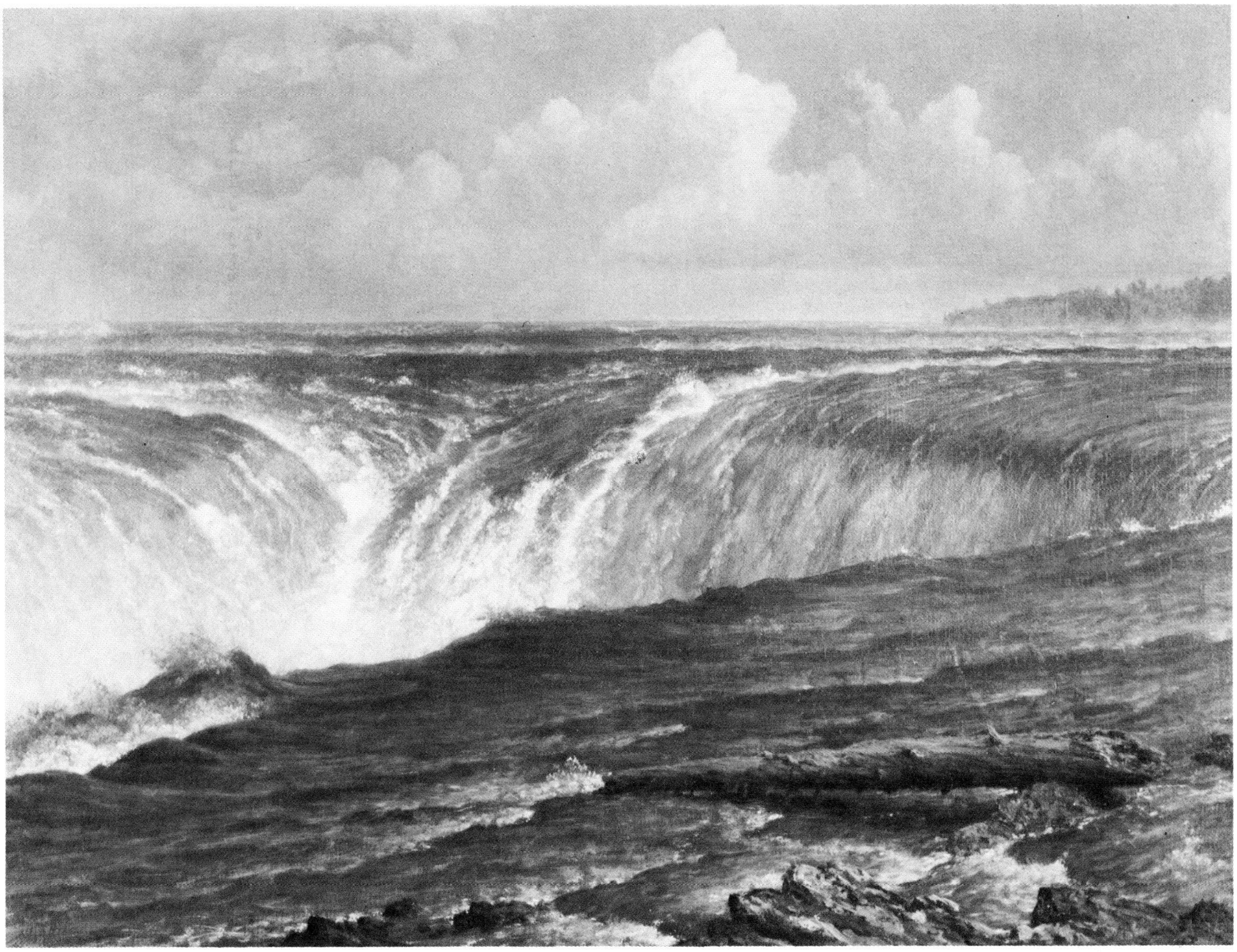

Albert Bierstadt

This is a study for the central group in Bierstadt's *Last of the Buffalo,* a large canvas which exists in two versions, one in the Corcoran Gallery of Art, Washington, and the other in the Whitney Museum of Western Art, Cody, Wyoming. Bierstadt projected the scene back into the past, when buffalo herds were beyond counting and Indians hunted on horseback with bow and spear. The artist had seen that wild, primitive life himself and summoned up from his memories a vivid image. The action is furious, the touch free, the whole done with splendid vigor.

When he submitted the large picture, 6 by 9 feet, to the jury of selection for the American section of the Paris Exposition of 1889, the jury of Paris-trained artists, holding the ideals of another generation, rejected it. Bierstadt went on painting but never returned to the old subjects. This was his farewell to the West.

Canvas: 24-15/16 x 36-1/16 inches. Signed at the lower left, *A. Bierstadt.*

44 *Indians Hunting Buffalo   ca. 1888*

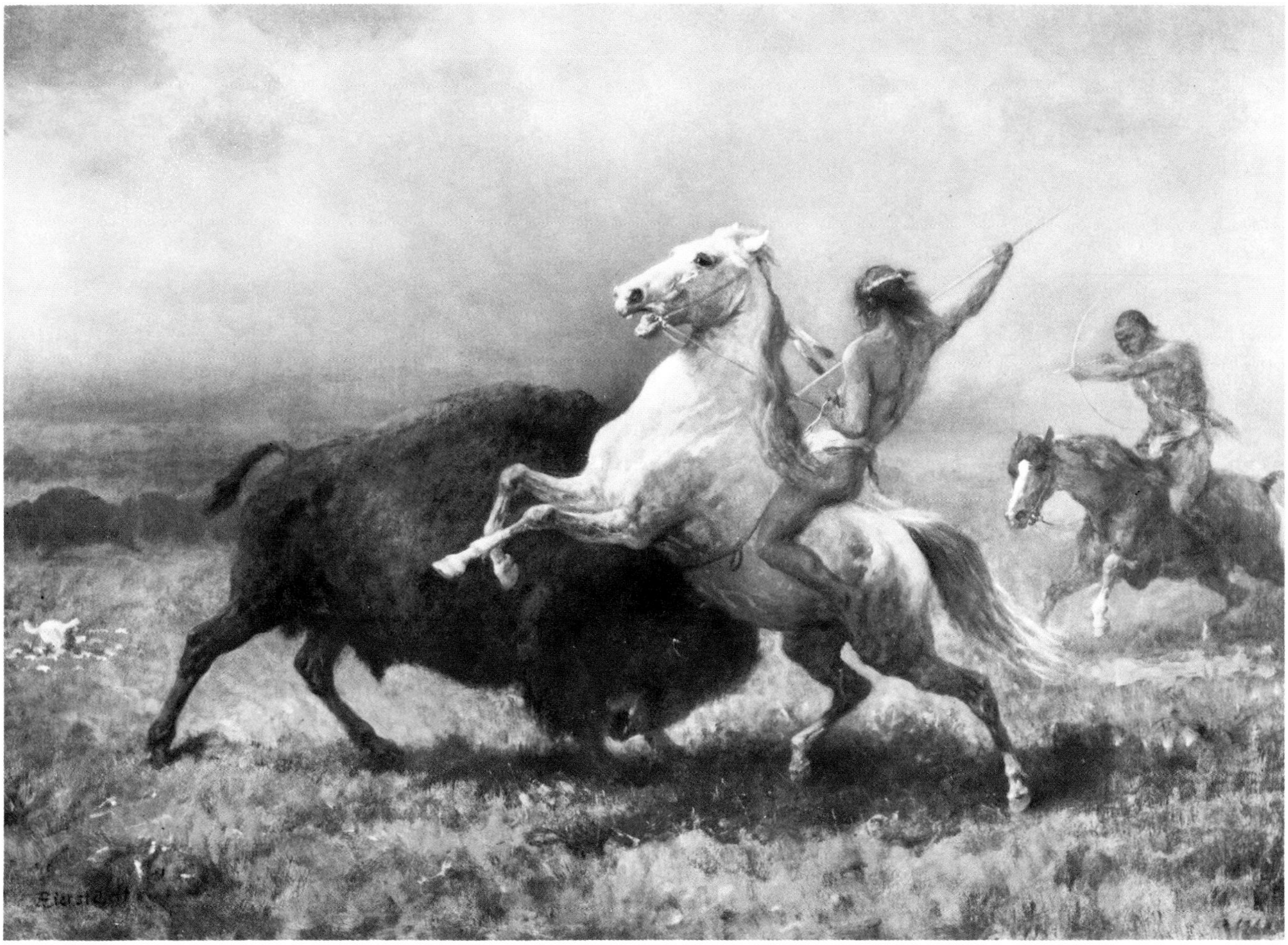

Frederic E. Church 1826-1900

Born at Hartford, Connecticut, the son of well-to-do parents who encouraged his bent toward painting, Church studied first with two Hartford artists, Benjamin A. Coe and Alexander H. Emmons. At 18 he went to Catskill, New York, and was taken into Thomas Cole's home as pupil and friend. After Cole's death in 1848, Church moved to New York City. His exceptional talent was recognized early. He exhibited at the National Academy of Design at age nineteen, became an Associate at twenty-two and a full member at twenty-three. Reading Humboldt's *Cosmos* and *Personal Narrative of Travels to the Equinoctial Regions of America* provided the inspiration to test himself against the greatest landscapes of the continent. He visited Ecuador in 1853 and 1857, painted the icebergs of Labrador in 1859, visited Jamaica in 1865, and in 1868 went to Europe, not to study its picture galleries but to paint in Greece, Syria and Palestine. The Islamic world fascinated him, and the home he built for himself on the Hudson is a dream of its exotic splendors.

Church's theme was the grandeur and awe-inspiring powers of Nature. To that imaginative vision, he brought a phenomenal skill of hand, a scientific naturalism of eye and mind, and a poetic sense of light and space. He was the greatest of our artist-explorers. In his fifties rheumatism crippled his right hand; he taught himself to paint with his left but that too became crippled. The last twenty years of his life he lived in summer at "Olana," his home on the Hudson, and spent his winters in Mexico. Under the impact of the European-trained American artists who brought back in the eighties an entirely different ideal of art derived from their schooling in Munich and Paris, American taste swung to the opposite pole from Church's heroic and naturalistic art. Now, after a hundred years, we see him again as a great figure of powerful imagination and an intuitive rather than a learned, or borrowed, technique.

Twilight, an early work, shows how far he had already surpassed his teacher Cole in luminosity and in resonance of tone.

Canvas: 24 x 36 inches. Signed at lower left:
F. E. Church.

45 *Twilight ca. 1856*

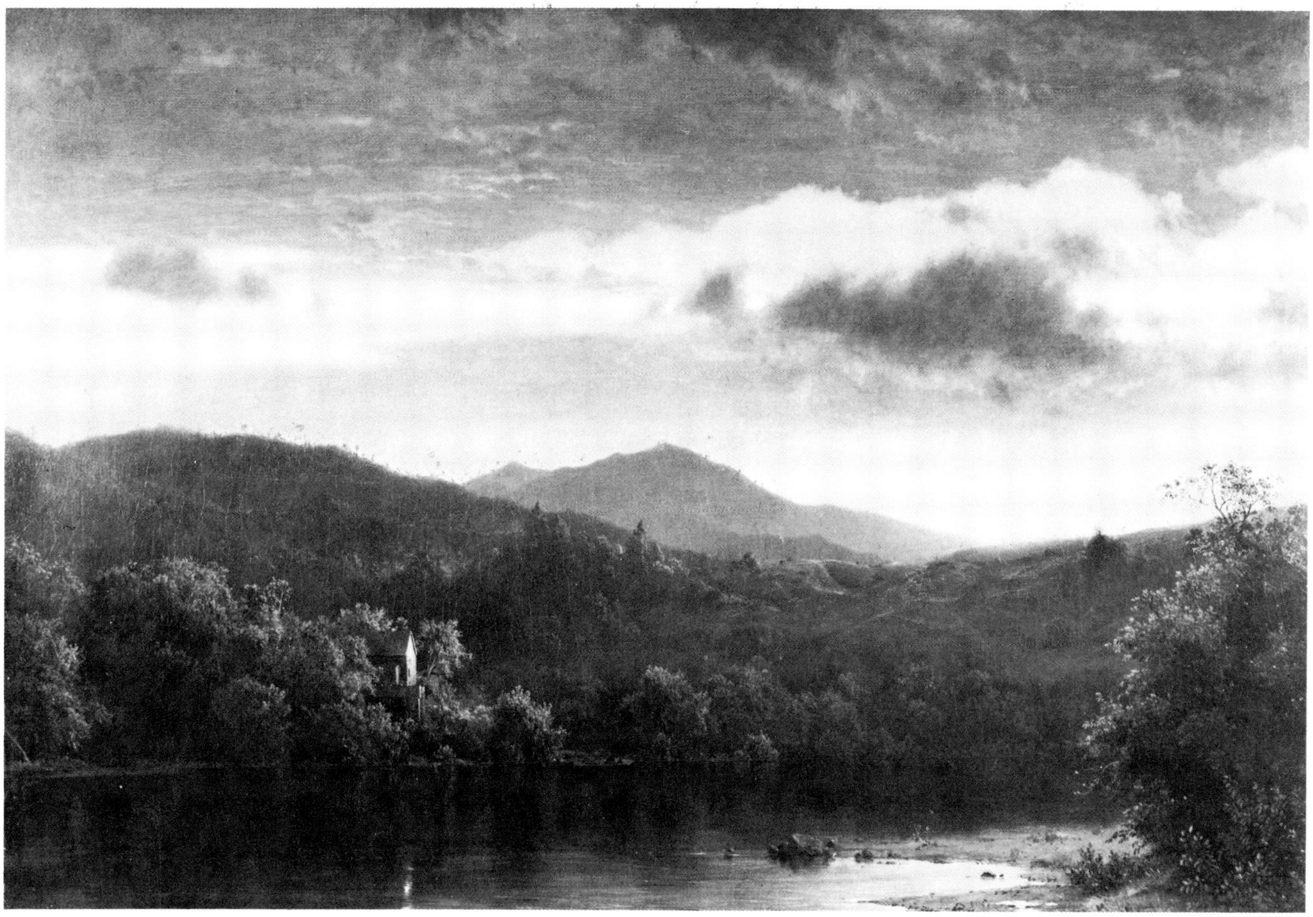

Frederic E. Church

In the 1860's Church began acquiring land on Mount Merino across the Hudson from Thomas Cole's home at Catskill. On a high point 500 feet above the river and commanding wide views of the Hudson and of the Catskill Mountains, he built in the 1870's his home "Olana." This sketch from the hilltop, dated February 1871, is done with superlative skill of eye and hand, recreating in the simplest, most direct manner a vast sweep of air and sun and the frozen world. It is a little masterpiece of the poetry of nature and the observing eye that make Church memorable.

Canvas: 12½ x 19⅝ inches. Signed and dated at the lower left, *F. E. C. Feb. 71*.

46 *Snow Scene, Olana 1871*

FEC. Feb/71

Sanford R. Gifford 1823-1880

Gifford grew up in Hudson, New York, a city on the river of the same name about twenty miles below Albany. He studied painting under John Rubens Smith in New York City and kept a studio there from 1846 until his death, but he was a great wanderer. Setting out on sketching trips with little baggage but a knapsack and paint box, he traveled over much of the world. In 1855 he went to Europe for three years. The travel diary of this trip is the record of a sensitive, articulate, independent mind. In 1870, with Kensett and Whittridge, he accompanied Dr. Ferdinand V. Hayden's U.S. Geological Survey expedition, traveling the Oregon trail up the Sweetwater through the South Pass to Fort Bridger and camping for three weeks in the Uinta Mountains before returning by the Overland Trail.

The theme of Gifford's art is sunlight and air. With his friends Kensett and Whittredge, he gave us a period of Luminism. The Luminists represented the poetry of air and light in nature by means of tone; their color was often luminous and bright but it was combined with an exquisite precision of outline. As Gifford traveled up and down the Hudson River between New York and his family home, he saw the river at all times of day and in all seasons: it was part of his life. The aerial unity of this scene, the delicate gradations of tone on sails farther and farther in the distance, and the stillness are characteristic of Gifford. His contemporary, Henry Tuckerman, said of his works, "They do not dazzle, they win; they appeal to our calm and thoughtful appreciation." (Tuckerman, 1867.)

Canvas: 18½ x 34⅛ inches. Signed at the lower right, S. R. Gifford; inscribed on the reverse, Presented to the Hudson Academy by S. R. Gifford June 1879 / A Sunset on the Hudson / by S. R. Gifford.

47 *Sunset on the Hudson*

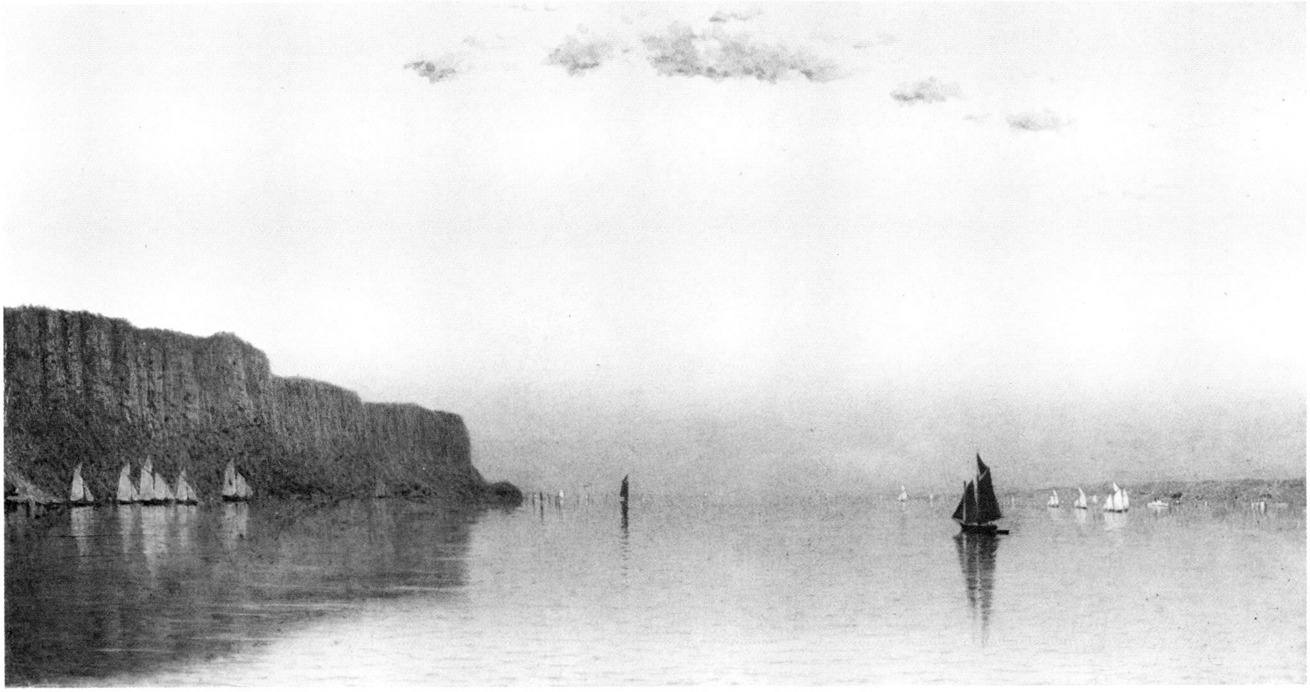

Martin Johnson Heade   1819-1904

Heade, born at Lumberville, Pennsylvania, on the Delaware River, died at Saint Augustine, Florida, where he lived form 1881 to 1904. In between these dates he was almost constantly on the move, wandering over most of the United States, Europe and South America. Henry Tuckerman, who knew him in New York City where Heade maintained a studio for many years, observed, "He began his artistic career as a portrait painter; but the love of travel was strong within him, and few of our artists have roved more about the world." (Tuckerman, 1867)

As an artist, Heade belonged to the group of American Luminists who combined sensitivity to light and color with a delicately precise outline. In this twilight landscape of the New England coast, the calm sky reflected upon the still surface of the water, the waves slowly rolling over and spreading thinly upon the sand, create an effect of almost uncanny silence. Heade painted many times the effect of light over water or over marshes as the sun slips below the horizon. But he never caught that moment with greater effect than in this painting.

Oil on board: 19½ x 36⅛ inches, sight. Signed at the lower left, *M. J. Heade, 1863*.

48   *Twilight, Spouting Rock Beach   1863*

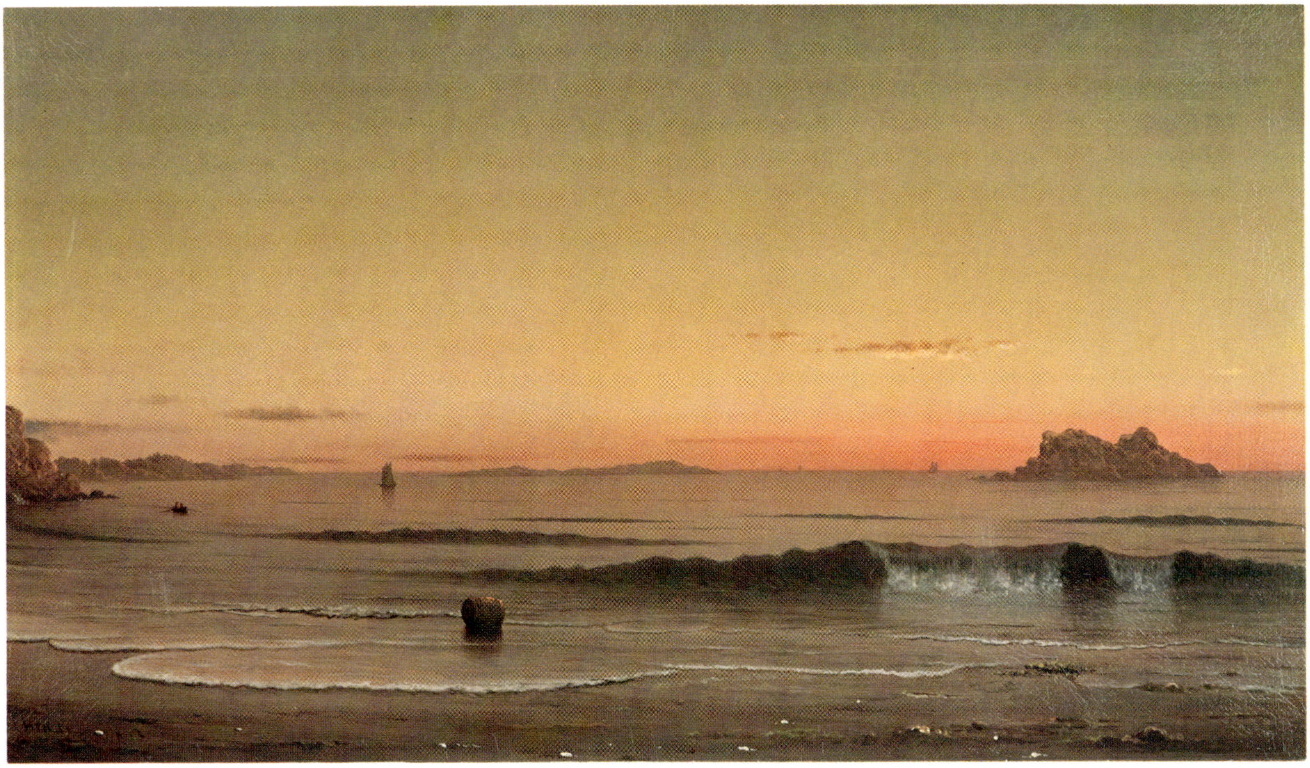

Martin Johnson Heade

The often repeated theme of sunrise or sunset over wide-spreading salt marshes appealed to two sides of Heade's nature. The poetry of light and space and solitude meant a great deal to him. But he was also a sportsman, with a life-long passion for shore bird shooting. To the gunner, dawn and sunset are the best moments of the day. Perhaps the double inspiration may explain why he could paint the subject so frequently with undiminished pleasure. This example belongs to the years 1867-68, which his latest biographer believes saw his highest achievements in landscape (Stebbins, 1969). Although it is hazardous to select one moment from so long a career, especially from one devoted to painting the same favorite themes again and again, certainly Heade never painted light and silence in a more moving way.

Canvas: 14½ x 29½ inches. Signed at the lower left, *M. Heade '68*.

49   *The Great Swamp* 1868

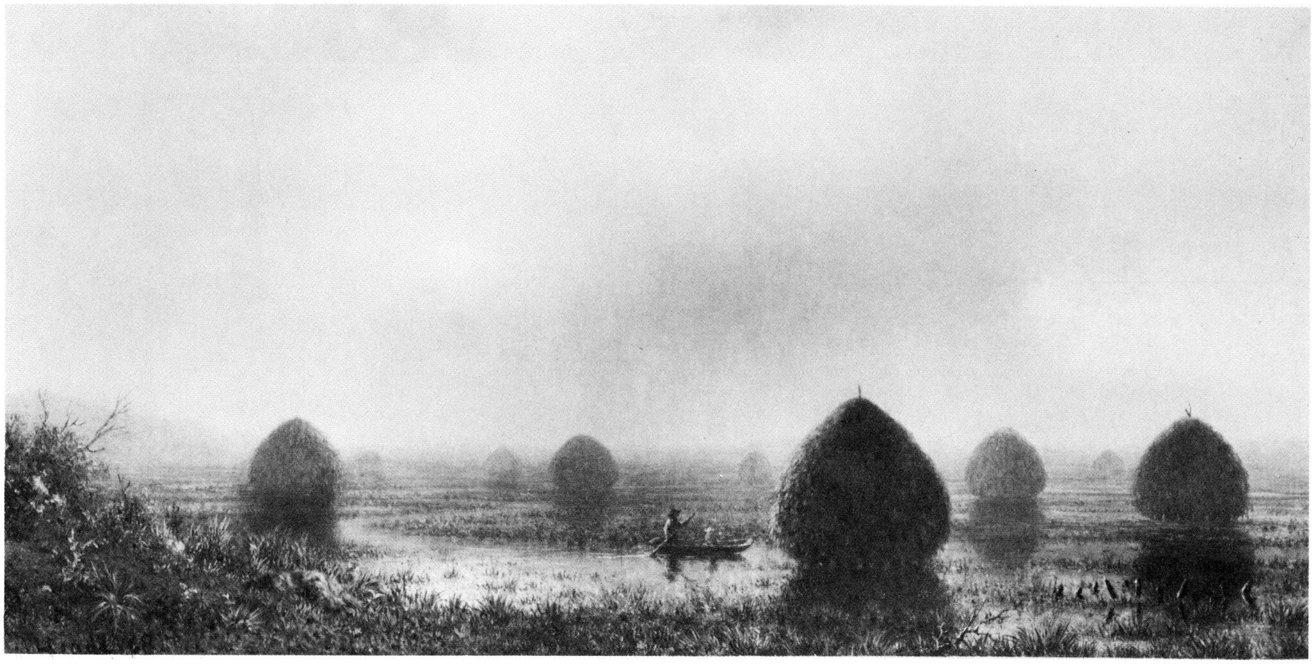

Fitz Hugh Lane 1804-1865

Lane was of a family long established in the fishing port of Gloucester, Massachusetts. Crippled by illness in childhood, he went through life on crutches. His training in art was as apprentice to Pendleton, the lithographer, in Boston. About 1835 he formed his own lithographic firm with J. W. A. Scott, a marine painter; the firm was active until 1847. Under the influence of Robert Salmon, he began to paint in oil in the 1840's. In 1849, after the dissolution of his firm, he returned to Gloucester and devoted himself to marine painting, visiting Maine, New York, and possibly Puerto Rico. His works enjoyed great popularity among the maritime population of Massachusetts. His art evolved from lively ship and harbor scenes, inspired by Salmon, to paintings in which the real theme is the aerial poetry of space and light. In these later landscapes of mood, a stillness seems to reign over all nature, and the sky and light are dramatic actors. This is one of the finest paintings he ever did.

Canvas: 24 x 39⅝ inches. Signed at the lower right, *F. H. Lane 1860*.

50 *Ships and an approaching storm off Camden, Maine 1860*

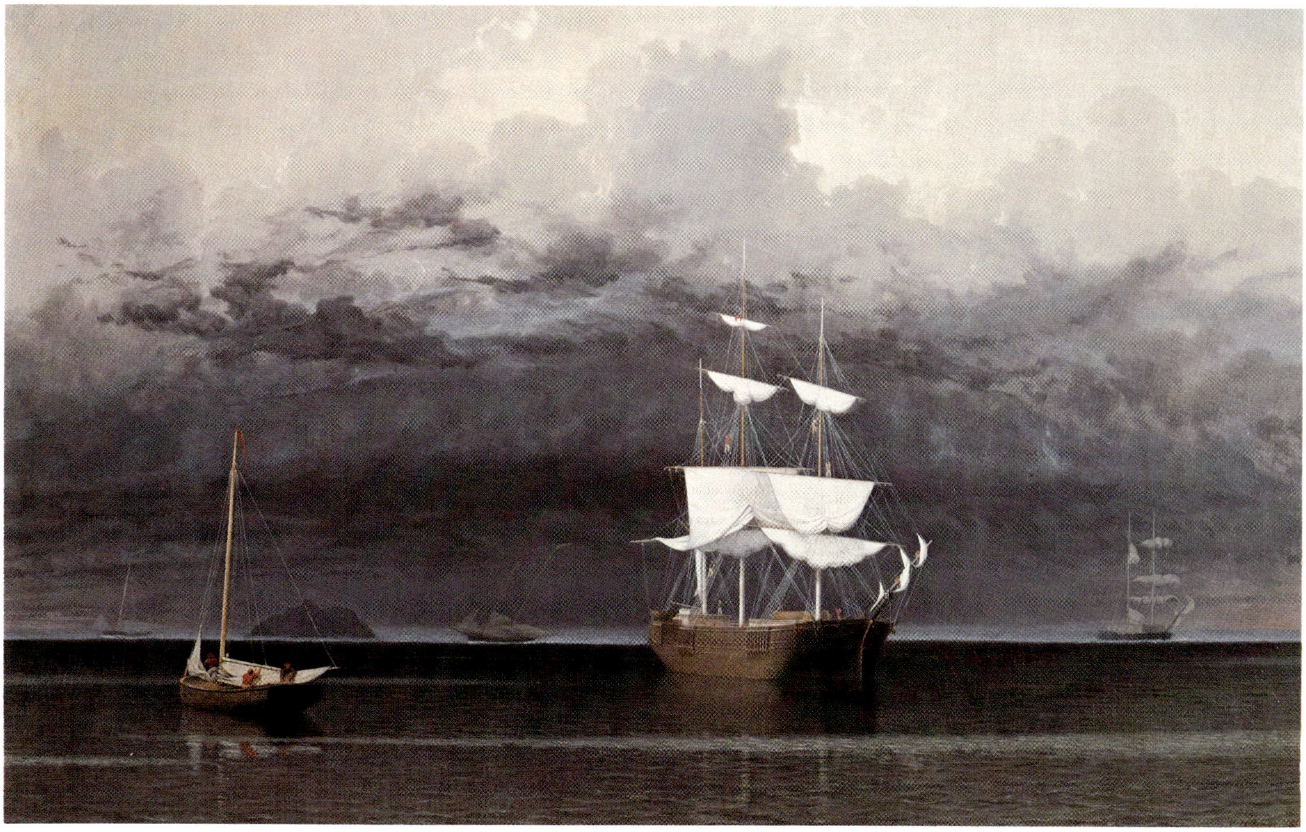

William Page 1811-1885

William Page was born at Albany, New York, in 1811 and spent most of his life in New York City. From 1844 to 1847 he was in Boston, where he did some distinguished portraits; the years 1849 to 1860 were spent in Italy, where he was a prominent figure of the Anglo-American colonies in Rome and Florence. He was one of the most experimental and controversial artists of his generation. Although he had little formal education, his thoughtful and deeply complex mind won him the friendship and admiration of poets and writers like Lowell and the Brownings.

One of the most discerning collectors and critics of that day, James Jackson Jarves, writing in 1864, thought that the most important accomplishment of American painting, and the best hope for its future, was the establishment of a sense of color based on the Venetian mode of painting, giving it the best color sense of any contemporary school. Jarves referred to the deep-toned style introduced by Allston, of which Page was the leading exponent at mid-century. But before Page's death in 1885 the trend of taste turned wholly against him, and he fell into complete obscurity. The revival of his name did not begin until 1937 when his grandson made a gift of Page's portraits of himself and his wife to the Detroit Institute of Arts (Richardson, 1938).

Cupid and Psyche is an example of both the originality of his art and the controversy that he often aroused. Page's model was a cast in his studio of the classical marble in the Capitoline Museum. When submitted to the National Academy of Design in 1843, the picture was refused by the exhibition committee, although seven of Page's portraits were hung. The picture was shown at the Boston Athenaeum in 1843 and its rejection in New York led to its attack and defense (Taylor, 1957). What went wrong? To say that it shocked Victorian prudery is too simplistic. In *Rees's Encyclopaedia,* the standard American encyclopaedia of that day, two engravings of the Capitoline group illustrated the article on sculpture. Nude and semi-nude figures in paintings, engravings and book illustration were as common then as now; and the use of sculpture as a model, though rare in nineteenth-century America, had the precedent of centuries of artistic practice behind it. The explanation lies, I believe, in the brooding power of Page's imagination that makes these ancient shadows alive.

Canvas: 10⅞ x 14¾ inches.

51   *Cupid and Psyche 1843*

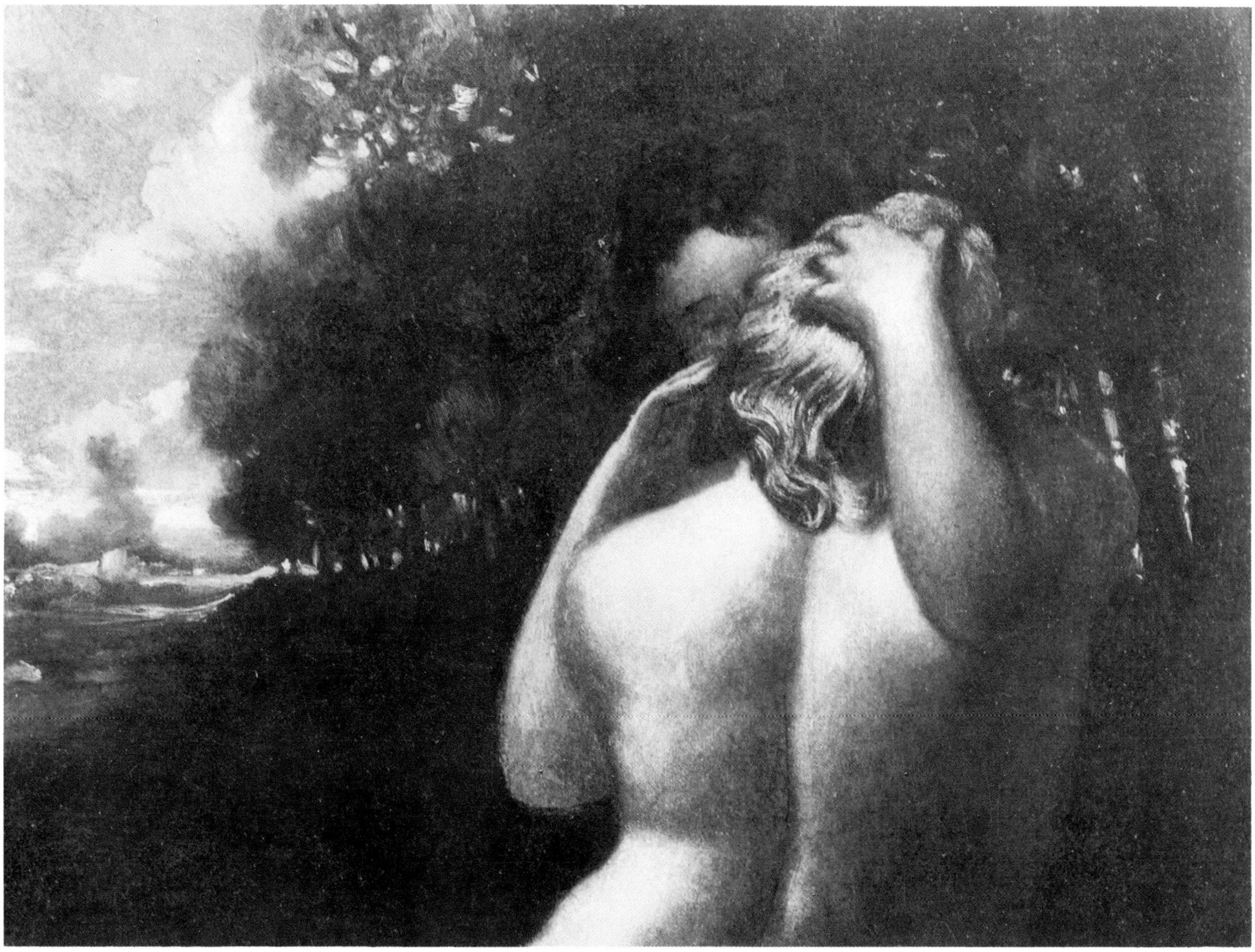

William Page

Page found in his mind a new vision of this ancient subject. The figures move in procession into the picture from the right. They come to a cliff's edge in the twilight. The land of Egypt opens vast and mysterious before them—a wide empty valley, a pyramid dimly visible. Page's use of sculptural models is subtler than in the earlier picture. One cannot say that the Mother and Child are based upon Michelangelo's group in the Medici Chapel, or Joseph upon Cellini's Perseus; but the suggestion is there and the grandeur and melancholy of the one and the tense energy of the other echo in his figures. It is an exceptional picture in its composition, its deep shadowy tone, its grave mood.

Canvas: 36 x 71⅝ inches.

52 *The Flight into Egypt* 1859

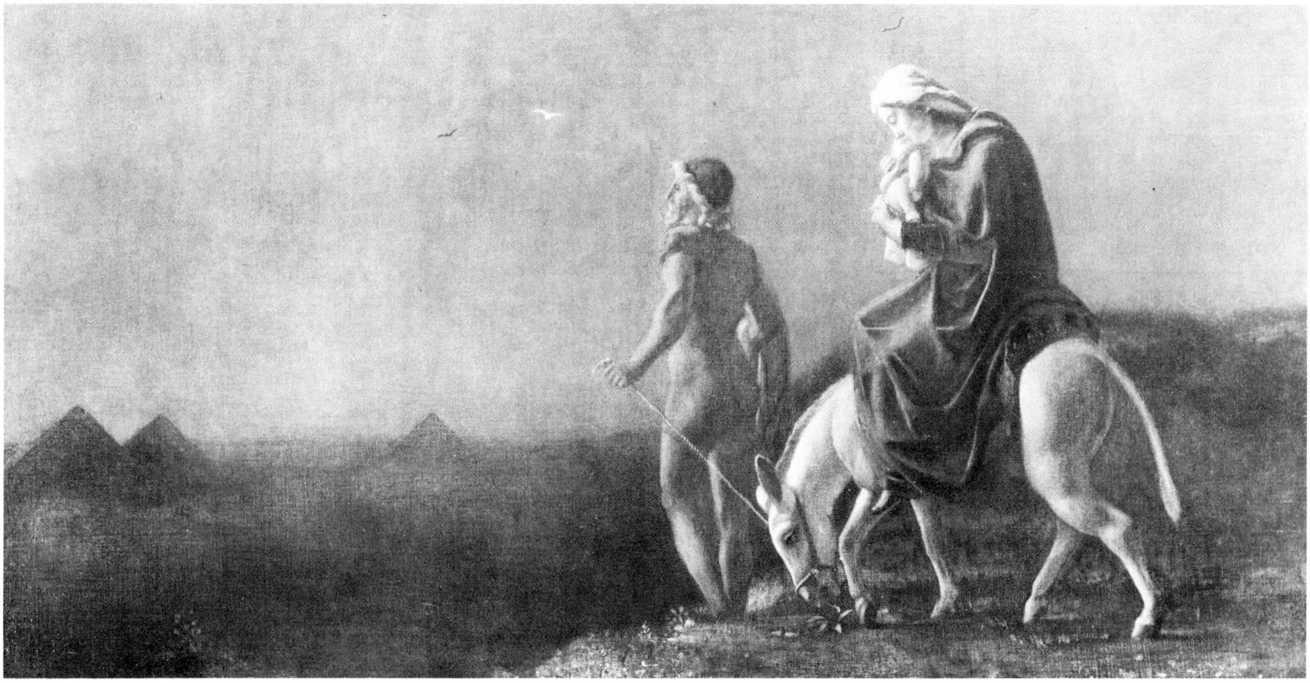

William Rimmer 1816-1879

The two sculptures in this exhibition, Eakins' *Arcadian* and Rimmer's *Dying Centaur*, have classical titles; but unlike so much other nineteenth-century sculpture, they do not derive their interest solely from their subjects. They create their own inner life and harmony—Eakins' an image of repose, Rimmer's a violent energy falling back upon itself. It is as if the two-thousand-year-old trunk of classical art had put forth two fresh leaves.

Rimmer firmly believed himself to be the son of the last Dauphin of France, a belief that partly explains the pride and isolation of his life. As a young man living in a poor suburb of Boston, he worked at a variety of occupations, painting signs, setting type, teaching music, making soap, cobbling shoes. He became a self-taught doctor, a self-taught painter, a self-taught sculptor. He was a teacher of anatomy in art schools of Boston and New York who influenced many younger talents; his book, *Art Anatomy* (1877), is still in use after a hundred years (Gardner, 1945). Yet he left few works either in painting or sculpture that express his stature. This one does.

Its story is typical of the fragmentary and incomplete nature of his career. The *Dying Centaur* was not cast in bronze in Rimmer's lifetime. The plaster was deposited with the rest of his artistic estate in The Museum of Fine Arts, Boston. In 1906 a single bronze was cast from it for the Metropolitan Museum of Art (Gardner, 1965). The original plaster was subsequently acquired from his estate by Gutzon Borglum, the sculptor, who took it on his travels while he worked in the Black Hills and on Stone Mountain, Georgia. When acquired from Borglum's son by the Kennedy Galleries in 1967, the model was in three pieces. It was carefully repaired by Joseph Ternback, and fifteen bronzes were cast from it. The original plaster is now in the Yale University Art Gallery.

Bronze: height 21⅞; width of base 23¾, depth 17¾ inches. Signed *W. Rimmer*. Cast number one.

53   *The Dying Centaur ca. 1871*

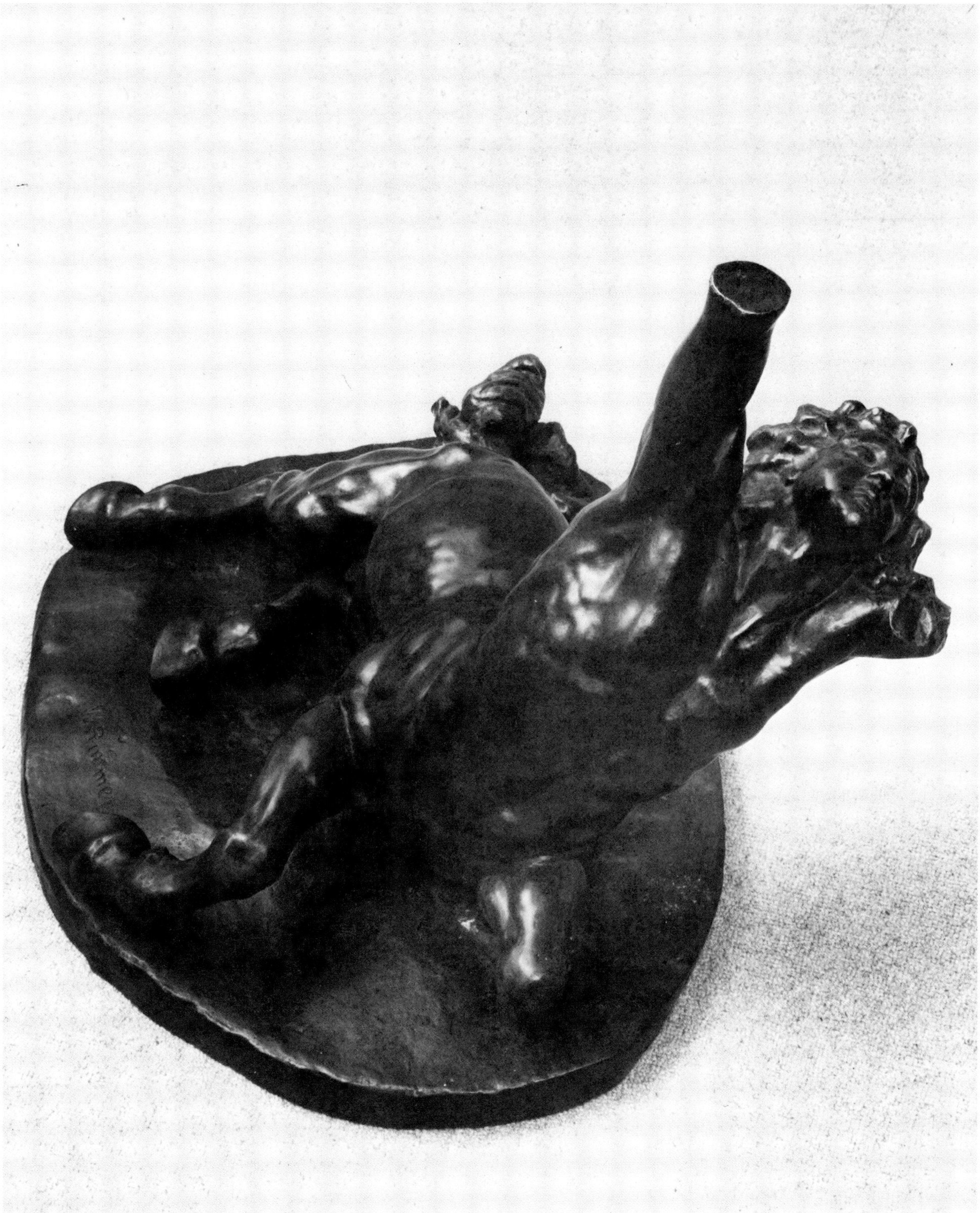

Worthington Whittredge 1820-1910

Whittredge was one of the earliest artists of note to appear from the newly-settled region west of the Alleghany Mountains. Born on a pioneer farm in the forests of southern Ohio, he found his way to Cincinnati, where he taught himself to be an excellent landscapist. He spent ten years in Europe, studying in Brussels, Düsseldorf, Rome and the great picture galleries; yet he returned doubting the value of long foreign study for an American artist. Upon his return he settled in New York City.

From the first, his instinct was that light was the great source of poetry in landscape. He was a luminist, using few colors but a rich, subtle range of tone. In this rare night scene, painted with characteristic subtlety of tone, he showed his sensitivity to the mystery of a moment.

Canvas: 14⅜ x 18½. Signed at the lower right: *W. Whittredge 1851.*

54 *Herons on the Marsh in Moonlight 1851*

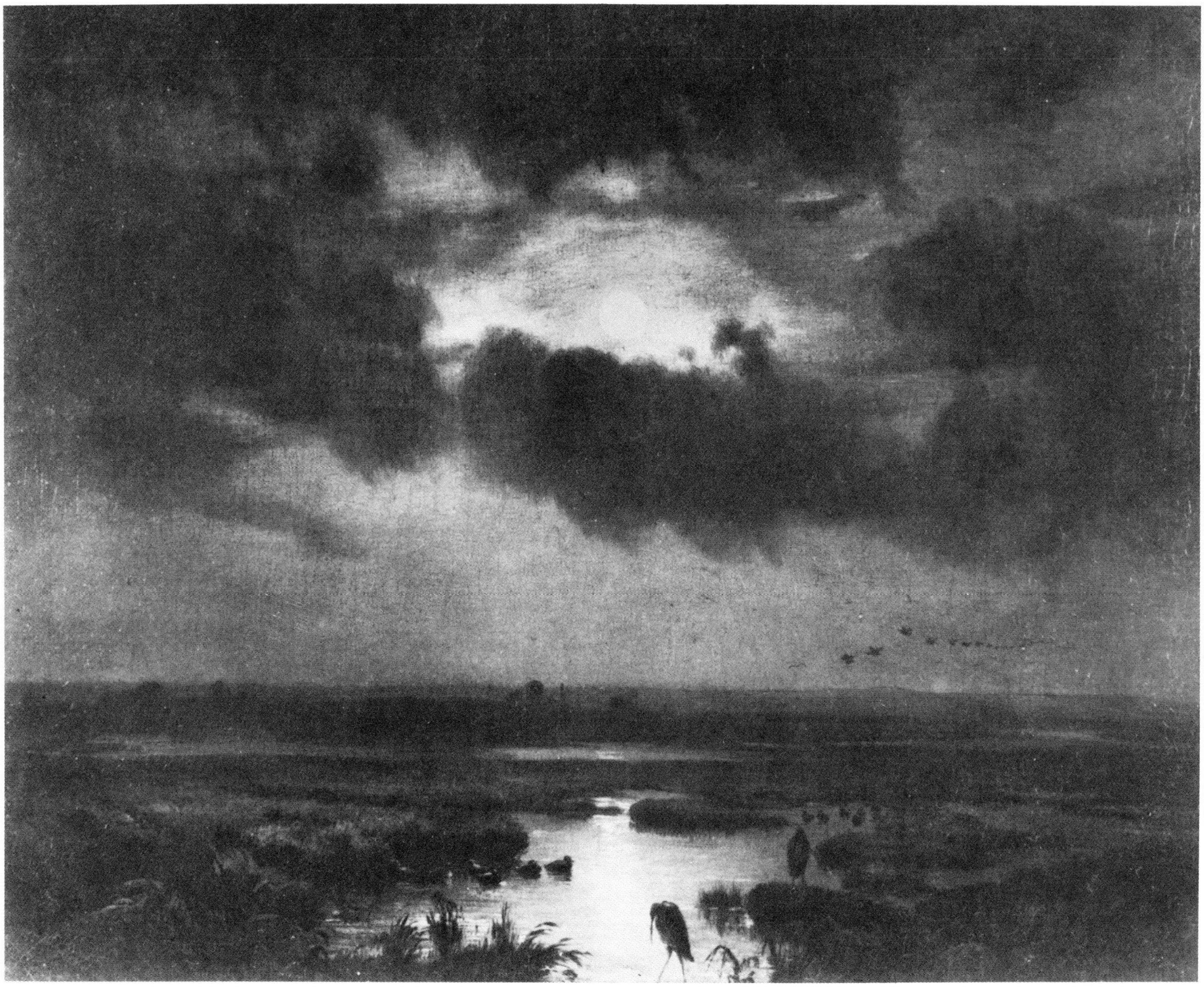

VIII

The Flowering of the Nineteenth Century: After the Civil War

A continuing surge of travel after the war carried a great many young artists to Europe to study in Italy, France, England, and Germany. Some returned, bringing a variety of European contemporary styles to America; some remained, becoming expatriates. A new type of traveled, cosmopolitan life appeared. At its best it produced highly cultured artists of wide horizon, like Sargent or La Farge: brilliant men and brilliant stylists.

Almost as if in reaction, others made the plain world of everyday America their subject. The secret poetry lurking beneath its prosaic exterior was their passion, and great art they made of it.

From the first deeply religious settlers in the seventeenth century, an introspective strain had touched American life, and made itself felt in artists as diverse as Fuller and Vedder.

This period has receded in time far enough from "only yesterday" into history. Our new perspective has brought re-evaluations and surprises. A remarkably strong and varied group of still-life painters, almost overlooked by their contemporaries, is one. The impressionist landscape painters are now widely collected and the subject of great affection; other landscapists and figure painters are only beginning to be re-studied. The realistic figure painters in this exhibition will show that Thomas Eakins was not an isolated figure, as he has often been regarded; he was one of a numerous and most interesting group of artists, all realists, and all worth study and appreciation.

Thomas P. Anshutz 1851-1912

It is said of the sculptor Flaxman that when asked where he found the handsome figures and poses depicted in his illustrations to Homer, he replied, "In the streets of London." Thomas Eakins, Eastman Johnson and Winslow Homer, sensitive as they were to the painter's vision of light and space, to time and weather and human feelings, also looked at the people around them and saw the human figure as sculpture. It is one of their great merits.

Anshutz was a pupil of Eakins and absorbed his lessons. At least once in this picture, almost his first independent composition, he did something that neither Eakins or Homer could or did do. While visiting his family's old home at Wheeling, West Virginia, he saw pictorial possibilities in an iron foundry and in the men on whose strong muscles the production of iron was dependent in those days. He made careful studies of both men and the foundry before painting this scene of muscular figures relaxing in the noon day sun. The frieze-like design, the rich but sober color, the contrasts of light and dark emphasize its monumentality. American artists in the nineteenth century painted few pictures of industry. This may well be the most important.

It was bought in 1883 by Thomas B. Clarke, one of the best collectors of American art at that time, and engraved by Frederick Juengling for *Harper's Weekly* (August 30, 1884). But it is said that the artist felt there was no interest in pictures of this sort, and he never painted this type of subject again.

Canvas: 17 x 24 inches. Signed at the lower left, *Thos. Anshutz.*

55 *Ironworkers—Noontime 1880-1881*

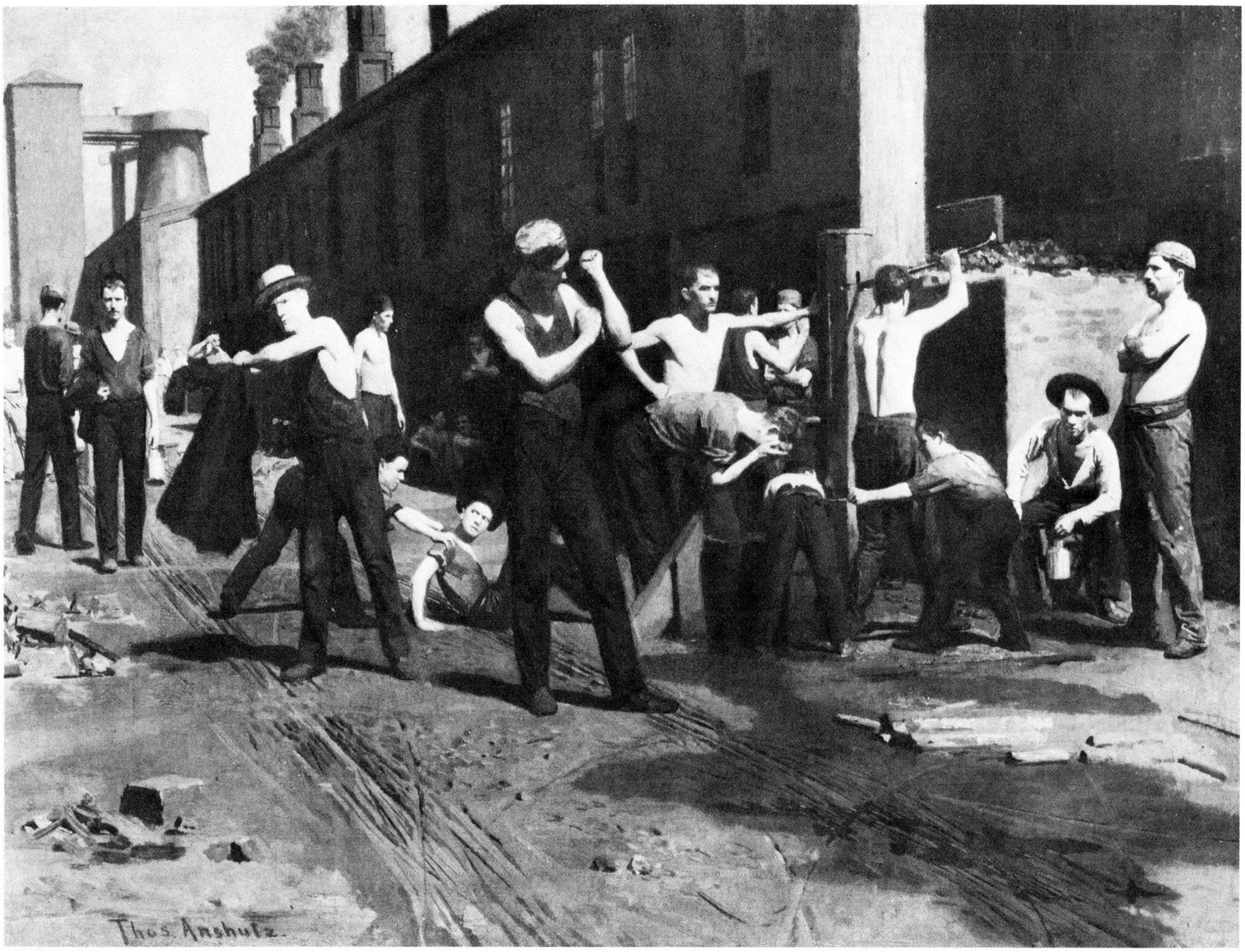
Thos. Anshutz

Alfred T. Bricher 1837-1908

This watercolor and Winslow Homer's *Backgammon* (No. 70) represent the first phase of watercolor after the founding of the American Watercolor Society in 1867 marked a new interest in that medium. Before that date watercolor was a form of colored drawing. It now began to play a significant part in broadening and loosening the technique of American painters. Bricher became a member of the Society in 1872.

  Bricher, born in Portsmouth, New Hampshire, worked first in Newburyport and Boston, carrying on the tradition of Salmon and Lane. In 1868 he abandoned New England for New York City, took a studio on Union Square and built a home on Staten Island. He was a painter of the seacoast, and most often of the sea and shore in moments of spacious calm. A mood of sunlit peace fills this watercolor.

Watercolor: 14½ x 20⅞ inches. Signed at the lower right, *AT Bricher 78* (the initials forming a monogram).

56 *Summer Enchantment 1878*

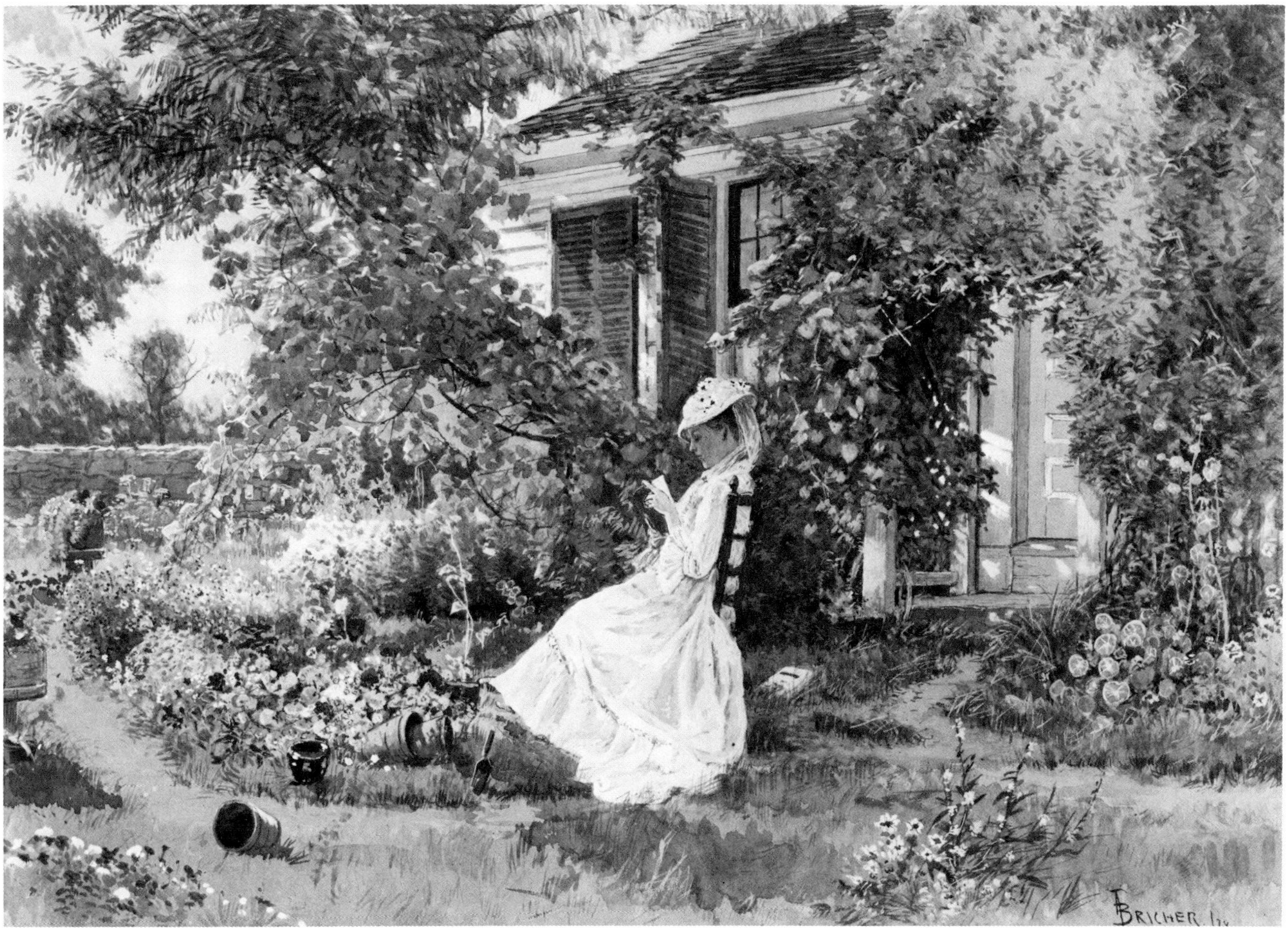
BRICHER

J. G. Brown 1831-1893

This scene on the Hudson River, so grand in scale, so rich in its disposition of light and shade, so pleasing in its aerial perspective, is the work of an artist not ordinarily thought of as a landscape painter. J. G. Brown was a genre painter, typed as a painter of boys of the New York streets. His newsboys and shoeshine boys were immensely popular in his lifetime. After the fashion of his day, he painted these ragged urchins as amusing and pleasant to watch, rather than as the discouraging social problem we see in children of the streets.

   Brown was, however, a painter of real gifts. To the traveler of today who approaches New York only by air, the Palisades may mean nothing. However, to one looking at them from the water, this wall of brown volcanic rock, rising from three to five hundred feet above the river and extending nearly thirty-five miles from Hoboken northward makes a grand and varied effect. Here and there little valleys break through the wall and give access to pleasant country behind; Snead's Landing is at the foot of one of these breaks. Brown's painting catches the qualities—the scale, the slanting light of afternoon, the animation of the river traffic—that lent charm to the river passage. A work of his youth, when his eye was fresh and his mind exploratory, it shows that there is more to J. G. Brown than we have supposed.

Canvas: 38¼ x 71½ inches. Signed at the lower left: *J. G. Brown/NY 1867*.

57   *View of the Palisades, Snead's Landing, Hudson River 1867*

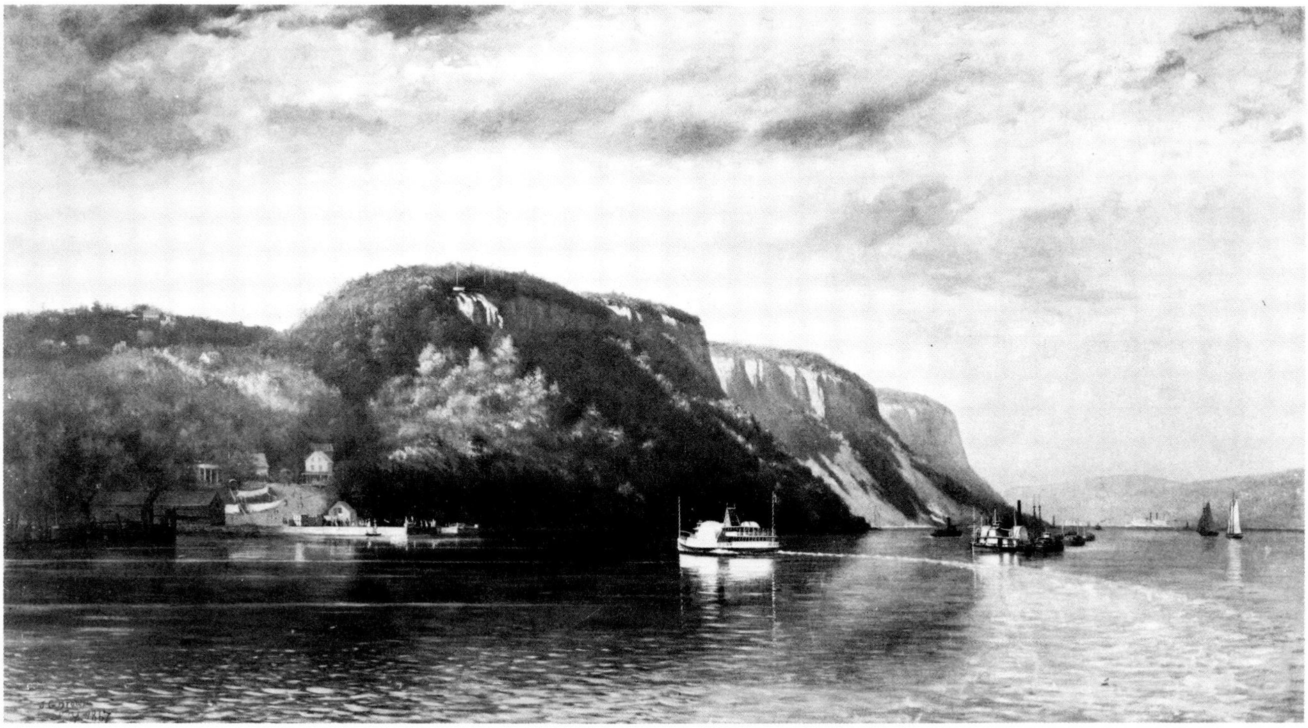

George DeForest Brush 1855-1941

In this pastel, Brush was working out of character. He was primarily a figure painter. Samuel Isham thought him one of the best figure painters the American school had produced (Isham, 1905). The opinions of that very discerning critic must always be taken seriously. In this still life the spare, disciplined design, the luminosity, the note of unconventionality are the mark of a gifted artist experimenting in a new vein with unusual and attractive results.

Pastel: 19½ x 13¾ inches. Signed at the lower right, *Geo. DeForest Brush.*

58 *Flowers*

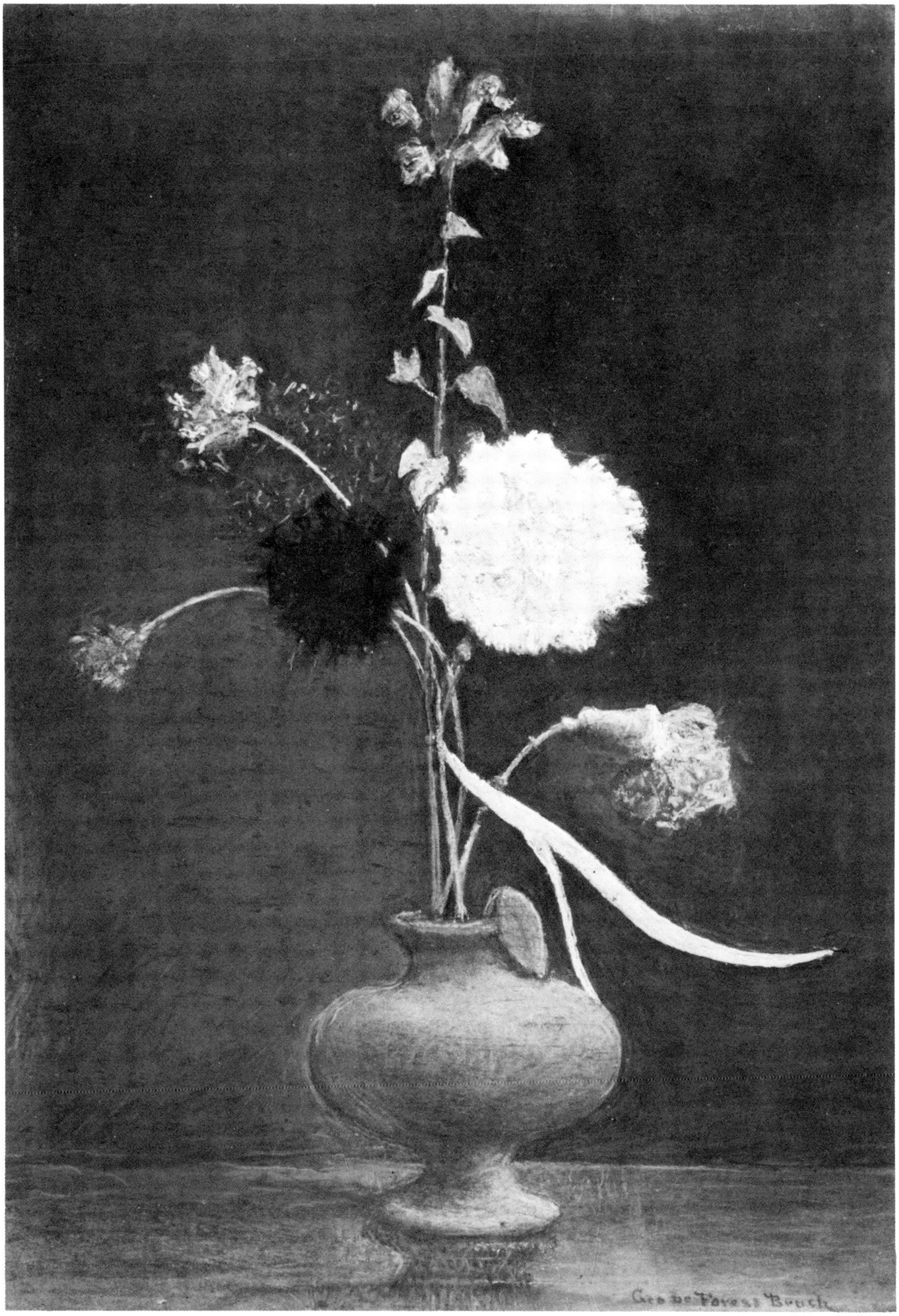
Geo De Forest Brush

Dennis M. Bunker 1861-1890

Bunker died at twenty-nine, leaving only a small number of pictures to show his talent. Born in New York, he studied at the National Academy of Design and with Chase at the newly organized Art Students League before going on in 1882 to Paris. There he studied under Gérôme, with whom Eakins had studied a few years before. Gérôme must have been a great teacher. His American pupils had unbounded admiration for him. And yet—and this is the mark of the rarest kind of teaching—they did not imitate him.

Bunker's brief career spans the divide in American painting between the warm, rich chiaroscuro of the seventies (to which Eakins remained faithful all his life) and the blonde, high-keyed palette that came in the eighties, first with *plein air* painting and later with Impressionism. Most of Bunker's landscapes, whether painted at Medfield or at Calcot in England (where he and Sargent spent a summer painting together) are in the clear, cool palette of *plein air*. *The Guitar Player* belongs to his earlier period. It was painted in New York City after his return from France in 1885, while he had a studio there for a time before going to Boston to teach in a private art school (Gammell, 1953).

Artist's studios in the eighties were of two kinds. One type was Chase's famous studio, familiar since he painted it many times, each picture a period piece. Chase filled his studio with souvenirs of taste and travel—antique furniture, oriental rugs, gold-framed pictures on the walls, a profusion of bric-a-brac from all over the world, a white cockatoo, a Russian wolfhound wandering about. It was a setting for elegant parties, when Carmencita danced for the guests or a visiting violinist played. People were flattered to be asked there. Bunker, on the other hand, shows us the studio of a bohemian artist (as such he thought himself), the rather bare work place of an artist proud of his poverty and detachment from all the world except his art.

Canvas: 26 x 36½ inches. Signed on the bench at the right, *Dennis M. Bunker/New York 1885*.

59 *The Guitar Player 1885*

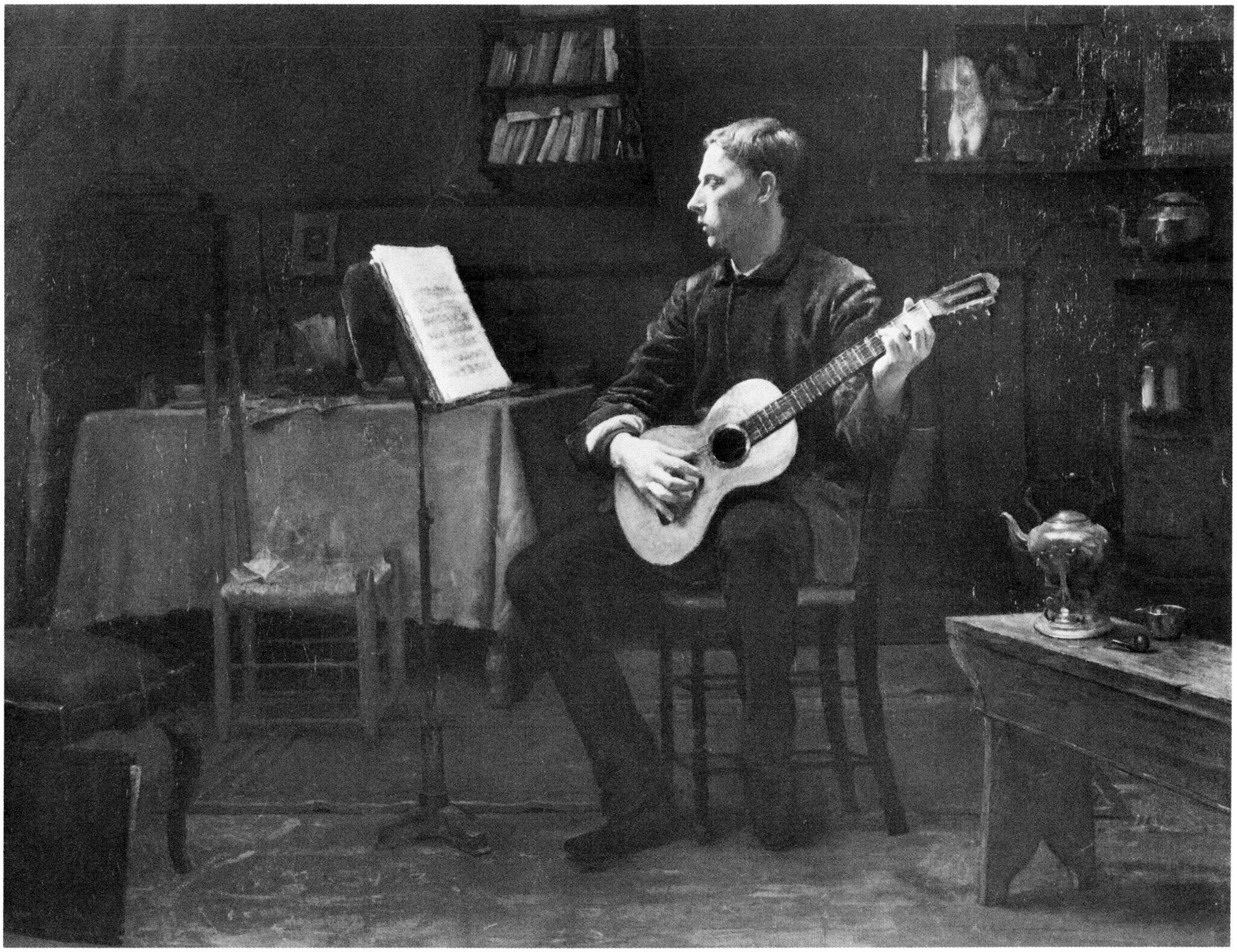

Jefferson Davis Chalfant 1856-1931

Wilmington, Delaware, and the valley of the Brandywine reaching north into Pennsylvania have produced a number of talented painters, from Howard Pyle to Andrew Wyeth, during the past century. Chalfant, who spent his life in Wilmington, was first a cabinetmaker. About 1880 he turned to painting still life, following the lead of Harnett but with qualities of his own. His genre paintings are rather rare. This, painted on an engraver's copper plate, shows his lustrous color, his precision and intense actuality, which make it almost a *trompe l'oeil*.

Oil on copper: 13⅛ x 9½ inches. Signed at the lower left, *J. D. Chalfant*. Dated *1899* on the reverse side and inscribed *The Clockmaker   J. D. Chalfant*.

60   *The Old Clockmaker 1899*

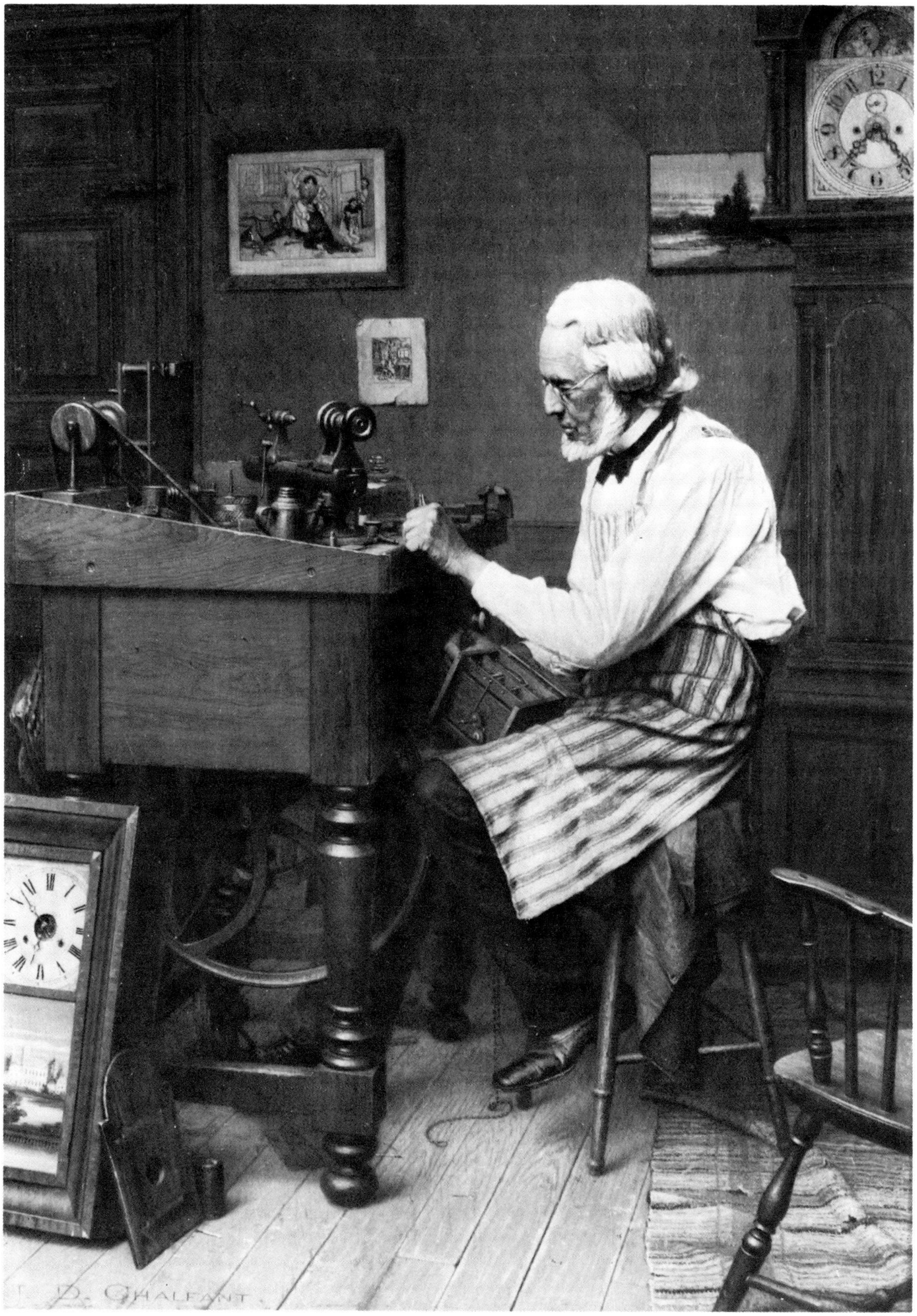
J. D. CHALFANT

William Merritt Chase 1849-1916

In 1891 Chase opened the earliest outdoor summer school of painting at Shinnecock near the outer tip of Long Island. During the eleven summers spent there he found an unending source of pleasure in the view of the path winding through the low beach growth toward the shore and the blue sea beyond. He painted it many times—never better than here. His awareness of the all-enveloping light of outdoors, his touches of the well-loaded brush to record nuances of luminous color in this very simple subject, illustrate his art in a particularly happy aspect.

Oil on panel: 9⅞ x 13¾ inches. Signed at the lower left: *Wm M. Chase.*

61 *Near the Beach, Shinnecock*

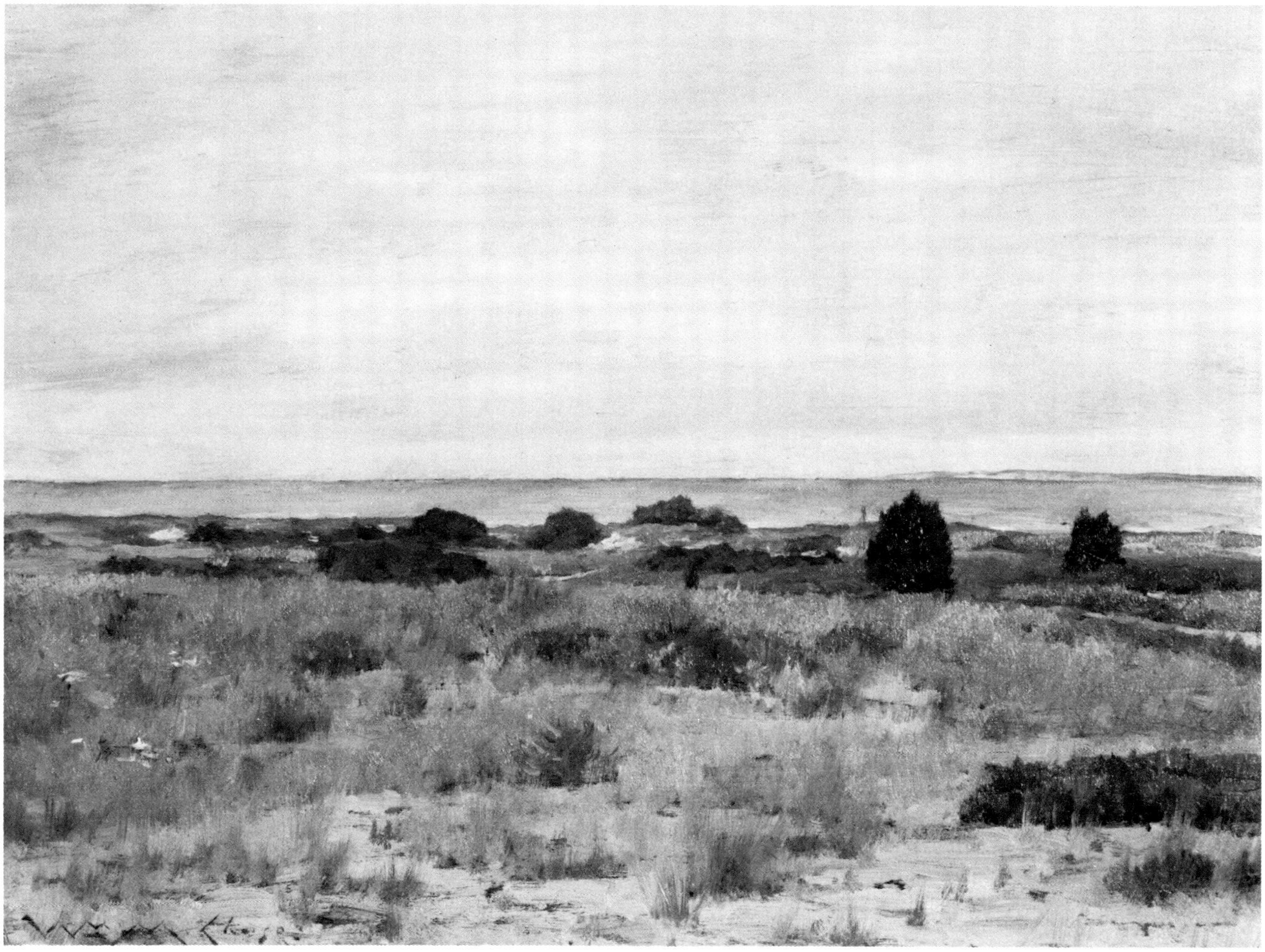

Samuel Colman 1832-1920

This charming little picture belongs to a distinctive moment of landscape painting at the end of the nineteenth century. Muted tones, a broad atmospheric touch, subjects such as one might find during a walk at twilight in a familiar locale, took the place of the great dramas of earth and sky and seasons. The century in which so many artists had explored so many aspects of nature closed on a note of quiet.

Colman was born in 1832, was a pupil of Durand, and first exhibited at the National Academy of Design in 1851 when he was only nineteen. His friends were men like Vedder and Sanford Gifford. Like them he loved the picturesqueness of foreign lands, traveled widely, and carried out his subtle studies of light in a warm and tonal palette. In 1867, after fighting in the Civil War, he and James Smillie organized the American Watercolor Society, which played an important role in raising that medium to the high place it occupied in the later part of the century.

The poetry of his work can be described in the words used by Samuel Isham to characterize the group of artists to which be belongs: "Their pictures on the wall of a room make no insistent appeal to attention, but their presence is felt half unconsciously like that of old and sympathetic friends whose real value can only be comprehended after long acquaintance." (Isham, 1905)

Canvas: 8-3/16 x 14⅞ inches. Signed at lower left, *Sam. Colman*. On the reverse, a label of the American Art Association, New York, sale of March 25, 1903. *November, Irvington*.

62 *November, Irvington, New Jersey*

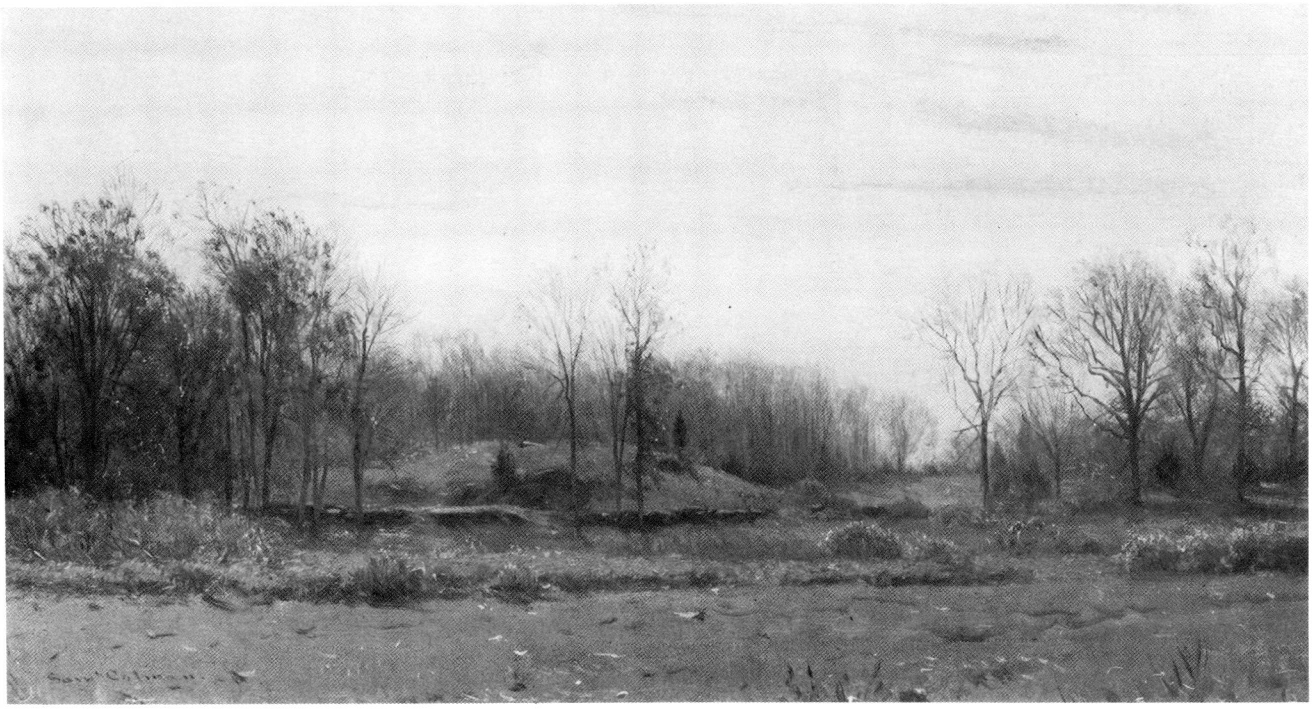

Susan Macdowell Eakins   1851-1938

Susan Macdowell was a pupil of Thomas Eakins at the Pennsylvania Academy of the Fine Arts. She married her instructor in 1884 and moved into the family home on Mount Vernon Street, where she and her husband each had a studio on the top floor. She continued to paint until the end of her life. Although her husband considered her the best American woman painter, she exhibited little. Her work is different in feeling from her husband's, yet in tune with it in quietness of statement, in unity and depth of mood. She was to outlive her husband by twenty-two years and paint in this quiet feeling to the end. (Adelman & Casteras, 1973.)

Canvas: 15½ x 17½ inches. Signed at the upper right, *S. H. Macdowell 1880* and below with the initials, *S. M. E.*

63   *Woman Seated   1880*

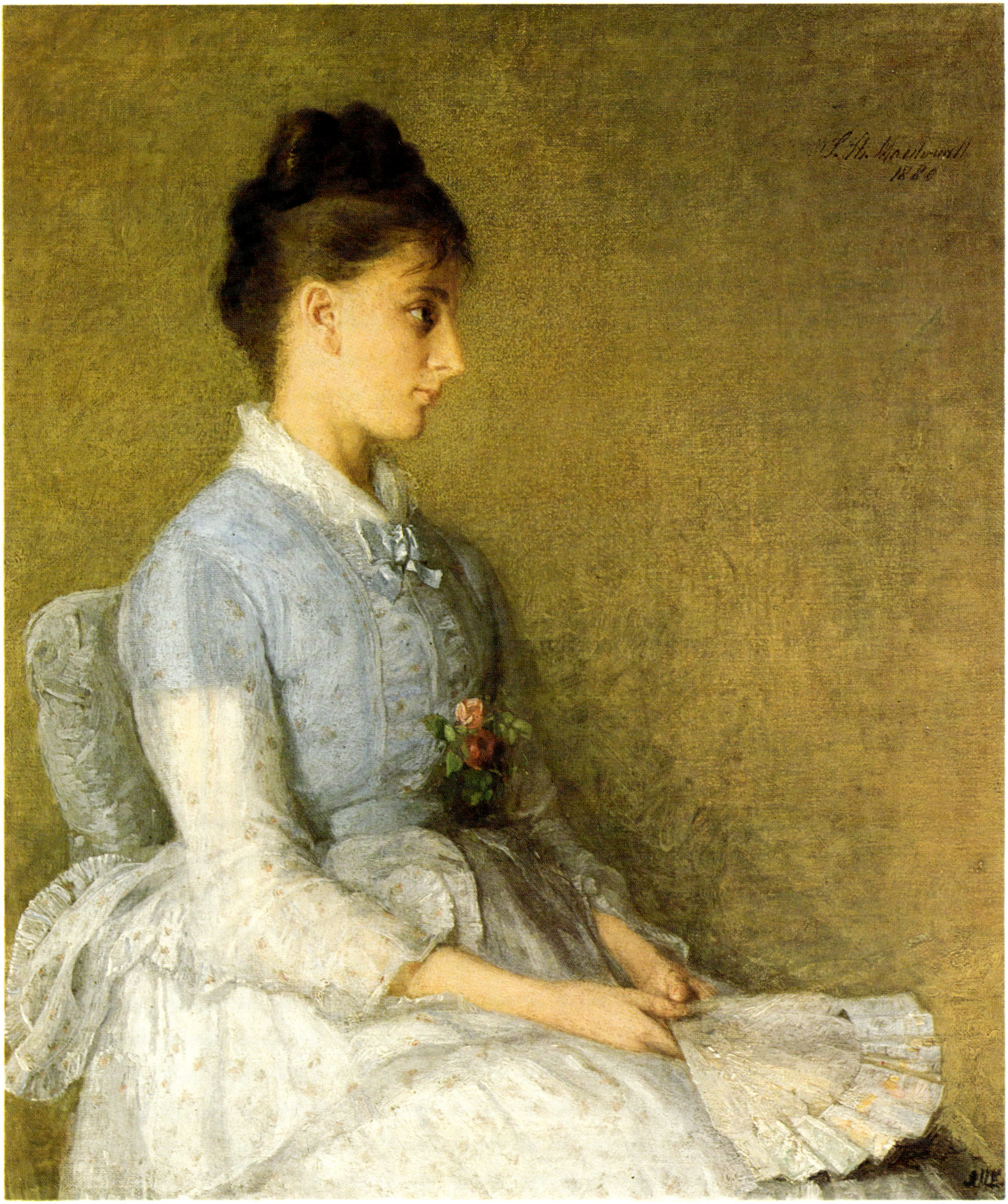

Thomas Eakins 1844-1916

Few American artists have been so closely identified with their native city as Eakins with Philadelphia. Except for his student years abroad and a brief visit to the western plains in 1886, he did not travel. He painted the people, the home life, the sports and recreations of his own city; as a portrait painter he recorded its doctors, scientists, scholars and clergy. He was born in 1844, the son of the "Writing Master" whose portrait is in The Metropolitan Museum of Art. He studied first at the Pennsylvania Academy of the Fine Arts; from 1866-69 was a pupil of Gérôme, Bonnat and the sculptor Dumont in Paris; and spent a year in Spain before returning home. His art of disciplined, objective realism and warm, dark tonality evolved independently and, in many ways, opposed the growing movements of French Impressionism, post-impressionism, Fauvism and other international currents of his lifetime. In the 1880's he became deeply interested in photography and in relief sculpture, which, he said, "holds a place between a painting or drawing on a flat surface and a piece of full sculpture." In 1884 he married Susan Macdowell, a student at The Pennsylvania Academy. He taught painting and lectured on anatomy at the Academy until 1886, when a disagreement on policy forced his resignation. He then continued his teaching at the Art Students League of Philadelphia.

A sculptor's understanding of the human body was at the center of Eakins's art. He taught his painting students to draw with the brush—that is, in the round, with light and shadow—and to learn the bones and muscles by anatomical dissection. When opportunity offered, he executed monumental reliefs in bronze—one for the Trenton Battle Monument (1893) and, in collaboration with William R. O'Donovan, another for the Memorial Arch in Prospect Park, Brooklyn (1891). For his own study and pleasure he did a number of small reliefs in the early eighties when he was making photographic studies of girls wearing Greek costume. This study of the rhythmic movement of the human figure and its drapery is classical sculpture in the true sense, although its richly pictorial effects of light and shadow show the painterly side of his art.

This is apparently a unique casting in bronze. At the time of the exhibition of gifts and loans of Eakins's works from Mrs. Eakins and Miss Mary Adeline Williams at the Philadelphia Museum of Art in March 1930, the relief was still in plaster. In a letter to Fiske Kimball, director of the museum, on March 4, 1930, Mrs. Eakins wrote, "The relief of figures in Arcadia and the relief of (a) single figure, which I had to send in plaster, I hope later on to have cast in bronze." The form of the signature is explained by a sentence in a letter to Henri Marceau, curator, April 25, 1930: "Mr. Ricardo Bertillo (of the Roman Bronze Works) will send a man to sign all the bronzes that are not signed." (Letters in the Philadelphia Museum of Art, through the kindness of Mr. Theodor Siegl). The bronze was in Mrs. Eakins's possession in 1932 when Lloyd Goodrich saw it (Goodrich, 1933, No. 507).

Bronze bas relief: 8¼ x 5 inches. Signed at lower right: *Thomas Eakins*. Foundry mark at lower left, *Roman Bronze Works, N.Y.*

64 *An Arcadian 1883*

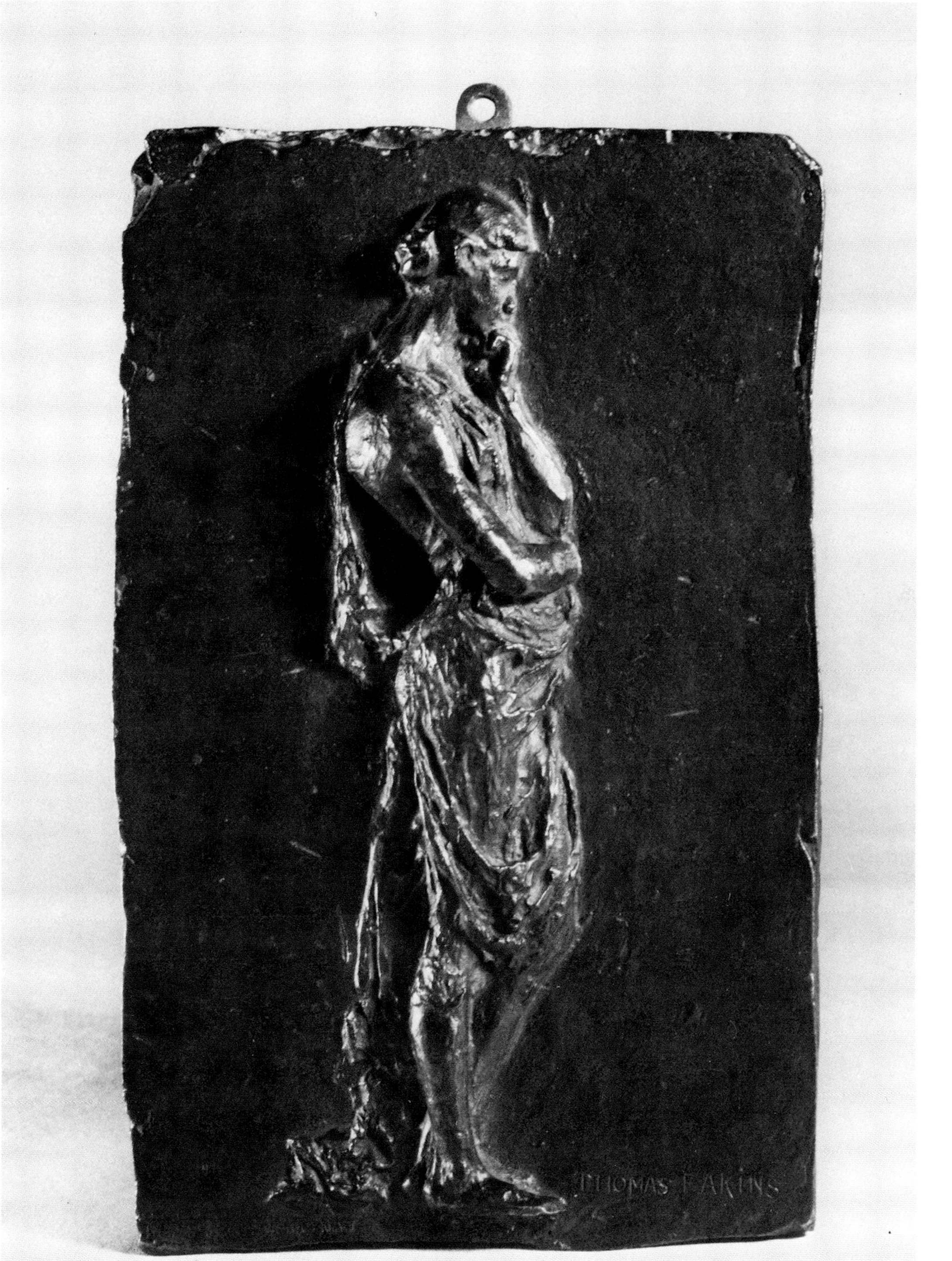
THOMAS EAKINS

Thomas Eakins

This portrait is a reminder of Eakins's preference for painting his sitters in old clothing that looked as if it had been lived in and had assumed the character of the sitter. Mr. Leslie W. Miller, a painter and head of the School of Industrial Art (now the Philadelphia College of Art), recalled that when he was painted by Eakins, "he not only wanted me to wear some old clothes but insisted that I go and don a little old sack coat—hardly more than a blouse—that he remembered seeing me in in my bicycle days, and which I certainly never would have worn facing an audience, which the portrait represented me as doing. He did much the same thing with Dean Holland. He made the poor Dean go and put on a pair of old shoes that he kept to go fishing in, and painted him shod in this way when he faced a distinguished audience on a very impressive occasion." (Lloyd Goodrich, 1933). Frank Jay St. John was a business man, a coal dealer. We know nothing of how Eakins came to paint him, but every detail—his face, hands, the way he sat and held his head, his pince-nez—show how much meaning and character Eakins saw in each. Something in this rather obscure and unsuccessful man appealed strongly. Eakins made him a figure one does not forget.

There is a photograph of Eakins's friend, the sculptor Samuel Murray, modeling a bust of St. John at the time he was sitting for Eakins (Hendricks, 1969).

Canvas: 24 x 20 inches. Signed at middle right: *Eakins 1900*.

65 *Frank Jay St. John 1900*

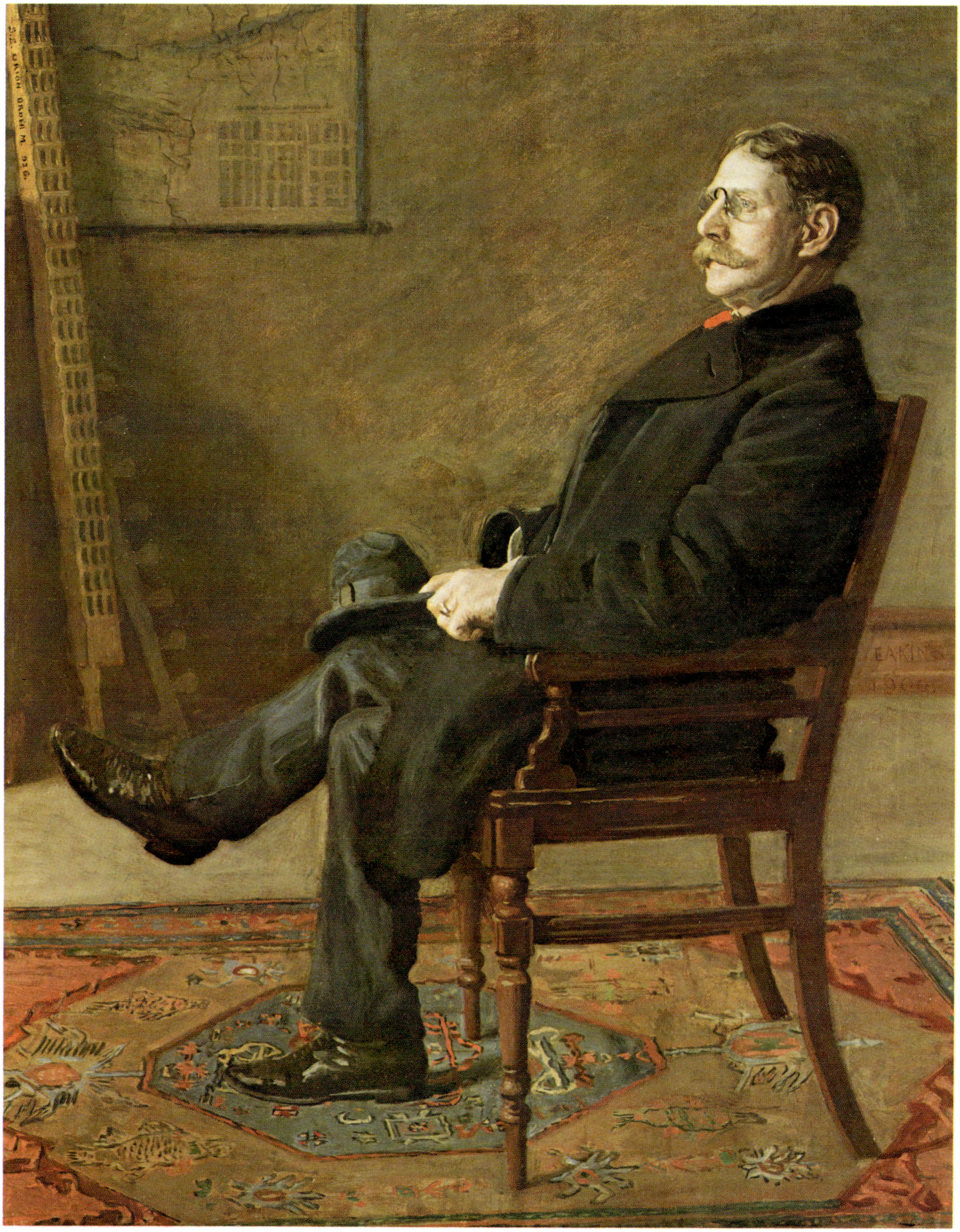
EAKINS

Henry Farny 1847-1916

Farny, born in Alsace in 1847, was brought to the United States in 1850. The family settled first in a wild region of western Pennsylvania, then moved to Cincinnati. Farny began his career at the age of eighteen as a black-and-white illustrator. Study abroad in Rome, Dusseldorf, Munich and Vienna in 1866-69 and again in 1870 made him an accomplished painter. From 1881 onward he made many journeys to the West. He first attracted notice by his illustrations for Frank H. Cushing's memoir of his life among the Zuni (*The Century Magazine,* 1882-1883), which led Joseph Pennell to name Farny as one of the artists whose technique should be studied by students. Farny spent most of his mature years in Cincinnati, where he died in 1916. His work was so greatly appreciated at home that his pictures have only recently begun to find their way into collections elsewhere.

Farny was a painter of the West. The march of explorers and settlers across the continent, the life of plainsmen and Indians, have been painted in many ways. Some artists depicted picturesque costumes, chases, fights, adventures, cowboy-and-Indian stuff: good fun but not very deep. Others, like Farny, brought great qualities of imagination, observation and style to the interpretation of his subject. He began as a black-and-white illustrator for *Harper's, The Century,* and *Leslie's.* These magazines demanded illustration on a very high level and Farny never lost the illustrator's aim to be true, to show how people actually looked, to catch the exact flavor of a place. As a painter in oils he shows great gifts of atmosphere and observation, giving us most convincingly the sense of a day, a place or a moment in the life of nature. When he paints an Indian camp in summer beside a river in Wyoming, one feels the fierce heat on the baked earth and the vast emptiness around. When he paints Indian women bringing firewood at the end of a winter day, one feels the bitter cold, the fading light and the harshness of primitive life.

Gouache on paper: 6 x 8½ inches. Signed at the lower left: *Farny 1912.* Pasted to the back of the mount is a photograph of a painting by Farny showing an Indian hunt for bear in a winter landscape.

66 *Bringing in the Firewood* 1912

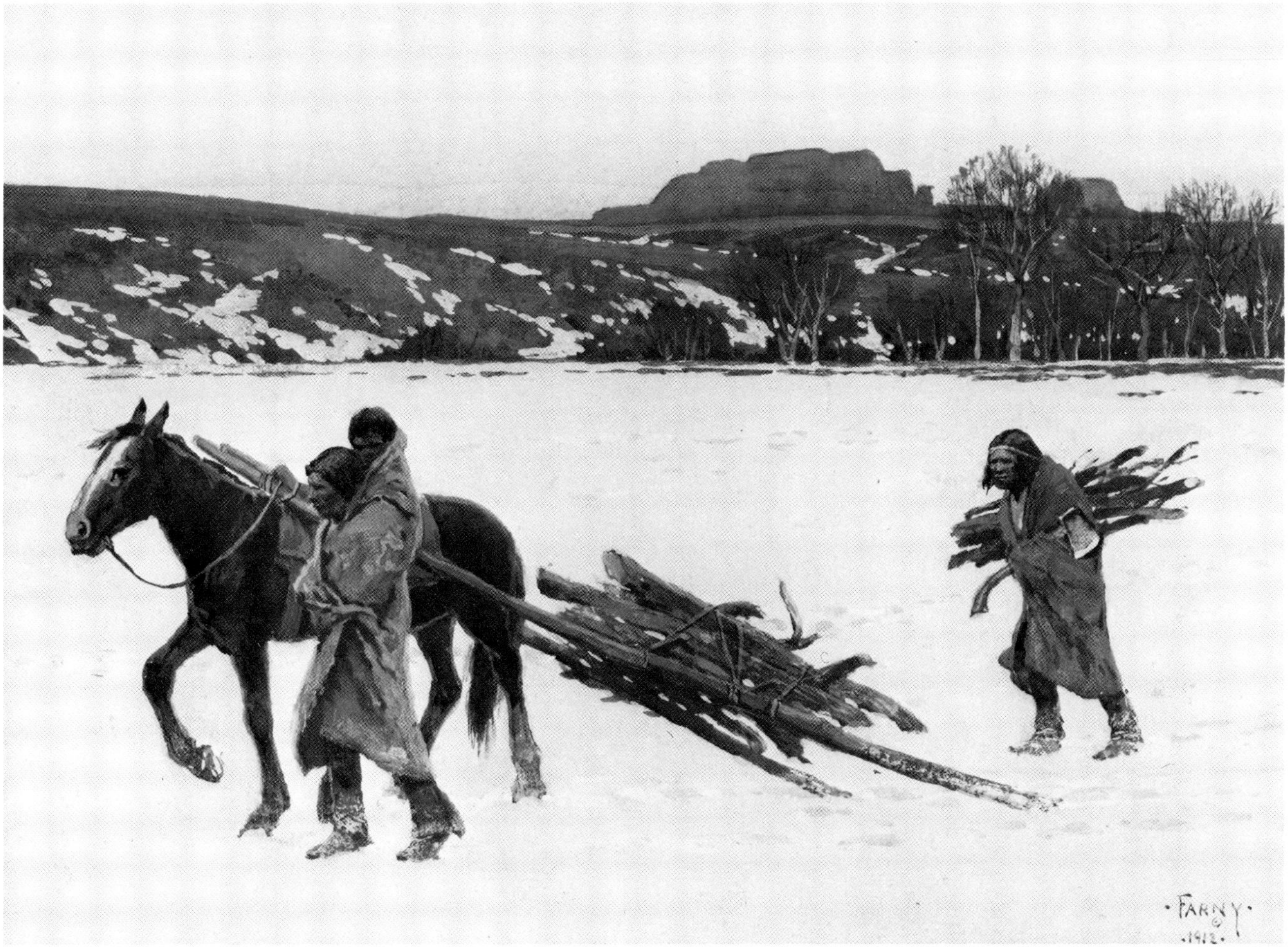
FARNY
©
1912

William Michael Harnett 1848?-1892

The group of *trompe l'oeil* still-life painters, of which Harnett was the chief, is now considered to form one of the interesting chapters in American painting. Fifty, even forty years ago, they were all forgotten. Such are the vagaries of taste. Harnett's early years as an artist were passed in Philadelphia, where the Peale tradition of still life was still felt (cf. No. 27). In 1880 he went to Europe where he lived for six years, chiefly at Munich; in 1886 he returned to New York. After his death he was forgotten until a picture, *The Faithful Colt,* in an exhibition at the Downtown Gallery in 1939 roused curiosity about him. The surrealism of Dali and the "magic realism" of German painters of the twenties had prepared the way for a new taste in which Harnett's remarkable gift for realization of the actual was again appreciated.

In European museums Harnett discovered the profuse splendor possible in still life in the work of Dutch seventeenth-century painters like Kalf and van Beyeren. *Still Life with "Le Figaro"* shows his response. Its brilliant, precise style, its glowing colors like sealing wax or polished fruit, its apparently random but actually carefully contrived profusion of contrasting shapes, colors and textures, all contribute to Harnett's peculiar, haunting poetry of things seen.

Oil on canvas: 9½ x 12 inches. Signed at lower right, *Harnett/Munchen/1882.*

67 *Still Life with "Le Figaro" 1882*

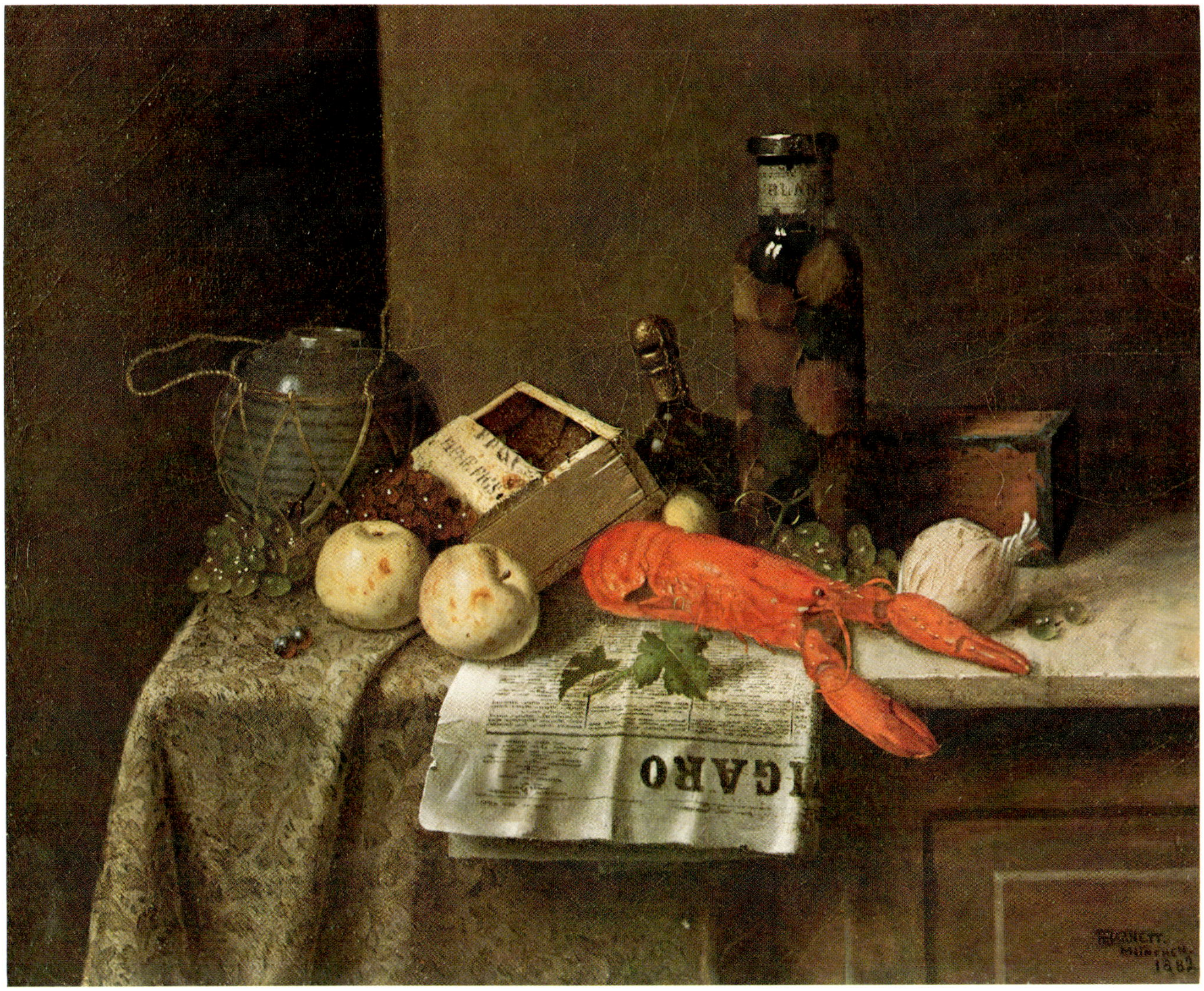
BLAN
IGARO

William Michael Harnett

Harnett returned to America enriched in technique and matured in his art. In *The Meerschaum Pipe* he returned to the subject matter that Alfred Frankenstein calls his "American vernacular" (Frankenstein, 1965), consisting of the simplest of objects—perhaps a pipe, a revolver, a horseshoe, or a plucked chicken—hanging against painted boards close to the picture plane. Nothing could be simpler than these images, yet the magic of Harnett's vision pervades them and makes them poetry.

Canvas: 16½ x 12 inches. Signed at the lower left, *W. M. Harnett 1886* (the W and M forming a monogram).

68   *The Meerschaum Pipe 1886*

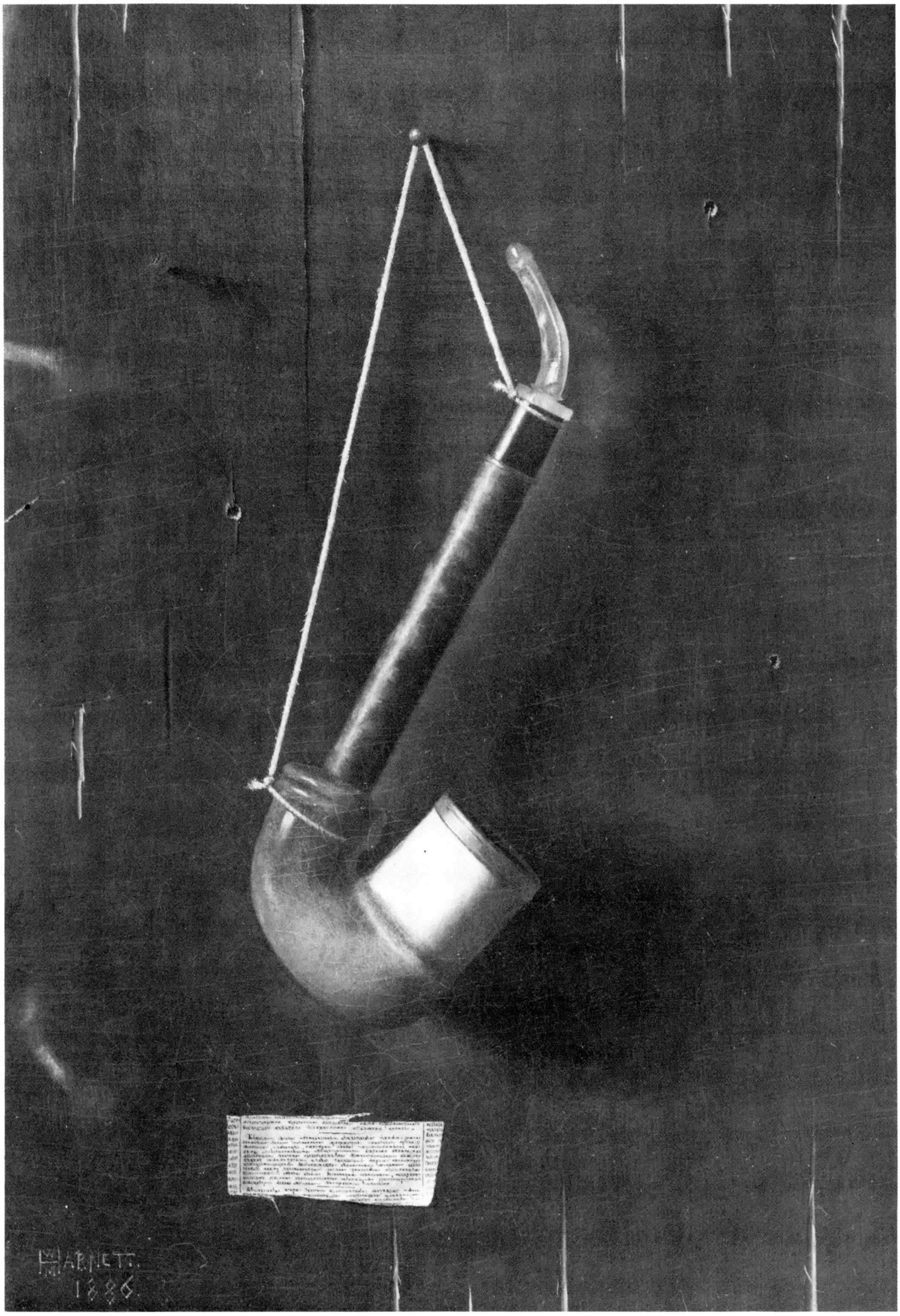
HARNETT.
1886.

Winslow Homer 1836-1910

During the Civil War, Winslow Homer, then a freelance illustrator in New York City, went a number of times to the battlefields and encampments of the Union army in Virginia, making drawings which were later engraved for *Harper's Weekly*. He began also in those years to paint in oils and watercolors, developing his sketches of the war into paintings that were shown at the annual exhibitions of the National Academy of Design.

Homer was a different kind of war artist from those who sent back scenes of armies on the march and regiments charging into battle. For the most part Homer drew the life of the common soldier in camp, his amusements and boredom, his moments of homesickness and his rough comforts. He observed these things with a keen eye, so that after a hundred years his illustrations leap out from the page with a realism that says, "You are there—this is how it was."

The Bright Side was exhibited at the National Academy of Design in 1865. For a lifetime, while an interest in Homer's early work was steadily growing, it hung in the home of an artist, Miss Julia Peck, in Port Huron, Michigan. Consequently, it is one of the least familiar of his wartime pictures. It is also one of his most interesting and original.

Canvas: 13 x 17½ inches. Signed at the lower left: *Winslow Homer 1865*.

69 *The Bright Side* *1865*

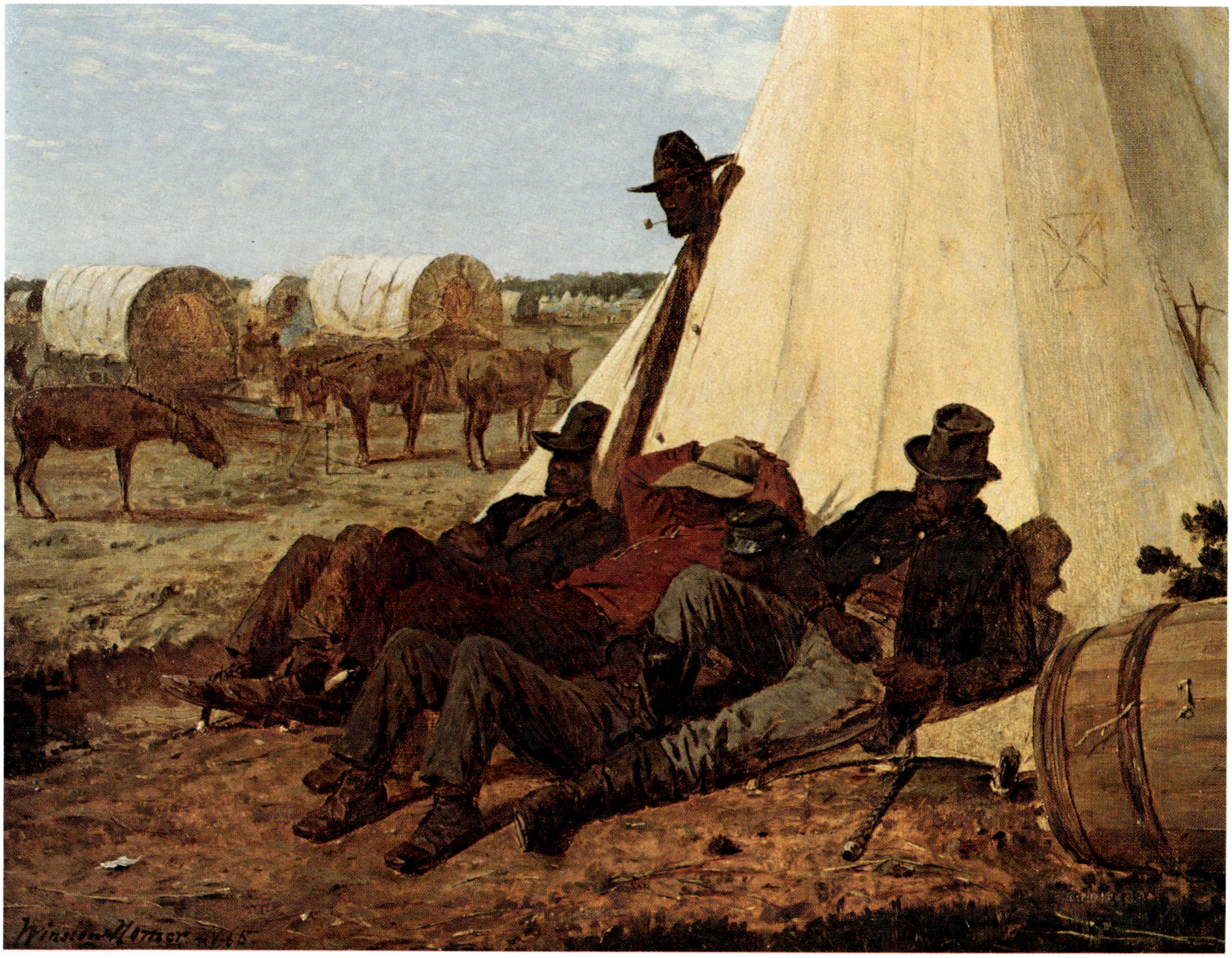

Winslow Homer

One of the merits of an unjustly neglected book on Homer by Albert Ten Eyck Gardner (1961) was that it placed the artist squarely among the artistic movements of his time. One of the most important of these was the discovery by western artists of Japanese prints in the fifties and sixties of the last century. Homer's first biographer, Downes, knew him as the solitary of Prout's Neck and wrote of him as a man so independent that he never looked at the work of another painter. It is true that he was an independent and an artist of strong individuality, but he was also a painter of great knowledge and sophistication. Gardner showed how much Homer learned from Japanese prints that helped him turn his observation of familiar things in the life around into boldly planned, unhackneyed, subtly organized works of art.

There is nothing at all Japanese about the subject or the details of *Backgammon* except a fan and the unusual form of the signature. But the qualities that separate Homer's watercolors from those of his contemporaries, the broad simple areas of color, the elimination of all unnecessary detail, the subtle placing of the figures within the area of the paper, show what he had learned from the *ukiyoye* manner. The awkward tenderness with which he painted these two young girls is entirely his own.

Watercolor: 13 x 17½ inches. Signed at center right: *Homer 1877*.

70 *Backgammon* 1877

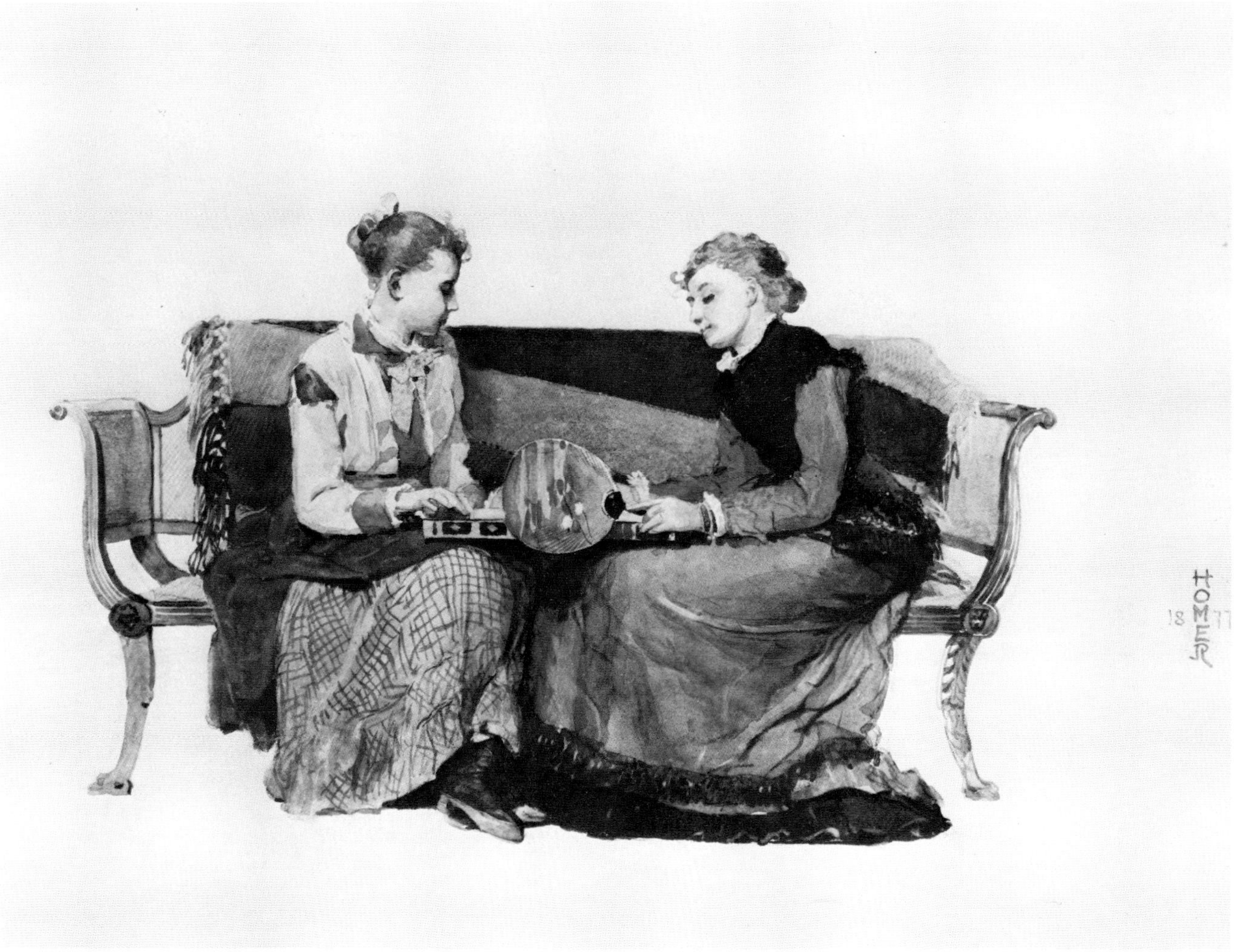
HOMER
1877

Winslow Homer

The turning point in Homer's career came in the years 1881-83. He left New York City in 1881 to spend the better part of two years in England at a fishing village near Tynemouth on the North Sea coast. On his return he settled at Prout's Neck, on the Maine Coast, where his family had built a summer home. The remainder of his life was spent in Maine, with sketching trips to the north woods or to the tropics by way of change.

The equinoctial storms that beat in autumn on the English coast seem to have stirred him deeply. His imagination turned to the elemental forces of earth, wind and sea and to the human beings who work and live among these forces. This watercolor is one of his first paintings at Prout's Neck; it was exhibited at Doll and Richards Gallery, Boston, in December of 1883. With a new largeness and simplicity of manner, it strikes just two notes: the power of the sea, and the strength and vigilance of the men who live upon it. Twenty years later Homer returned to this same idea in the famous oil, *Kissing the Moon* (1904).

Watercolor: 15 x 21⅜ inches. Signed at the lower left: *Winslow Homer 1883*. The mark of Doll & Richards' exhibition is on the reverse.

71   *A Swell of the Ocean 1883*

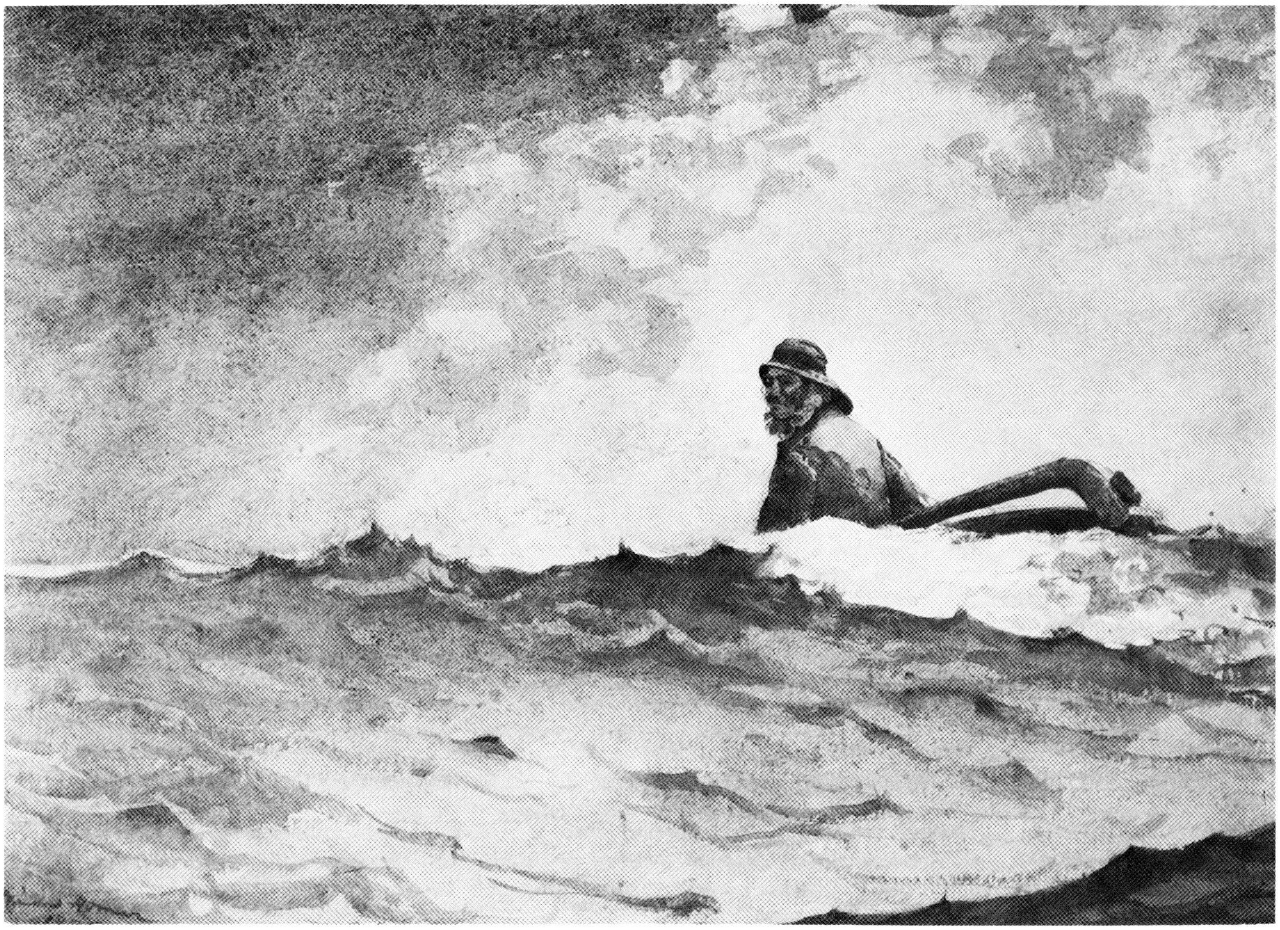

Winslow Homer

Most of Winslow Homer's watercolors were done on trips away from Prout's Neck. He went south for the first time in the winter of 1884-85, spending several months painting at Nassau in the Bahamas and at Santiago de Cuba. The following winter took him to Florida, first to Key West, then to Tampa. In the Caribbean he saw a new guise of the great forces of nature—sun, sea, weather, man—which he was studying in his oils of the Maine coast. In this image of wind, rain and palm trees, he has concentrated an impression of elemental power.

Watercolor: 14 x 20 inches (sight). Inscribed on the reverse: *"A Norther" Key West, Florida.*

72   *A "Norther," Key West* 1886

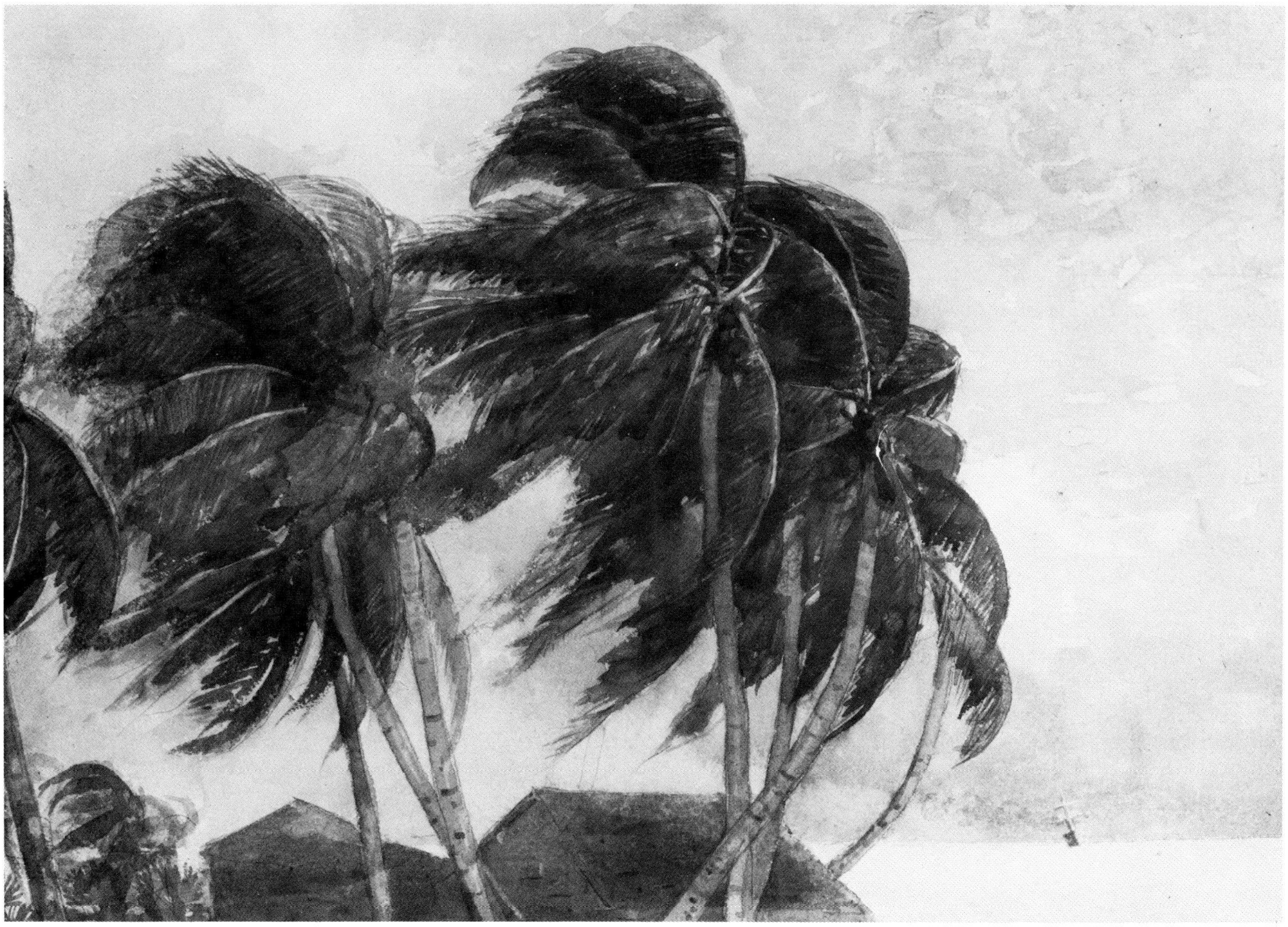

Winslow Homer

One of the early, discerning collectors of Winslow Homer's watercolors was Mr. Charles R. Henshel of Knoedler & Company, the firm that from 1899 on acted as his agents in New York. During their years of business association, Henshel formed his own private collection of Homer's watercolors, among which this is an outstanding example. It was to Henshel that Homer made the remark quoted by Lloyd Goodrich (1959): "You will see, in the future I will live by my watercolors."

In the late eighteen eighties Winslow Homer and his brother Charles began to spend several weeks of each summer at a fishing camp in a wild mountainous section of the Adirondacks around the headwaters of the Hudson River. The watercolors done on these trips are among his greatest achievements. Painted with great directness, they give the impression that we are seeing for ourselves the cold rushing streams, the light sifting through dense forest, the exhilaration of the open mountain top. In Homer's view the wilderness was not uninhabited. It contained men, dogs, deer, fish, not as intruders but as parts of the great whole of earth.

The Adirondack watercolors are original also in style. Homer had by this time fused luminous color with strong contrasts of tone, precise drawing and dramatic pattern with the overall flood of light of the sky, creating a marvelously rich, eloquent language of the eye.

Watercolor: 13½ x 19¾ inches. Signed at lower left, *Homer 1892*.

73   *Burnt Mountain*   1892

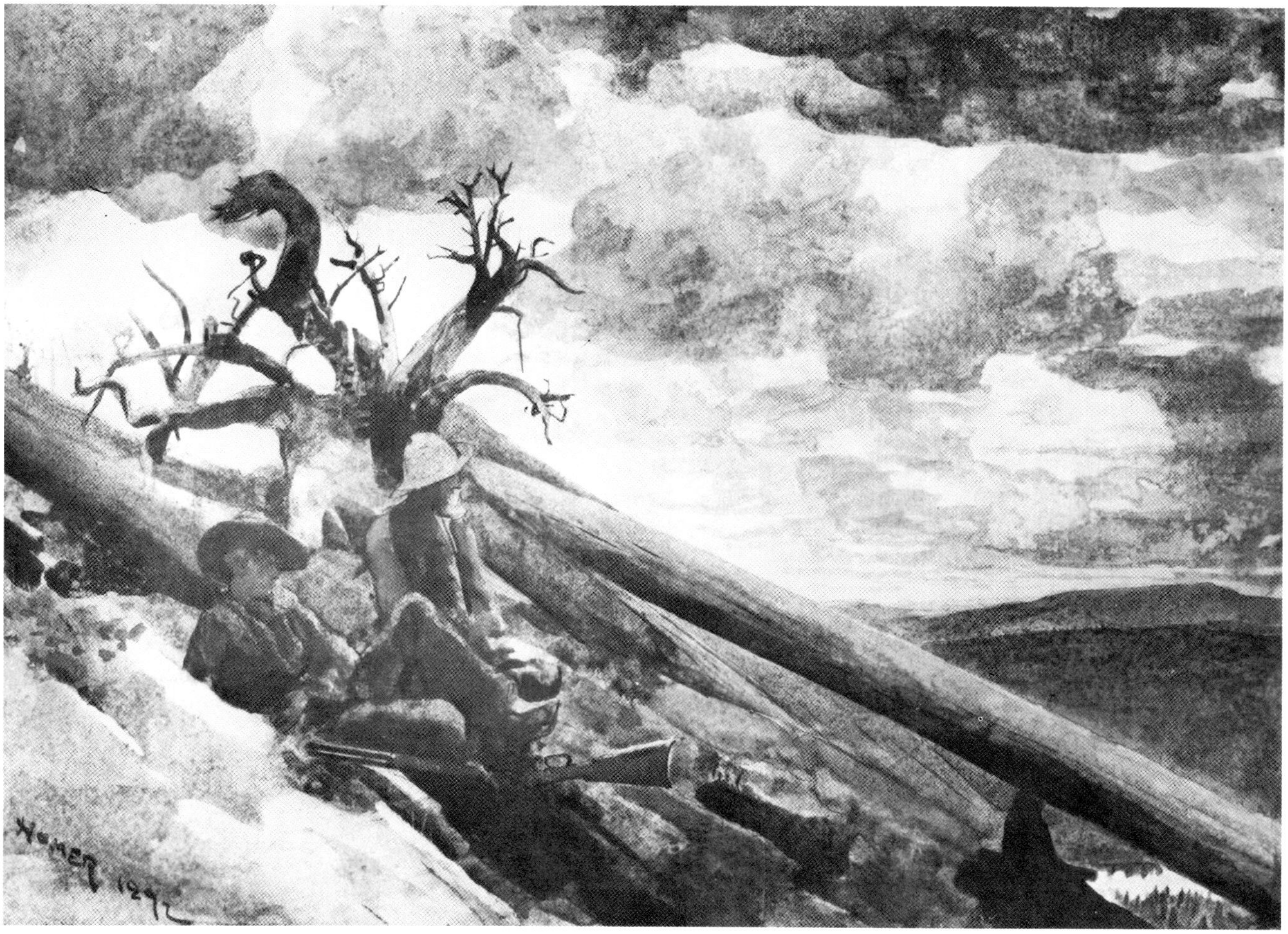
HOMER 1892

Thomas Hovenden   1840-1895

The year 1880 was the turning point in Hovenden's life. He had spent seven years in Paris studying under Cabanel, training himself to paint historical costume pictures such as were then bringing fortunes and world-renown to artists like his teacher and Meissonier. His works in that mode are extremely able exercises of skill and intellect, unwarmed by feeling. Returning to the United States in 1880, he married a Quaker wife (also a painter) and settled in a stone farmhouse belonging to her family in a hamlet, Plymouth Meeting, northwest of Philadelphia. In that pleasant countryside he discovered his own place and time. Leaving historic costume behind, he became a quiet, sympathetic observer of the country people around his home. *The Old Version* shows the dignity and restraint, as well as the human understanding, he brought to their study. The *Man Smoking* is one of a genial series of studies of Negro life, in many of which this same man appears.

74. *The Old Version. Canvas:* 23¾ x 18½ inches. Signed and dated 1881.

75. *Man Smoking a Pipe. Canvas:* 16 x 20 inches.

74 *The Old Version* 1881

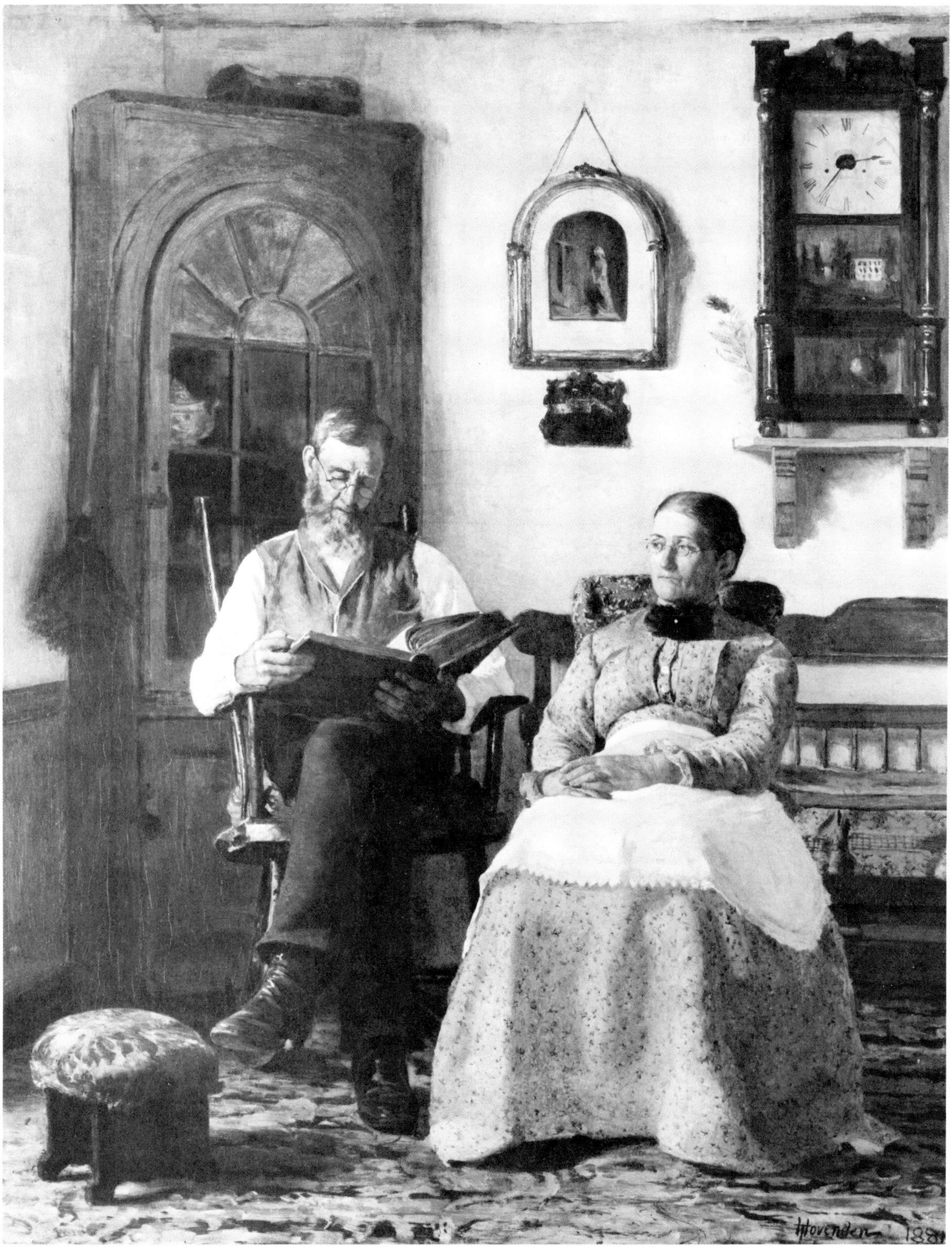

Thomas Hovenden

75 *Man Smoking a Pipe*

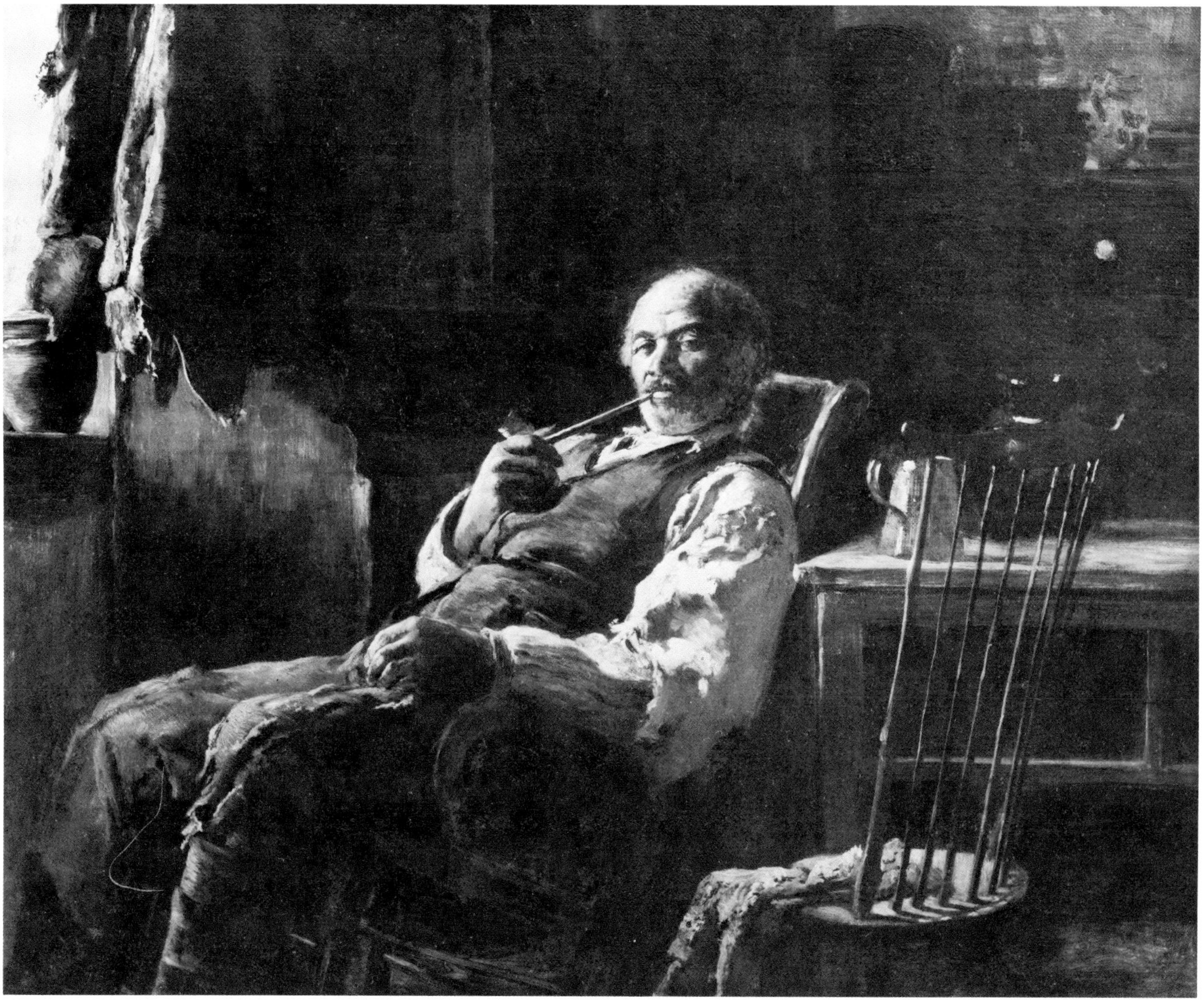

Thomas Hovenden

John Brown's stormy life illustrates the passions aroused by the question of slavery which brought the country to civil war. No one will ever be able to understand exactly what led him with only eighteen men to seize the United States arsenal at Harper's Ferry on the night of October 16, 1859, and to remain there inflexibly in the face of certain death. He was captured, tried in a Virginia court and hanged on December 5, 1859. On the day of his death he gave to one of his guards a paper on which was written, "Charlestown, Va. Dec. 2, 1859. I, John Brown, am now quite *certain* that the crimes of this *guilty land* will never be purged away but with *blood*. I had, as I now think, vainly flattered myself that without very much bloodshed it might be done." Within eighteen months of his death many northern regiments marched off to war, singing

> John Brown's body lies a-mouldering in the grave,
> But his soul is marching on.

On the scaffold he showed great fortitude. A reporter for the New York *Daily Tribune* (Dec. 5, 1859) wrote that as Brown was escorted from the courthouse, he stopped to kiss a baby held out to him by a Negro mother. The incident inspired a poem by Whittier that apparently led a New York manufacturer, Robbins Battell, to commission this picture about 1881.

The event had taken place only twenty-two years earlier but a great war had rolled over the country in the interval. Hovenden, trained in the same realism that Eakins learned in Paris, spent over two years of research on the reconstruction of the scene. He visited Harper's Ferry. The courthouse at Charleston (now West Virginia) had been destroyed during the war, but he learned its appearance, even the number of steps Brown must descend. He talked with Captain Avis, Brown's jailer, and with survivors of the Jefferson Guards who had watched over the scene. The likeness of Brown was taken from a photograph borrowed from Mr. Horace Howard Furness, a noted Unitarian minister and abolitionist of Philadelphia.

The picture was exhibited with great success in 1884 in Philadelphia, New York and Chicago, bringing the artist a national reputation. To a criticism that it was not dramatic enough, Hovenden answered, "I might have made it more dramatic, but I purposely refrained. I tried to give simplicity to the incident, and then paint the best I knew how." Mr. Battell treated the artist generously, not only paying $2000 more than the agreed price of $4000 but allowing the artist to copyright it—a privilege worth money. Photoengraving had not appeared; paintings were reproduced then by the time-consuming processes of etching or wood engraving. The artist made the present two-thirds size replica, there can be no doubt, in order to exploit the rights of reproduction after delivering his picture to Mr. Battell. A woodcut by Frederick Juengling appeared in *Harper's Weekly* and in a limited number of signed artist's proofs on Japanese paper. Hovenden himself made a large etching, published in 1885 in an edition of 1000 by George Gebbie of Philadelphia. The Battell picture was exhibited in the 1889 *Exposition universelle* at Paris and in 1897 was given by his daughter and her husband to The Metropolitan Museum of Art.

Canvas: 48 x 38 inches.

76 *The Last Moments of John Brown* ca. 1884

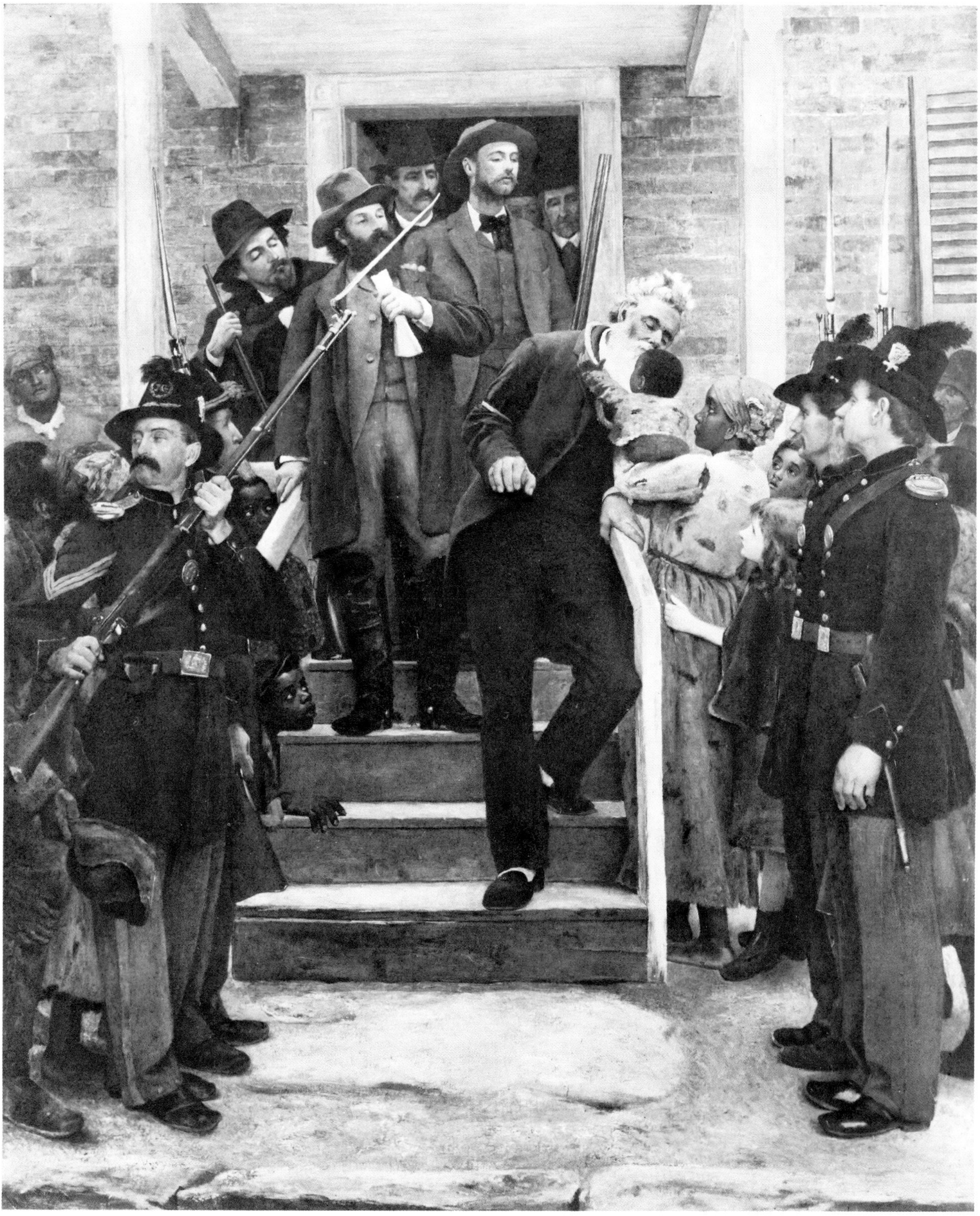

William Morris Hunt 1824-1879

Hunt was primarily a painter of the human figure in portraits, genre and murals. Landscapes are rare in his work; yet when he turned to nature, he showed the same traits that made Samuel Isham say of him, "He saw form simply, nobly, and in those great masses that give character, and he was besides a colorist..." (Isham, 1905).

After the Civil War a few people from the north, in search of a warmer climate, began to spend winters in Florida. Travel was by water—by sea to Jacksonville, then by river boat up the St. John's River to little, now-forgotten resorts like Mandarin (named for the mandarin orange introduced there from China), where Harriet Beecher Stowe settled in 1867. Florida was still an untouched tropical garden. Hunt, seeking health in the winter of 1873-74, found there this image of brooding quiet.

Canvas: 25½ x 39⅜ inches. Signed at the lower left with the monogram, *W.M.H.*

77 *Governor's Creek, Florida 1874*

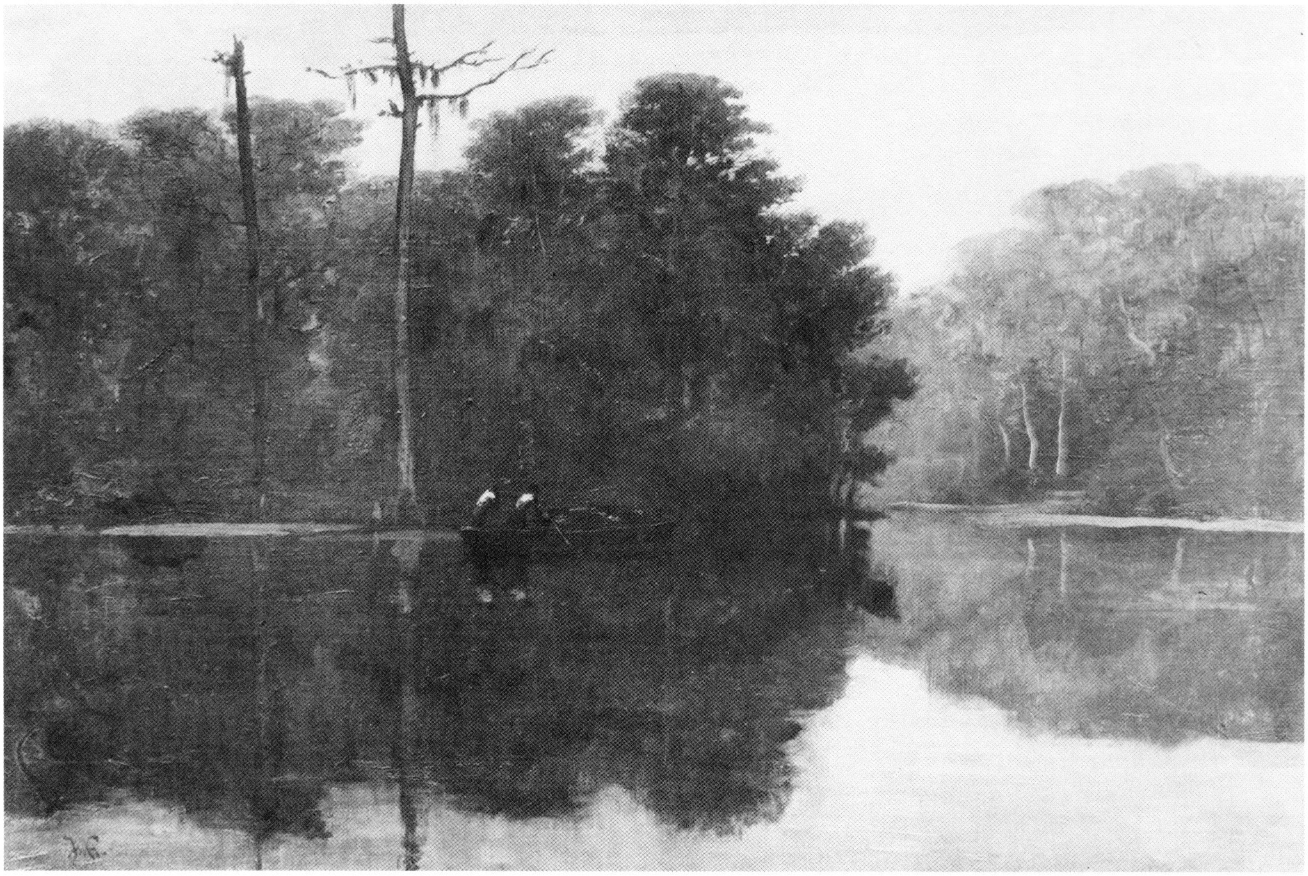

Eastman Johnson 1824-1906

Eastman Johnson was born at Fryeburg, Maine (where he later did many paintings), and spent his childhood there and in Augusta, where his father was Secretary of State. About 1840 or 1841 he was apprenticed to a lithographer in Boston (perhaps the same Bufford shop where Winslow Homer worked) but by the age of eighteen was home in Augusta, determined to be a portrait painter. His portrait drawings in pencil and crayon were an immediate success in Augusta, Washington and Boston. In 1849 he was able to go abroad to study painting. The decisive influence there came from three and a half years spent at The Hague, where he learned from Dutch painting the artistic values of everyday life. Returning to America in 1855, he first visited a married sister at Superior, Wisconsin, where he painted Indian life. He subsequently produced portraits in Cincinnati, painted his first famous genre *Old Kentucky Home* in Washington, and in 1859 settled in New York. His genre paintings were done before 1887; he painted portraits, often of great distinction, throughout his long career.

The "crayon portrait" was popular in the mid-nineteenth century. It was larger than a miniature, less costly than an oil, and less taxing upon the sitter's time and patience than a painting. This portrait of a ninety-two-year-old veteran shows Johnson's incisive touch and grasp of character.

Charcoal on paper: 21-7/16 x 15¼ inches. Signed at lower left: *1844 E. Johnson;* on the reverse, *Gen. Henry Sewall, Aged 92 | Augusta, Me. | Nov. 26, 1844 | E. Johnson, del.*

78 *General Henry Sewall 1844*

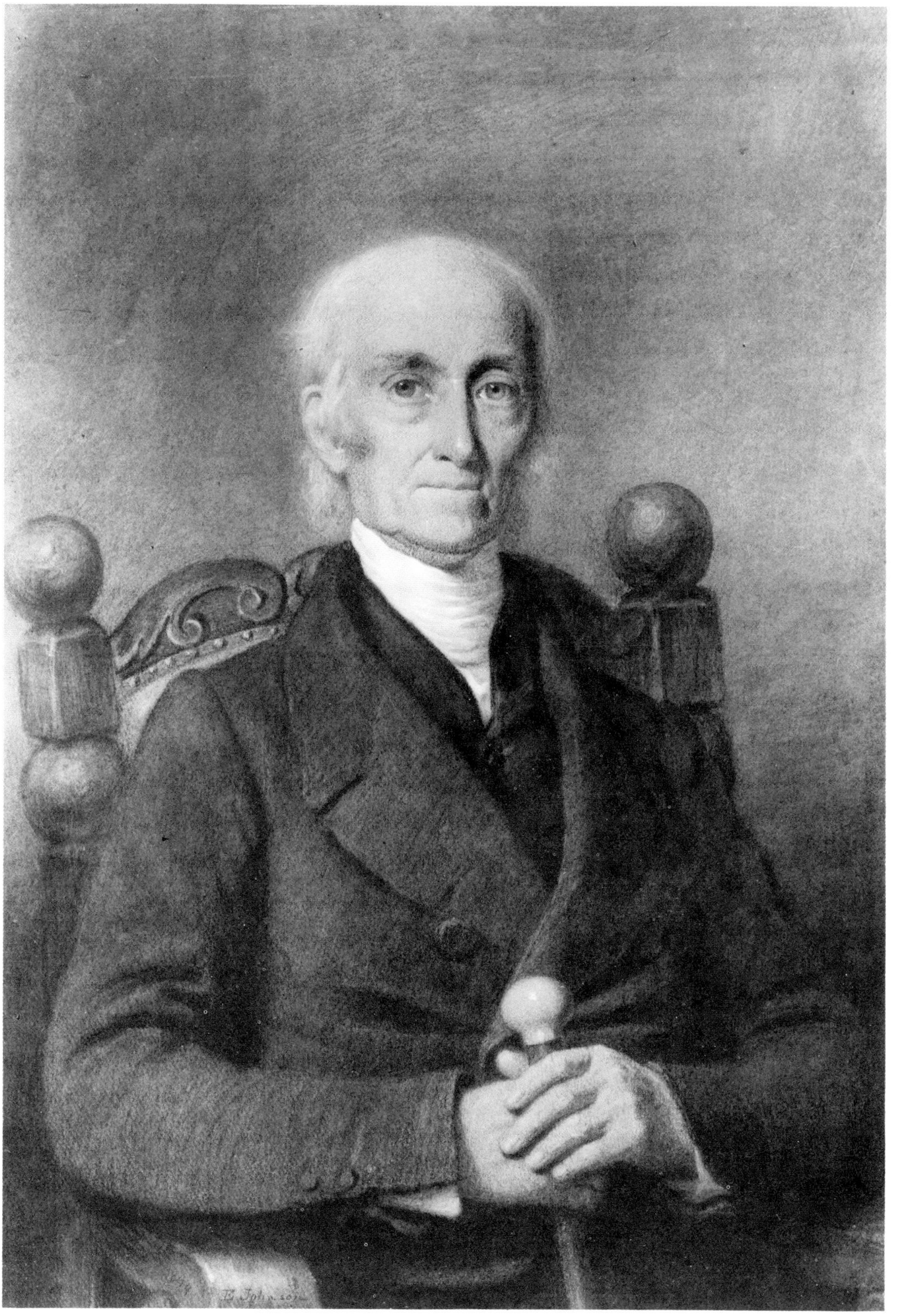

Eastman Johnson

James Brown was a New York banker with interests in railroads and shipping. In 1846 he had commissioned from a leading cabinetmaker and interior designer, Leon Marcotte, the decoration of the parlor of his home on University Place in the then fashionable French Renaissance style. In 1869 he commissioned this picture from Eastman Johnson partly, it would seem, as a memento of the old home, as the family was about to leave University Place for a new house on Park Avenue. Mr. and Mrs. Brown are shown with their grandson, William Adams Brown, in the parlor which was about to be dismantled so that portions of its decoration could be re-used in the new house (Howat, 1970).

Johnson rose to the challenge. This is a portrait of a family and a home. The Renaissance Revival walls, the furniture and furnishings, the light, the atmosphere of the room are preserved as if in amber. The people also are the work of a great genre painter. The excellence of genre lies not in painting a number of people or a scene from daily life but in the artist's ability, like that of a playwright who ties the action of his characters on stage into a psychological knot, to draw separate lives together so that they live a moment as one. Here is a moment in three long-past lives in a familiar room, alive still as clearly as affection could desire.

Canvas: 38½ x 32½ inches. Signed at the lower right: *E. Johnson / 1869*. The picture remained in family possession until offered to the present owner.

79 *The Brown Family* *1869*

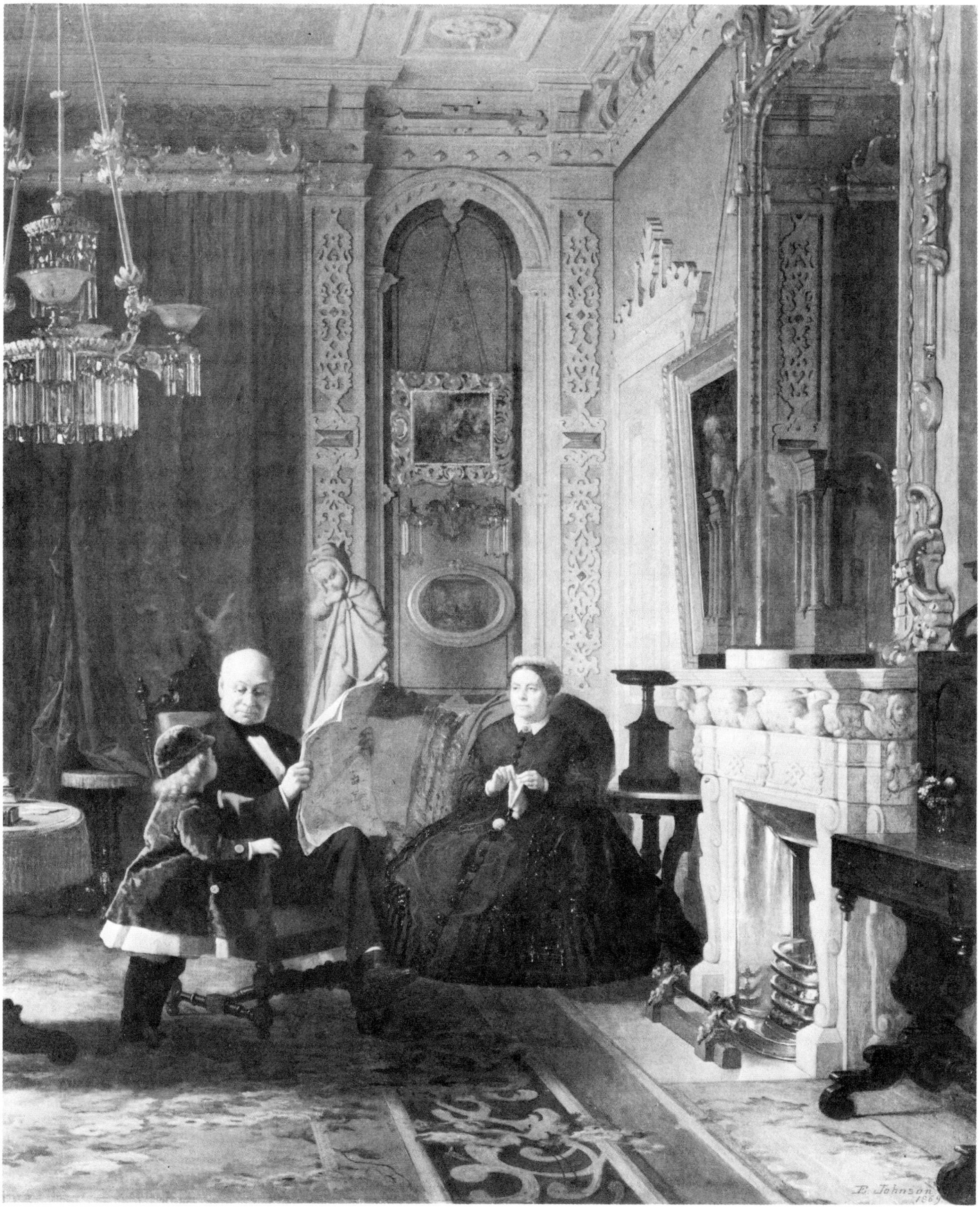
E. Johnson
1869

Eastman Johnson

One can understand that Johnson could learn from Dutch seventeenth-century painting to see meaning and poetry in every passing, unregarded moment of life. His three-and-a-half years in The Hague were well spent. But where and how did he learn to see a human figure like a Greek sculptor modeling a Tanagra figurine, making the movement of the whole body a single expressive gesture? He not only saw the human figure as a sculptor does; he added the painter's art of light and tone and rich visual harmony. What a pleasure it is to see such a painting!

Oil on academy board: 18⅝ x 14¾ inches. Signed at the lower right, *E. Johnson 1865.*

80 *Girl Picking Waterlilies 1865*

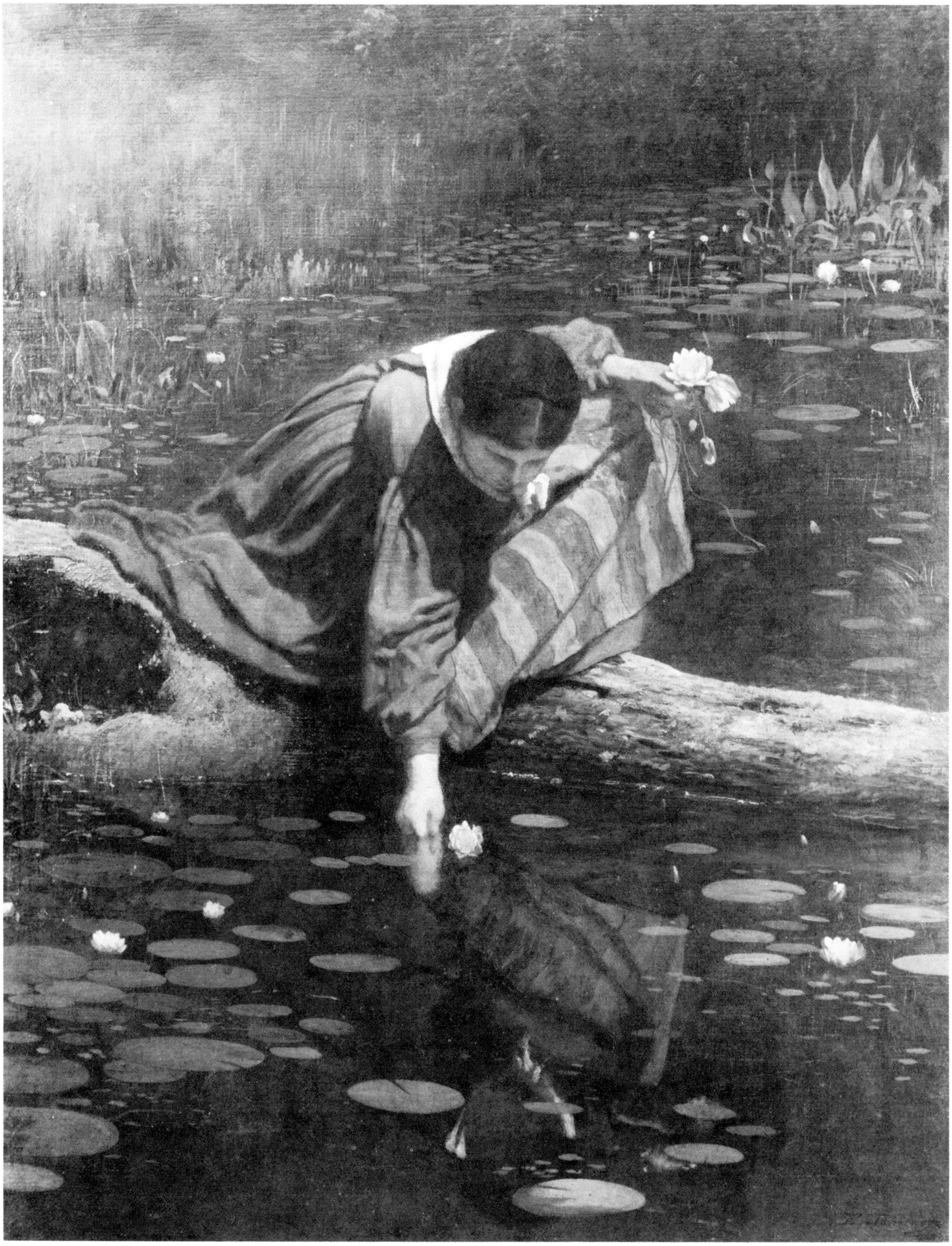

Eastman Johnson

It is the magic of painting to catch a fleeting moment and make it timeless. In this, as in No. 80, Johnson has preserved for us a single, graceful gesture. He surprises and touches us by his unsentimental tenderness toward life.

Oil on academy board: 24 x 12 inches. Signed at the lower left, *E. Johnson 77*.

81   *A Day Dream*   1877

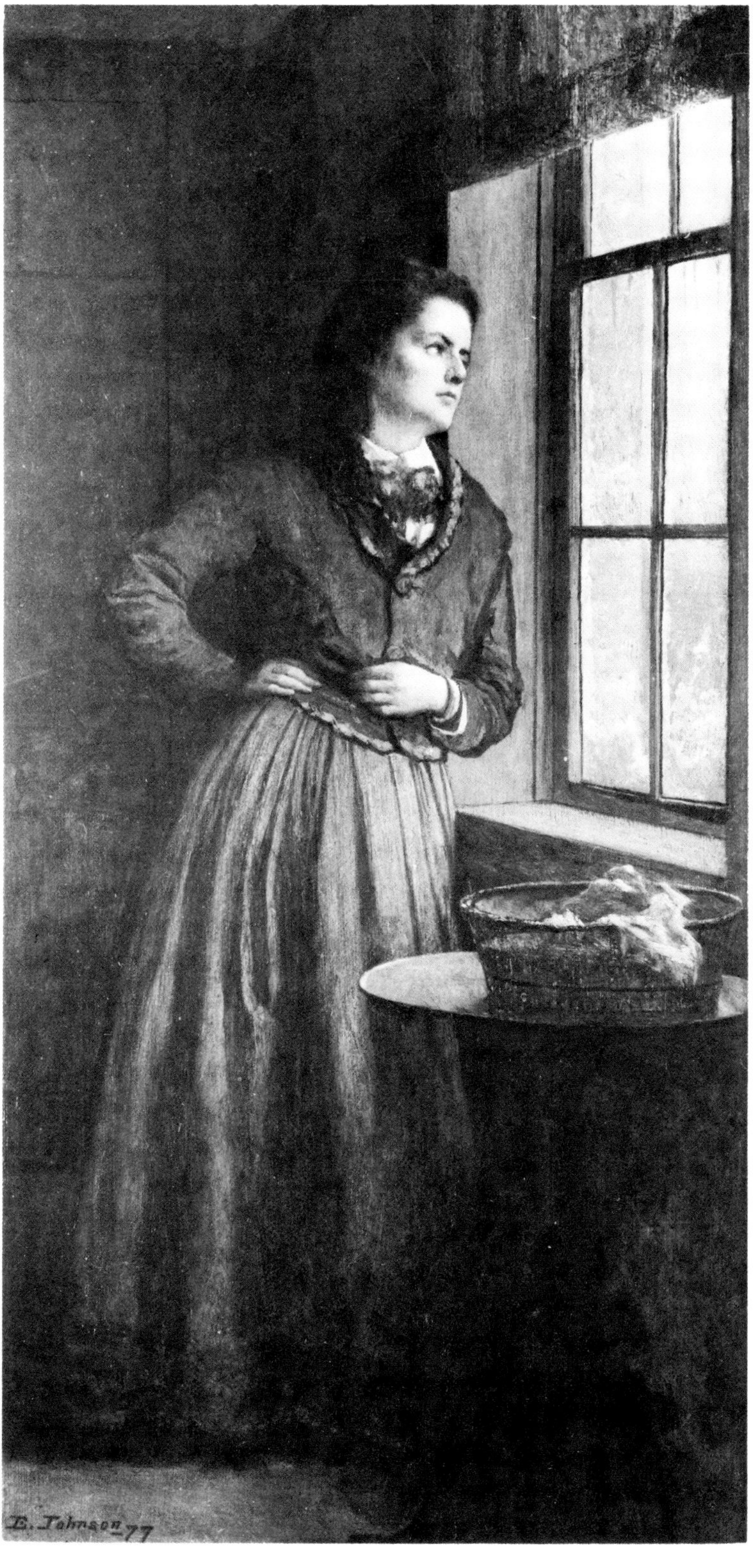
E. Johnson 77

Eastman Johnson

For several years in the early 1860's Johnson returned to Fryeburg, Maine, in early spring to sketch the maple sugar camp, when men were out tapping the trees and boiling down the sap to make syrup. There is a cheerful, festival feeling when the sap is running. The long New England winter is almost over; the first hint of spring in the air; it is good to be outdoors again. Everyone joins in to enjoy this moment of the New England year. Johnson made studies of the sugar camp at Fryeburg over a period of several years, trying different groupings of figures, dark against the snow, moving among the bare trees, standing, talking, gathered about the boiling kettle. This study may be the last, or nearly the last, before the final painting. He omits all detail: only a mosaic of subtle tones and colors suggests the size, placing and gesture of each figure in a long frieze stretching across the canvas. We are aware of the artist thinking, before our eyes, to form the people, the place, the season, the day into a whole. It is a summary of the subtle and delicate precision of his art.

Canvas: 17⅛ x 32 inches (sight). Signed at the lower left: *E. J.*

82 *Sugaring Off* ca. 1860-1865

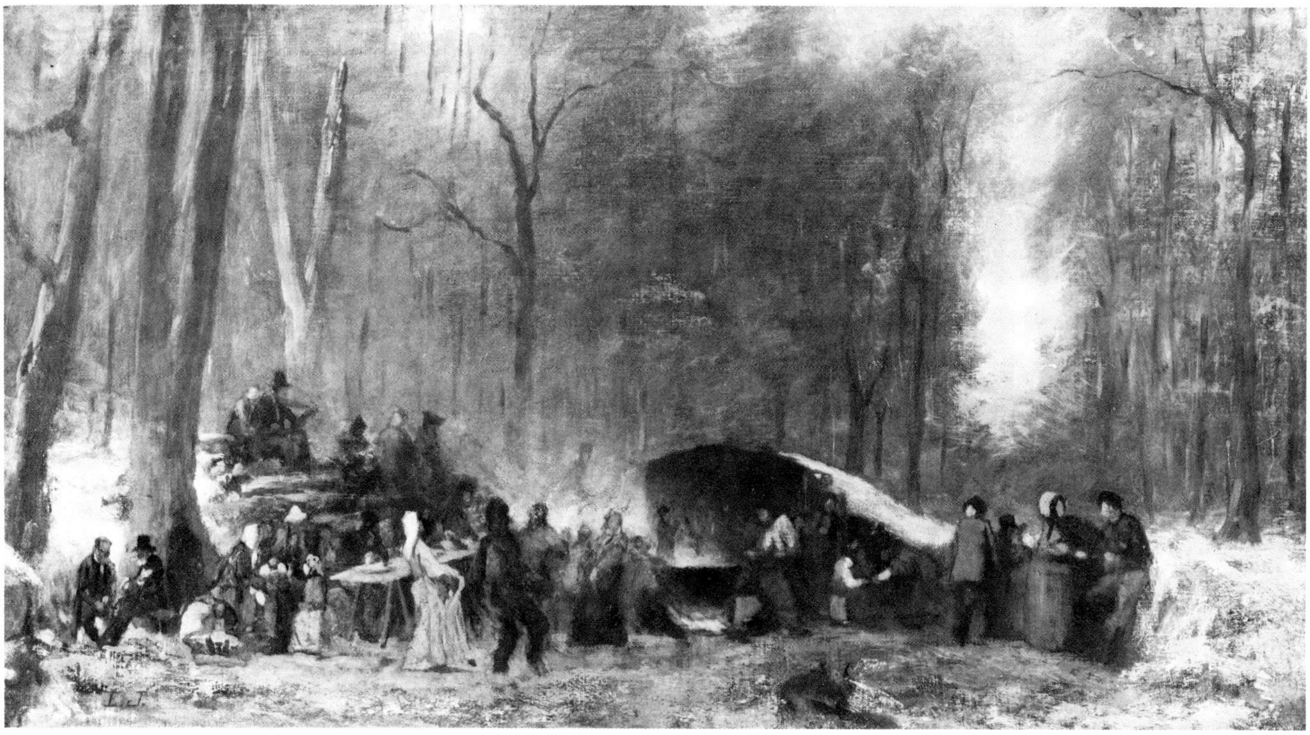

John LaFarge   1838-1910

LaFarge was an artist of great intelligence and distinction who had a national influence as mural painter, decorative artist, maker of stained glass, writer and lecturer. He left few easel paintings. In drawings, watercolors, and oil sketches such as this, one encounters the subtle mind and sensitive perception that make him memorable.

Oil on panel : 17 x 9 inches.

83   *Horse Chestnut Blossoms*

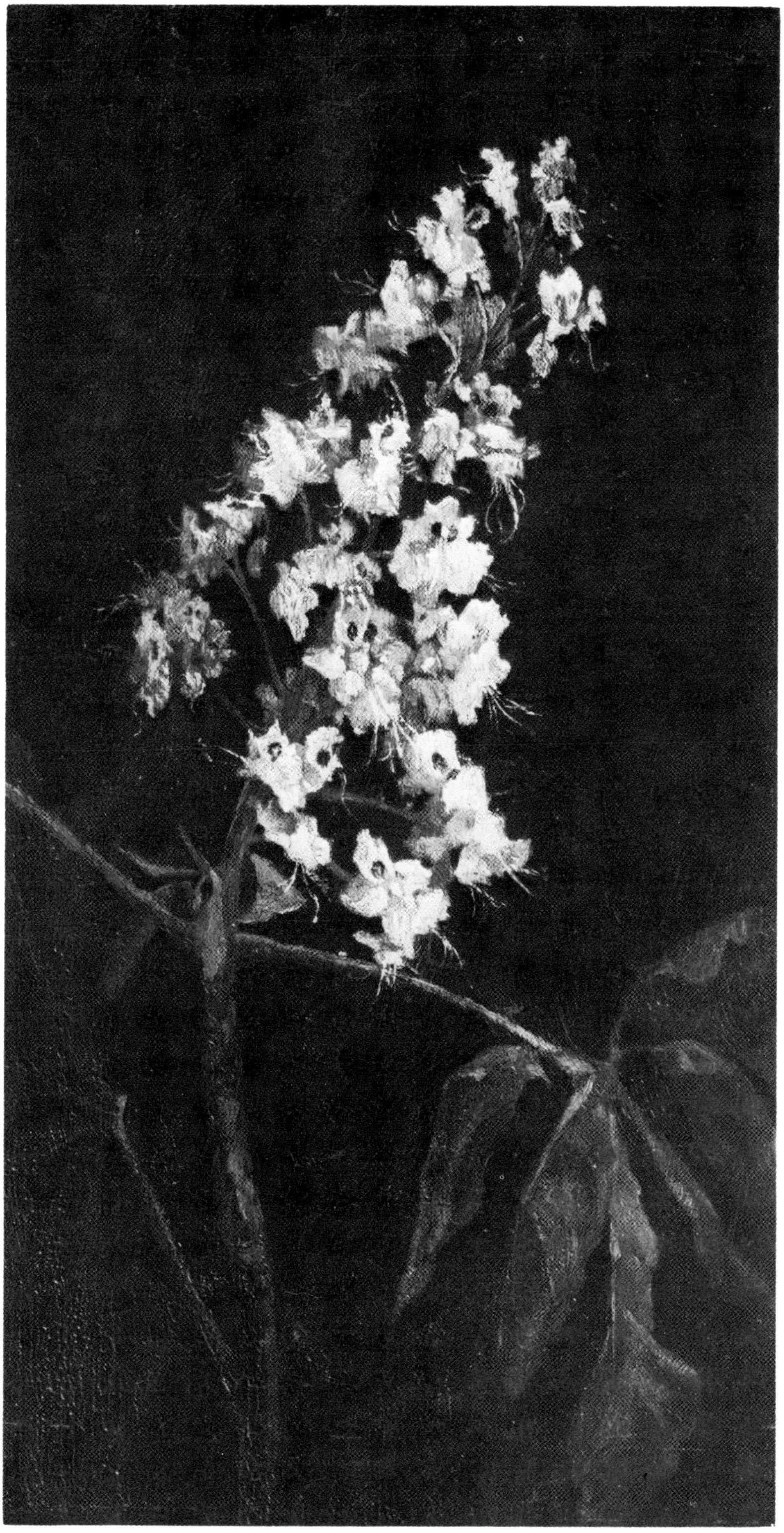

William J. McCloskey, active 1888-1891

It is tantalizing that this painter of fascinating *trompe l'oeil* still life should be so elusive. Almost the only facts known of him are that he exhibited still lifes of fruit at the National Academy of Design from 1888 to 1891 and a picture of *Tangerine Oranges* at the Brooklyn Art Association in 1891. Then he disappears. His works are very rare; I have seen four, all quite similar to this.

Canvas: 10½ x 17¼ inches. Signed at lower right, *William McCloskey*.

84 *Oranges in Tissue Paper*

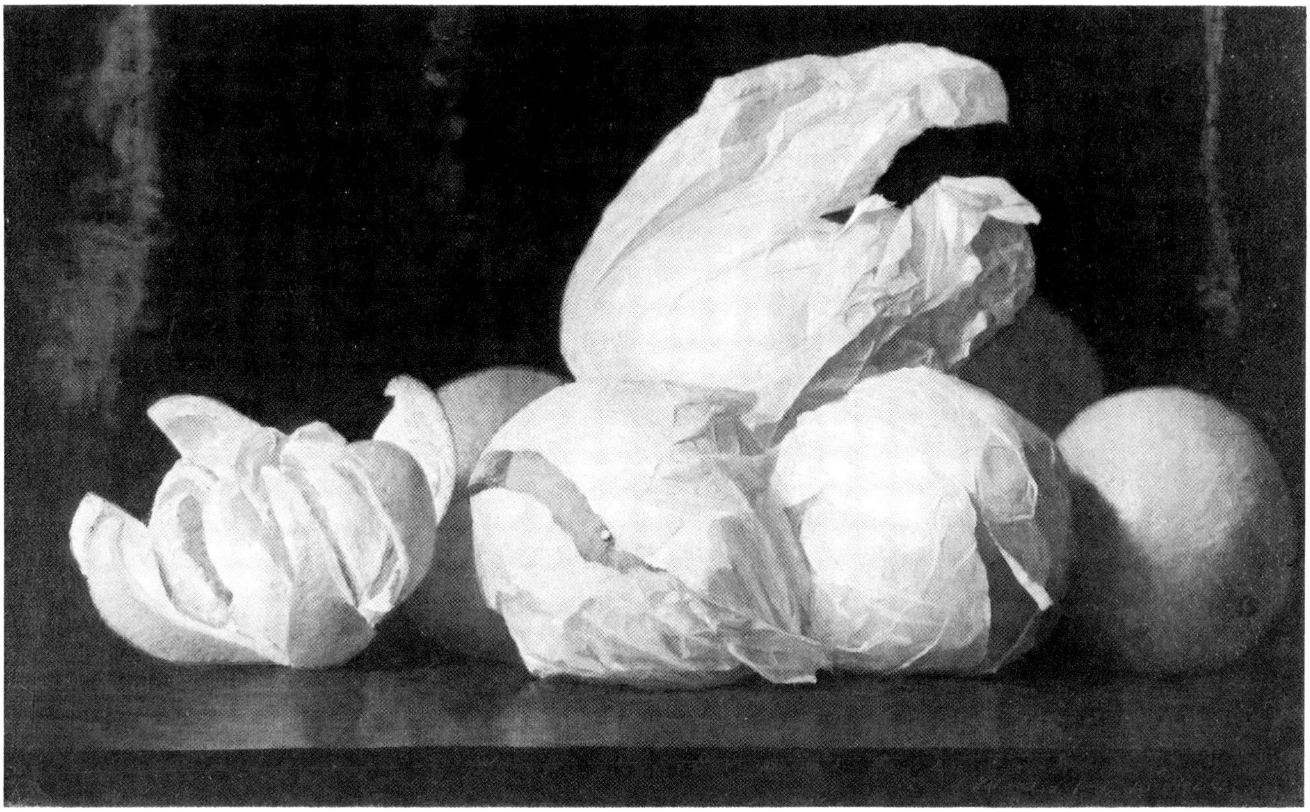

George W. Maynard 1843-1923

Maynard was one of the distinguished mural painters of his generation. Well-trained at the Academy in Antwerp, he returned in time to work with LaFarge on the interior of Trinity Church, Boston, 1875-76, which launched the mural movement. He also did murals at the World's Columbian Exposition, Chicago, the Library of Congress, Washington, and the Columbia University Library, New York. But it would seem that the fate of the painter of murals is to be forgotten as soon as the novelty of the building wears off. Maynard's name is unfamiliar today, like the names of others who took part in mural projects that once attracted national attention. His smaller works are seldom seen. *Grandfatherly Advice,* exhibited at the National Academy of Design in 1885, is the work of an excellent and sympathetic painter whose pictures will no doubt re-appear one day.

Oil on panel: 11¾ x 13⅞ inches. Signed at the lower center, *Maynard, 85*.

85 *Grandfather's Advice 1885*

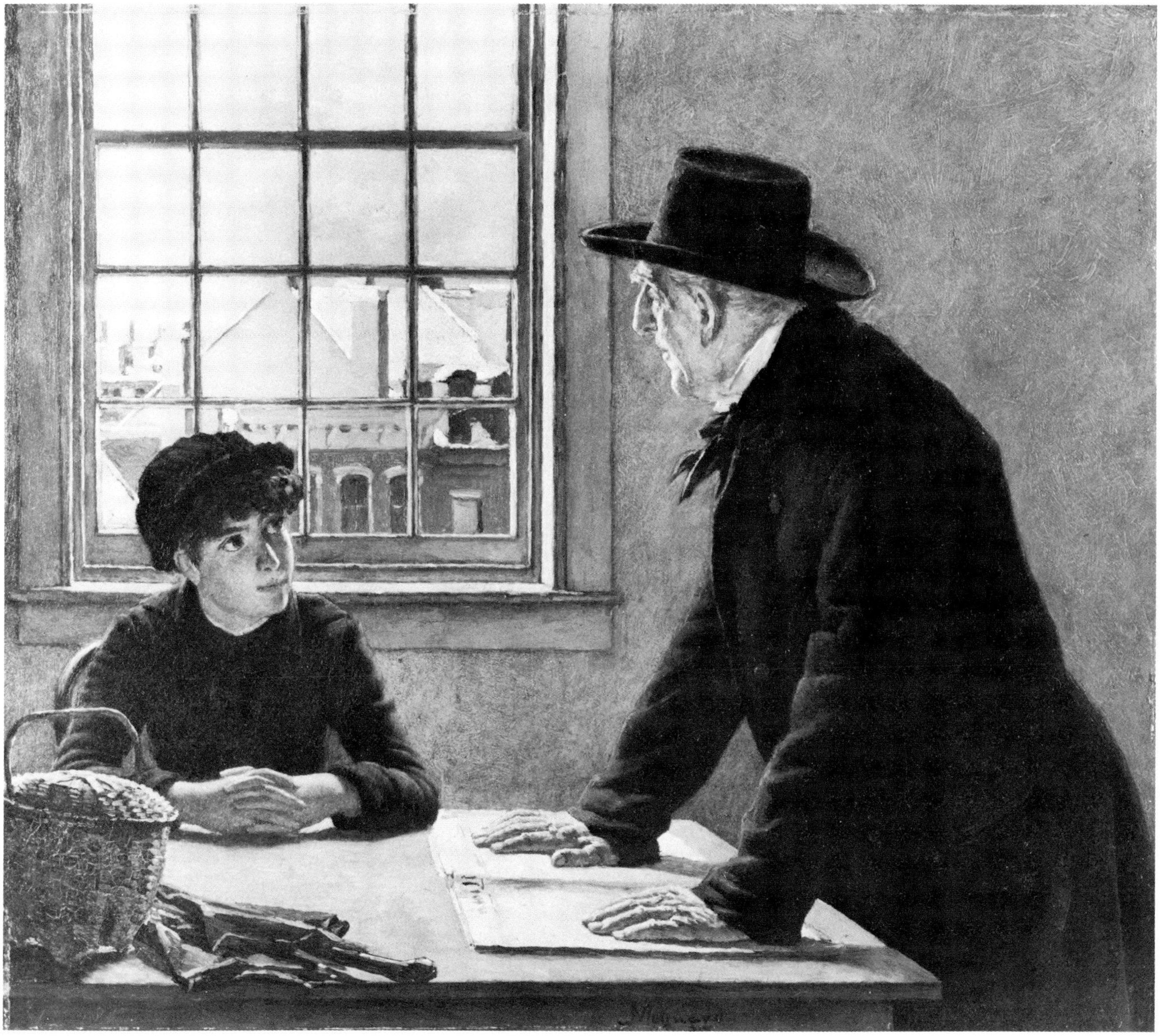

Thomas Moran   1837-1926

It is hard to realize how unexplored the American West was only a century ago. When *Scribner's Monthly* in 1870 accepted an article on "The Wonders of the Yellowstone" by N. Langford, and only some crude drawings by a soldier in the escort party were available, Thomas Moran was engaged to illustrate it. He had never been west but depended on his vivid imagination. As Wallace Stegner says, he drew the Grand Canyon of the Yellowstone looking "about four feet wide and four miles deep, and several of mud volcanoes in which the cones look as if they had been cut out of sheet metal with tin-shears." (Stegner, 1954.) But who then could tell the difference? The next year, Moran was so stirred by the article, which appeared in *Scribner's*, that he joined the Hayden survey party and finally saw the canyon. From his sketches came *The Grand Canyon of the Yellowstone* (1873), belonging to the Department of the Interior, and a career which, more perhaps than any other, made the wonders of the west known to the world.

Twenty years later in 1892 he revisited the Yellowstone and from new sketches painted a series of pictures. The colors of the rocks, the fantastic variations of the scene as one moved around the rim, the light that makes distant objects seem ethereal as the sky, were a challenge to which he returned again and again. One picture of 1893 was a vast canvas, 8 by 14 feet, now in the National Collection of Fine Arts, Washington. This small canvas, also done in 1893, seems jewel-like in comparison. Other pictures of the Canyon followed during the next eleven years. Thurman Williams, in his recent biography of Moran (1966), emphasized rightly that although he made studies from nature and used photographs, he did not paint literally. His aim was to give poetic visual form to the overwhelming impact of some of nature's grandest phenomena.

Canvas: 20 x 16 inches. Signed at lower right, *T. Moran 1893,* the T and M forming a monogram.

86   *The Grand Canyon of the Yellowstone   1893*

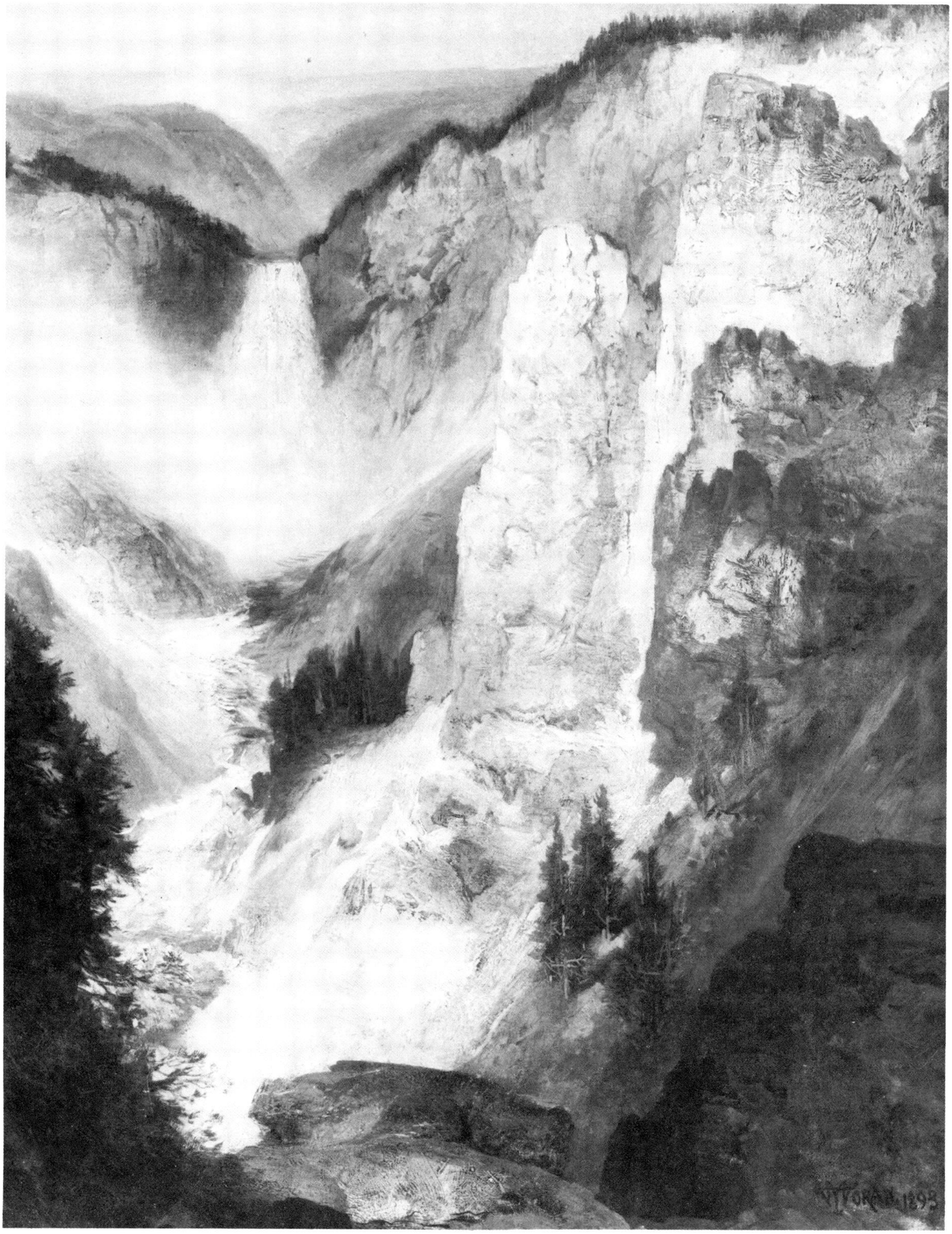

Thomas Moran

The best painters of the later nineteenth century were often also illustrators. The decades 1870-1890 were a remarkable period of book and magazine illustration; wood engraving offered the painter a process of reproduction that had high artistic quality of its own. This brush drawing shows the ease, precision and grace of Moran's work intended for reproduction by wood engraving.

Ink and Chinese white on paper : 10-3/16 x 17⅛ inches. Signed at the lower left with the monogram, *TM*.

87   *View of New York from across the Harbor*

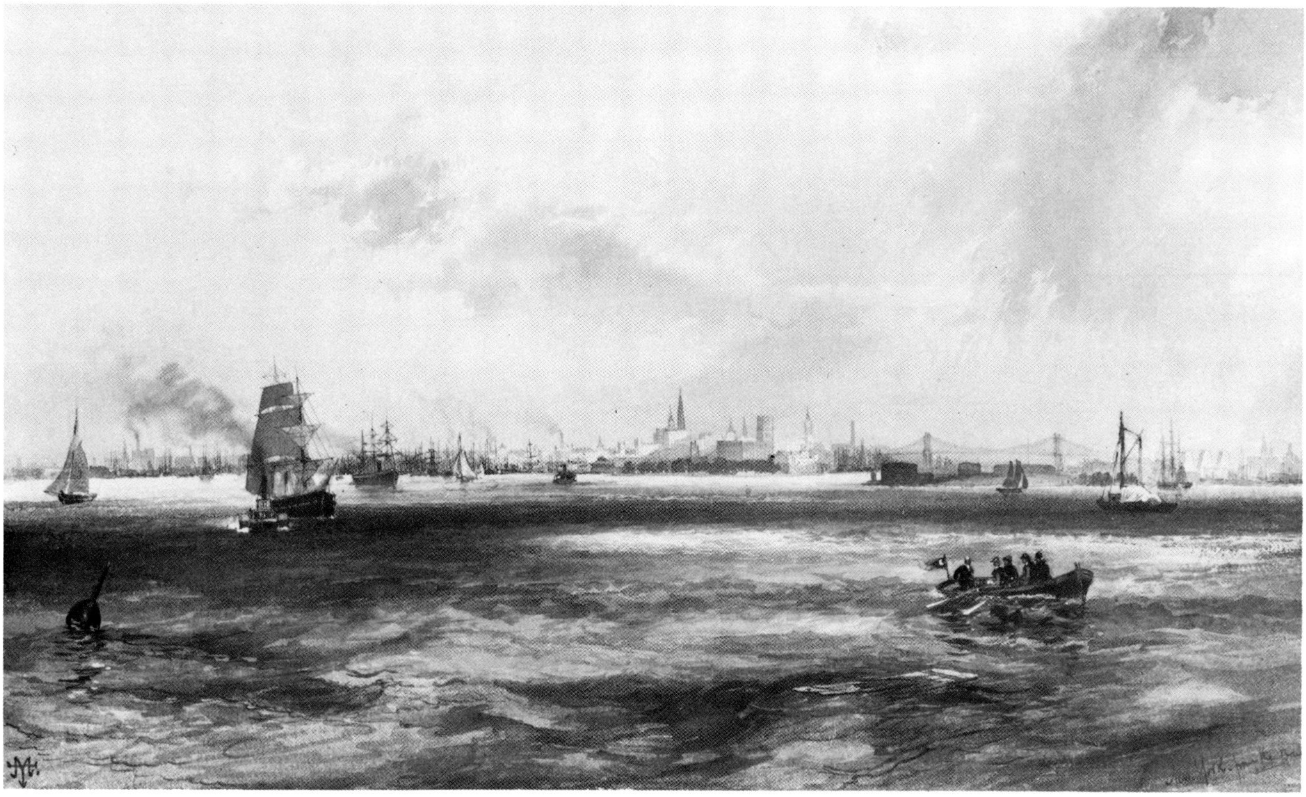

John F. Peto 1854-1907

One of the surprising discoveries of recent times was made by Alfred Frankenstein at the beginning of his study of Harnett. He found another artist in total eclipse behind the man he was investigating. The second artist was Peto. This discovery not only resurrected a forgotten artist but led, step by step, to the exploration of an entire *trompe l'oeil* school, as related by the author in *After the Hunt* (Frankenstein, 1953 & 1969).

Peto grew up in Philadelphia where he knew and admired Harnett, but from 1889 until his death he lived in a small religious resort on the Jersey coast named Island Heights. He continued to paint there but lost touch with the world of art so completely that his existence was forgotten; in time, Harnett's name was attached to many of his best pictures. In subjects, and even in the titles of his pictures, he followed Harnett closely; but his temperament was quite different. Where Harnett is brilliant and forceful, Peto is gentle and unworldly. His style is more atmospheric, more softly luminous than Harnett's. Instead of lustrous objects, Peto painted old, commonplace, worn-out things. There is a peculiar beauty and pathos, even a poetry of the discarded in Peto that is his special note, something of which one becomes very fond. *The Cup We All Race For* is an example of another note, which Frankenstein called "the fantasticality of the commonplace."

88. *Canvas*: 38¾ x 29¾ inches, sight. Signed at lower right, *J. F. Peto*.

89. *Canvas*: 25½ x 21½ inches. Signed at the top center: *John F. Peto*.

88 *Job Lot Cheap*

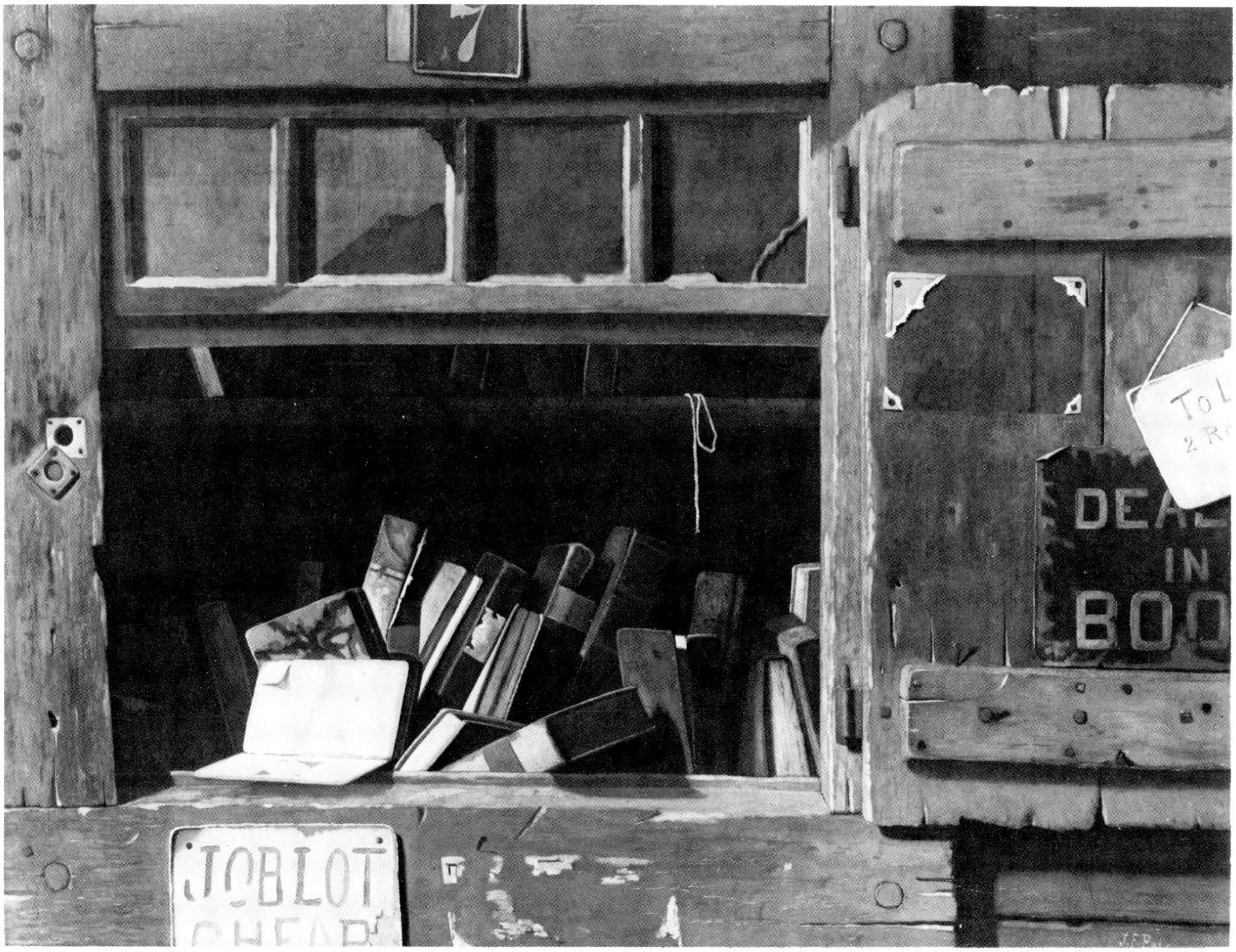
JOBLOT

John F. Peto

89 *The Cup We All Race For*

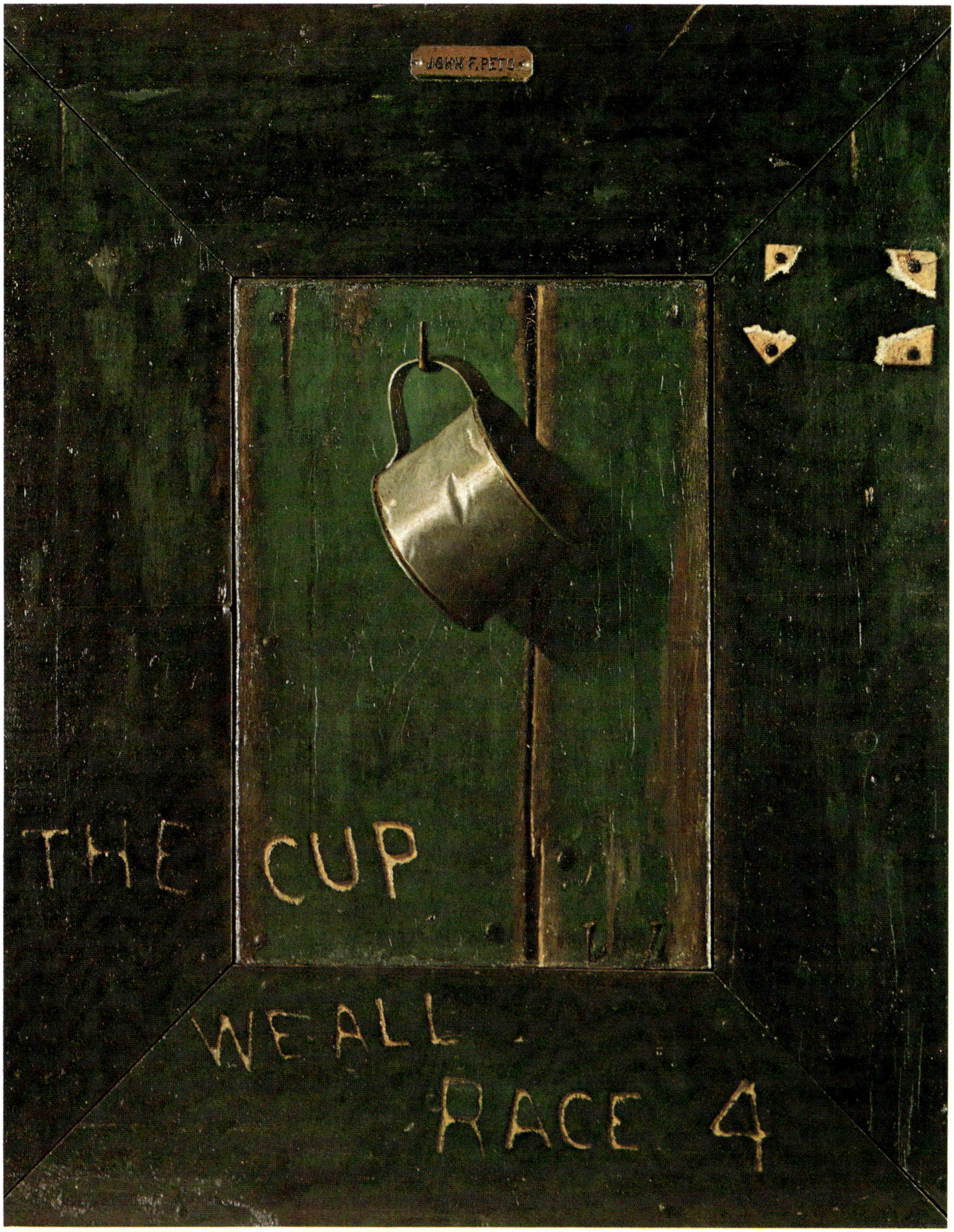
JOHN F. PETO
THE CUP
WE ALL
RACE 4

John Singer Sargent 1856-1925

Sargent combined skill of hand and an acute vision of the world about him to an extraordinary degree. Although his family were expatriates and he spent the better part of his life in Europe, he illustrates the same strain in the American temperament that gave us Winslow Homer, Thomas Eakins, William Harnett: all taciturn men passionately devoted to the poetry of fact. It is no accident that the examples of the Dutch and Spanish realists meant much to all of them.

This sketch shows how well Sargent could capture a fleeting movement with seemingly effortless ease. It was done in Brittany in the summer of 1877 as a preparatory study for *The Oyster Gatherers of Cancale,* which was exhibited in the Salon of 1878. (It is now in the Corcoran *Gallery of Art,* and a second, larger version is in the Museum of Fine Arts, Boston.) That was the opening of a long and brilliant career on both sides of the ocean. After Sargent's death, when his work went out of fashion, detractors said that his paintings were brilliantly observed and executed but lacked poetry. At the same time they objected to the brooding sense of religious mystery in his murals in the Boston Public Library. This only shows that if critics choose to dislike they can always find a reason.

Canvas: 11 x 10 inches. Inscribed at the upper left, *To my friend Rotch/John S. Sargent.* Signed at the lower right, *J. S. Sargent.*

90   *The Oyster Gatherer 1877*

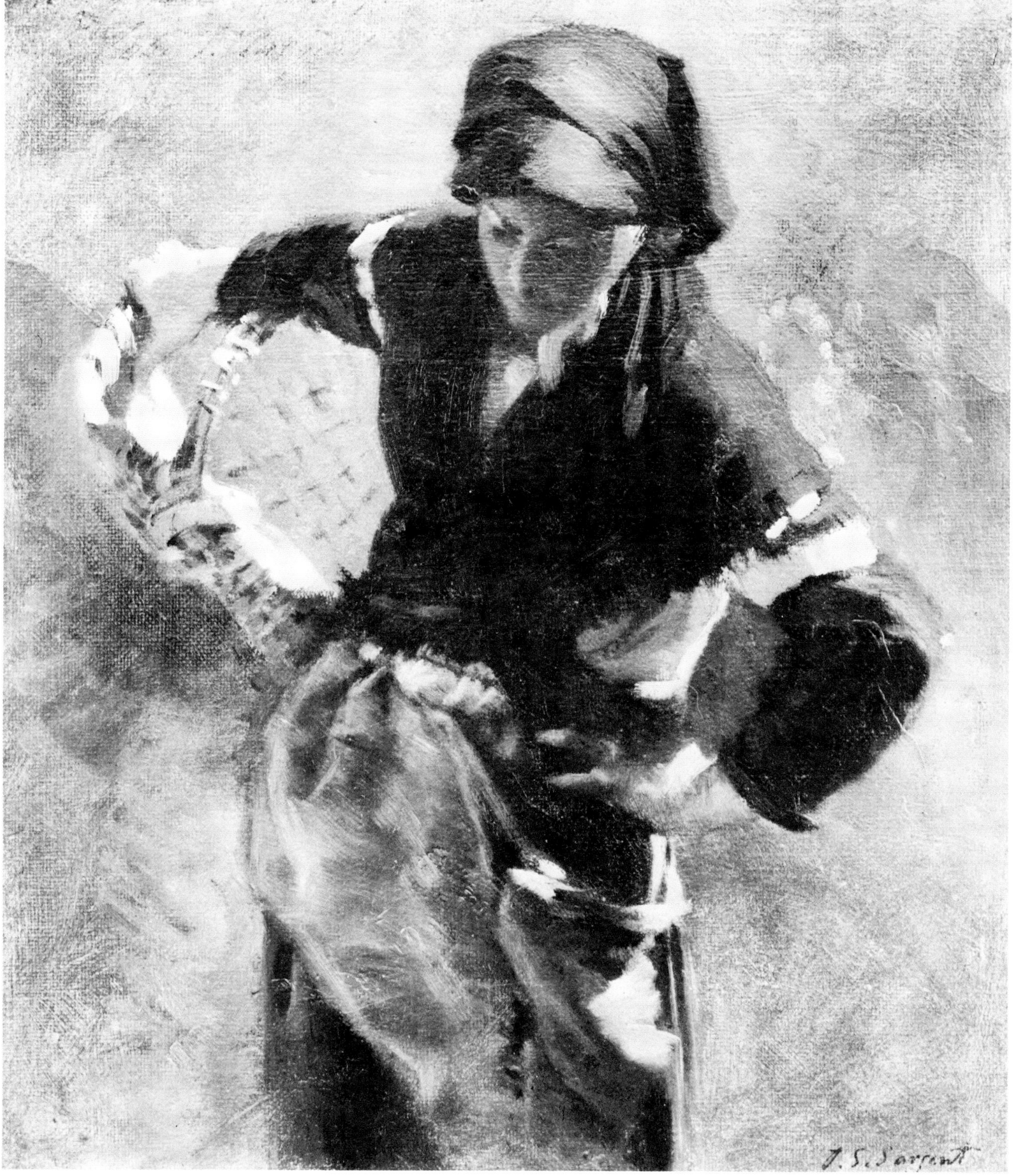
J. S. Sargent

John Singer Sargent

Sargent had an extraordinary eye; before the camera was able to do so, he could catch the fleeting moment, the casual movement, the glance that reveals the inner life. His brilliance so fascinated his contemporaries that in the end the demand for portraits grew burdensome and he sought release in watercolors and mural painting. But in the 1880's, before his interest in people had been dulled by repetition and his eye was at its freshest, what a painter he was!

Here is a young woman in the pride of her beauty and elegance, eyes alight, lips slightly parted, the clear skin of her throat and shoulders glowing above her low corsage as she throws back her enveloping evening cloak. She is the luminous vision of a moment against the darkness, about to sweep past on her way to the Opera. It is a mysterious power of art to make an instant timeless and to evoke by its presence a whole world.

Caroline Marie Eugenie Philippe Ghislaine de Bassano, Marquise d'Espeuilles, is a figure from a vanished world. Her mother was lady of honor to the Empress Eugenie and a great hostess in Paris of the Second Empire. Her father was a diplomat, senator, and *grand chamberlain du palais* to Napoleon III. The Bassano title went back only a generation further to a journalist and author, Bernard Hugues Maret, who became a confidant and chief civilian aide to Napoleon I, who rewarded his skill and loyalty by great estates and the title of duc de Bassano. On September 7, 1871, his granddaughter Caroline married a young cavalry officer, Marie-Louis Antonin, Marquis d'Espeuilles, of an old family of Nièvre, who had served in the war of 1870 and rose later to be Inspector General of cavalry. In 1878 the marquis was elected senator and took his place among the bonapartist group of the conservative majority. The list of his clubs given in Rovigny—Jockey, Cercle de la Rue-Royale, Société-hippique, Union, Union Artistique—gives a picture of his world.

At that time it was not easy for a young foreign artist to attract the patronage of conservative French society. Sargent's talent, since his first appearance in the Salon of 1878, had begun to win him a position as a portrait painter, but his portrait of *Mme. Gautreau* (now in The Metropolitan Museum) in the Salon of 1884 caused a storm. It is hard to understand why the portrait of this well-known beauty should ever have seemed suggestive or immoral, but it was so savagely criticized that Sargent moved to England. His career thereafter was centered in London and Boston.

Canvas: 62 x 41 inches. Signed and dated, *J. S. Sargent 1884*.

91 *Caroline de Bassano, Marquise d'Espeuilles 1884*

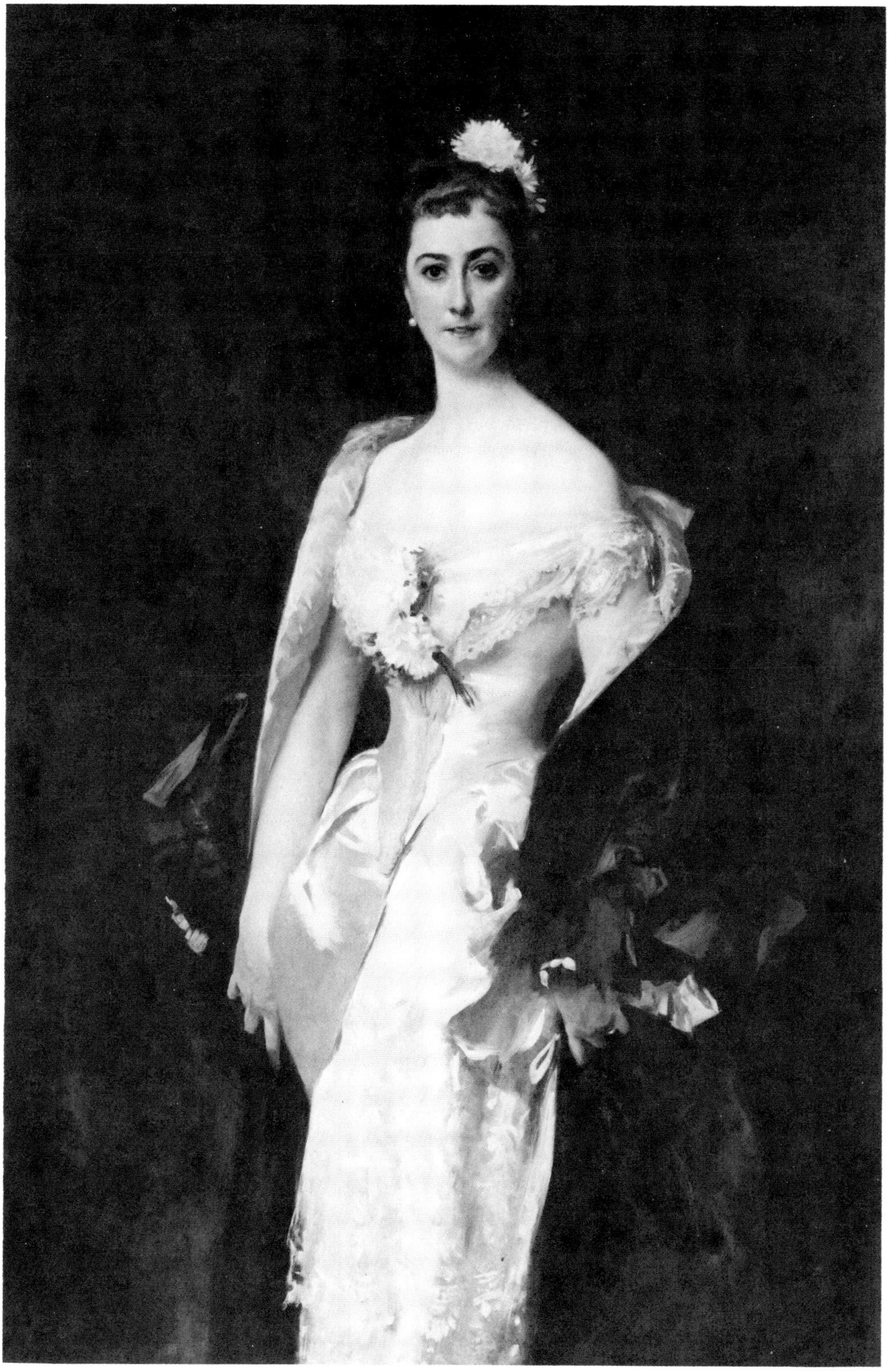

Charles Frederick Ulrich 1858-1908

The reviving interest in American impressionism has resulted in many rediscoveries in the landscape painting of the close of the nineteenth century, but Mr. Rockefeller has been exceptional in exploring the pre-impressionist figure painters. Ulrich was born in New York City, studied at the National Academy of Design and in Munich, and on his return exhibited in 1884 a large picture of arriving immigrants called *In the Land of Promise—Castle Garden* (Corcoran Gallery of Art, Washington), which was the first recipient of the Clark prize at the National Academy of Design. In 1886 a group of gentlemen gave Ulrich's painting of *Glass Blowers at Murano* to The Metropolitan Museum of Art.

This small picture of 1883 has the qualities that excited the admiration of these collectors—pure and lustrous color, exact observation, ability to capture the character of a moment. It was an age of music in the home, when every American family wished to have a piano. To the eye of an artist, the intimacy, the concentration and the charm of the subject offered many possibilities, which Ulrich has put to good use.

Oil on panel: 14⅞ x 19¼ inches. Signed at the lower left, *C. F. Ulrich, ANA 1883*

92 *Moment Musicale 1883*

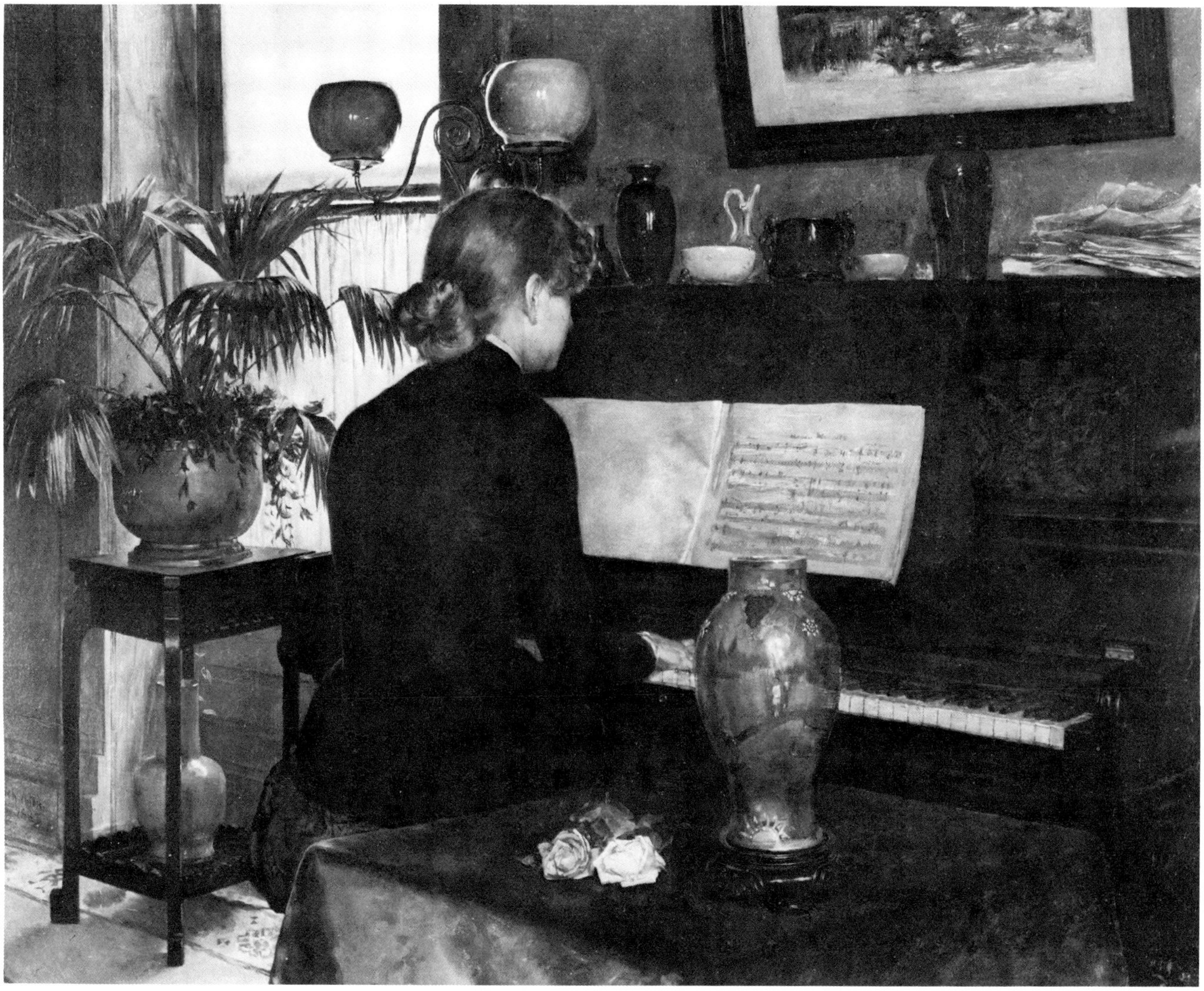

Elihu Vedder 1836-1923

Vedder came of the old Dutch stock of the Hudson Valley. His parents moved from Schenectady to New York City, where Elihu was born on Varick Street in 1836. He died at Rome in 1923. From 1856 to 1858, he studied in France; he went on to Florence for the following two years, where he was associated with the young and talented group of Italian artists known as the Macchiaioli. He returned to New York City in 1861. In 1865 he set up his studio in Rome but continued his activity in New York as book illustrator, decorative painter and mural painter. Vedder's fame in his lifetime came from his illustrations to *The Rubaiyat of Omar Khayyam* (1884) and from his mural paintings of the nineties in the Walker Art Gallery of Bowdoin College and in the Library of Congress. To our eyes his landscapes and visionary subjects have the greatest appeal. Ferris Greenslet, who knew him while he was writing his autobiography, *The Digressions of V,* said that his quality of imagination (a term thought by Greenslet to be more accurate than literary quality) combined "a steady sense of the melancholy mystery of the world with the genial temperament of an Anacreontic poet." The latter made him a favorite member of The Century Association: the former, out of fashion for fifty years, is today of great interest.

Three Monks at Fiesole is one of his first impressions of Italy and an astonishing achievement for a young American dealing with an experience so novel and profound. It is, he wrote, a sketch made on a dark, stormy day, with the road and cypresses coming down from Fiesole, into which he inserted three Dominican friars "whose black and white garments carried out the feeling seen in hillside and sky" (Soria, 28-29). Vedder thought the picture had been destroyed by the collapse of a building at Madison Square Garden during a loan exhibition, but it survived and belonged early in the century to Prosper Guerry.

Panel: 12¼ x 10¼ inches. Signed at lower left, *Vedder.*

93 *Three Monks Walking in a Garden at Fiesole* 1859

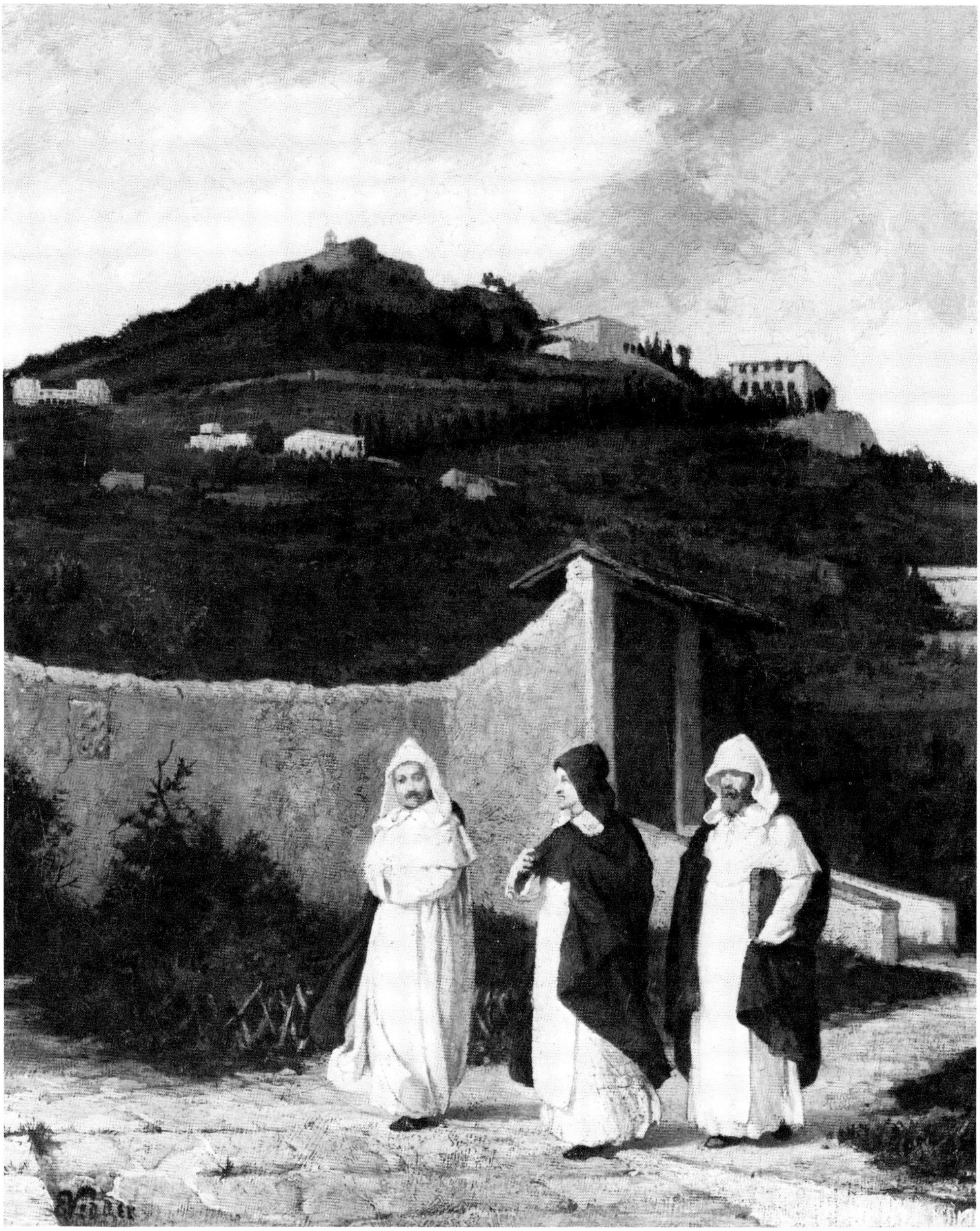

Elihu Vedder

Vedder was a passionate lover of landscape. The haunted solemnity of Italy with its mingling of ancient buildings and austere natural forms stirred his deepest feelings. The torrent Mugnone, within easy walking distance, gave him subjects for two of his finest early landscapes. An insignificant stream except during flood, it winds down out of the hills north of Florence, below the height of Fiesole with its villas and gardens, and enters the Arno just below the city. Vedder painted it first looking south toward the greener hills along the Arno (now in Detroit) and afterward produced this austerely beautiful view looking northward into the bare hills. Its harmony of delicate nuances of greys and sand colors shows Vedder at his best.

Academy board: 6 x 15½ inches. Inscribed on the reverse: *Painted for Mrs. R. W. Sanford by Elihu Vedder, 1864.*

94 *The Bed of the Torrent Mugnone 1864*

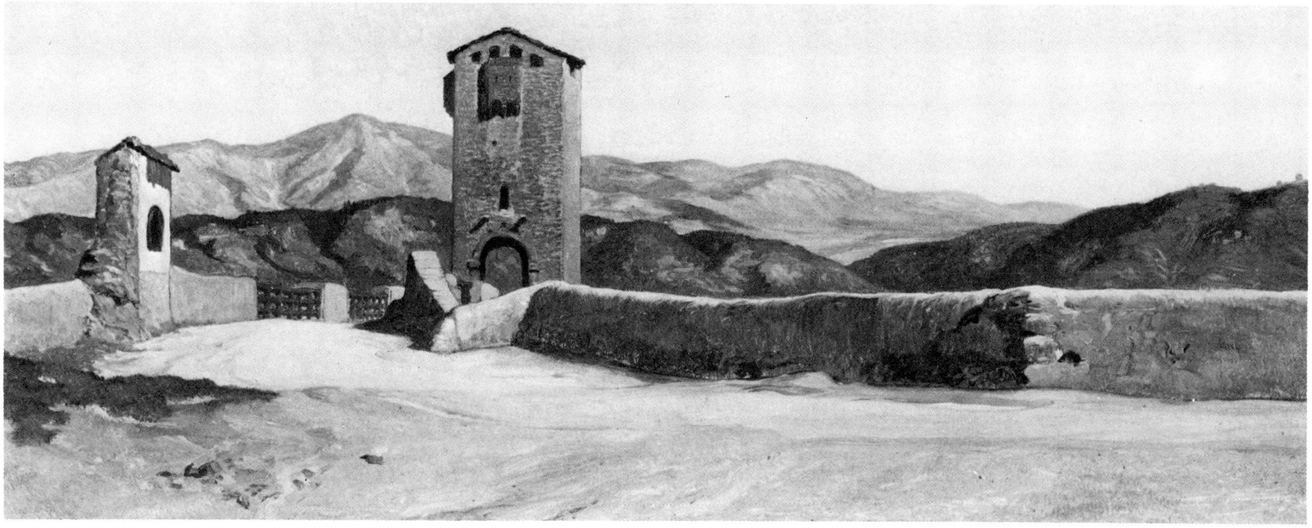

IX

The Twentieth Century

In our century there have been many movements and styles of painting; but the broad underlying currents of imagination that showed themselves before 1900 remain the same; and we still have the brilliant cosmopolitan artist, the artist who finds his poetry in the everyday face of America, and the visionary. To the first belong stylists like Demuth or Hartley, who distill from a few fruits bought in the farmer's market at Lancaster, or the view of a wooded hillside in Maine, visions that belong to no country except the world of art. Others are spiritual heirs of nineteenth-century realism: Henri painting a New York City workingman, Burchfield finding grand landscapes in the industrial suburbs of Buffalo, Wyeth painting the people and hillsides he has known all his life. The few works shown were chosen by a thoughtful collector; each, in its own way, has deep roots in the imaginative life of America.

Charles Burchfield 1893-1967

The cataloguer of Burchfield's work, Charles Trovato, says that the year 1933 was one of self-examination in the artist's life. He was dissatisfied with his recent work, feeling that he had lost touch with nature and that he needed fresh impressions.

If that was his feeling, his action was most characteristic. Instead of seeking novelties, he turned to his oldest sources of inspiration—the unpainted wooden houses around his home (1933 was the depth of the depression), the railroads, the sun over all—to study them with a new intensity. Watercolors of that year, like this, are remarkable for their austere economy of subject and for their power.

Watercolor: 28 x 42 inches. Signed at the lower right with monogram and date *1933*.

95 *Railroad in Spring 1933*

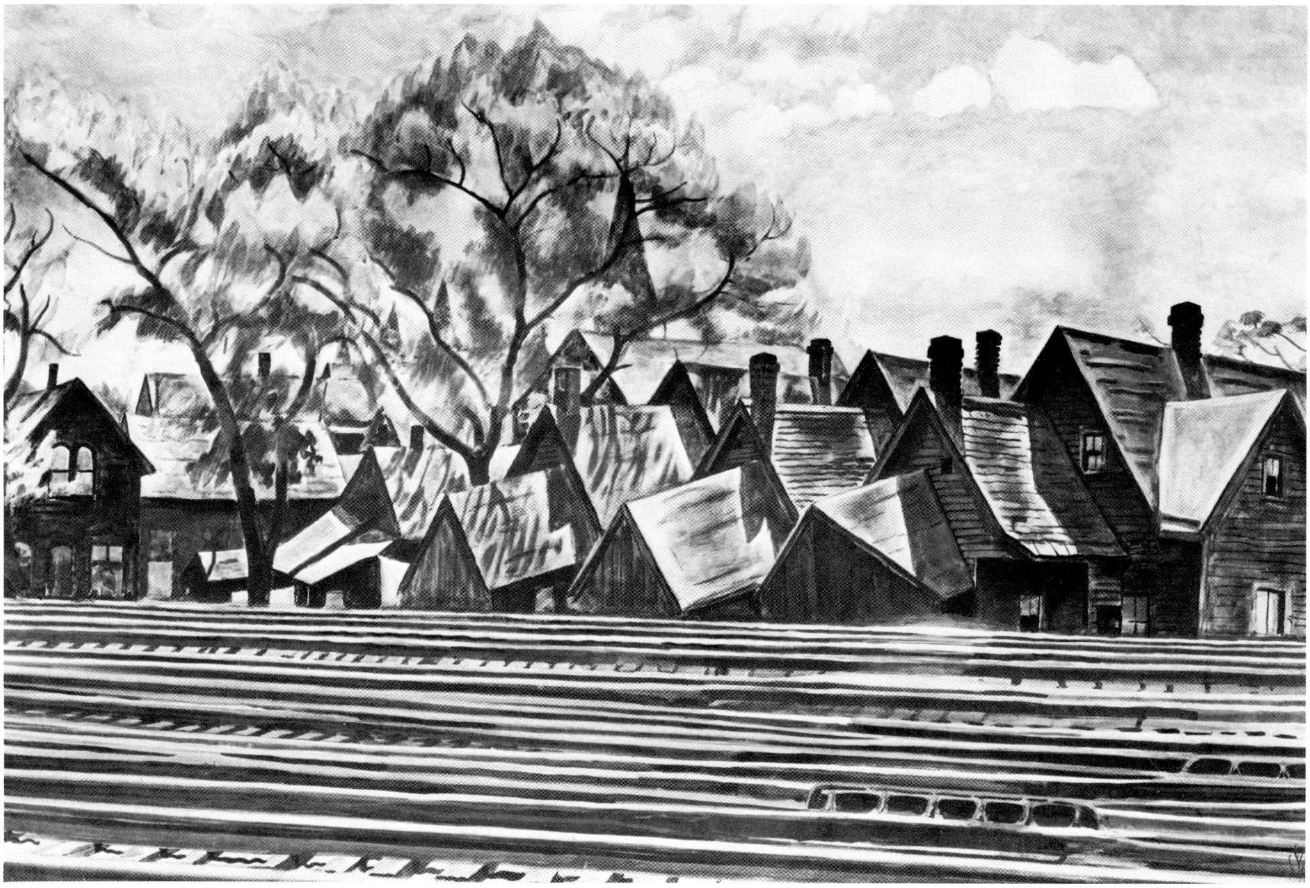

Charles Burchfield

In the 1920's the most important new influences on American art came from Paris. The Armory Show had established as dogma that learning the lessons of Cézanne and of the new movements in painting in Paris was the highroad all painters should follow. The atmosphere of the decade was dominated by expatriates. A group of writers living in Paris if they could (if not at least in New York), and filled with ardor from the backwash of the 1914 war, proclaimed that the United States had no soul and that life there stifled the human spirit. (Any resemblance to the 1960's may illustrate that those who know no history are doomed to repeat it.)

Burchfield cannot be said to have contradicted these expatriates because there is no evidence he gave them a moment's thought. Growing up in a small village in Ohio, studying art in Cleveland, he saw in the Cleveland Museum the Chinese scroll paintings that inspired his development. He created his own watercolor style in solitude, half from introspection, half from study of the world about him. In the 1920's introspection ruled. In the thirties he turned outward (he was then living in a small village outside Buffalo, New York) to find in the houses and gardens around his home, in the grey skies of March and November and the hot sun of August, in the railroads, viaducts and harbor of Buffalo, materials for an art of deep poetic mood and affirmation. In this painting of the two bridges where the Erie and New York Central railroads crossed the black waters of the Buffalo River, he gave us an image of the power and grandeur of American technology.

Watercolor: 29 x 41 inches. Signed with monogram, at the lower left, dated *1935*.

96 *Black Iron 1935*

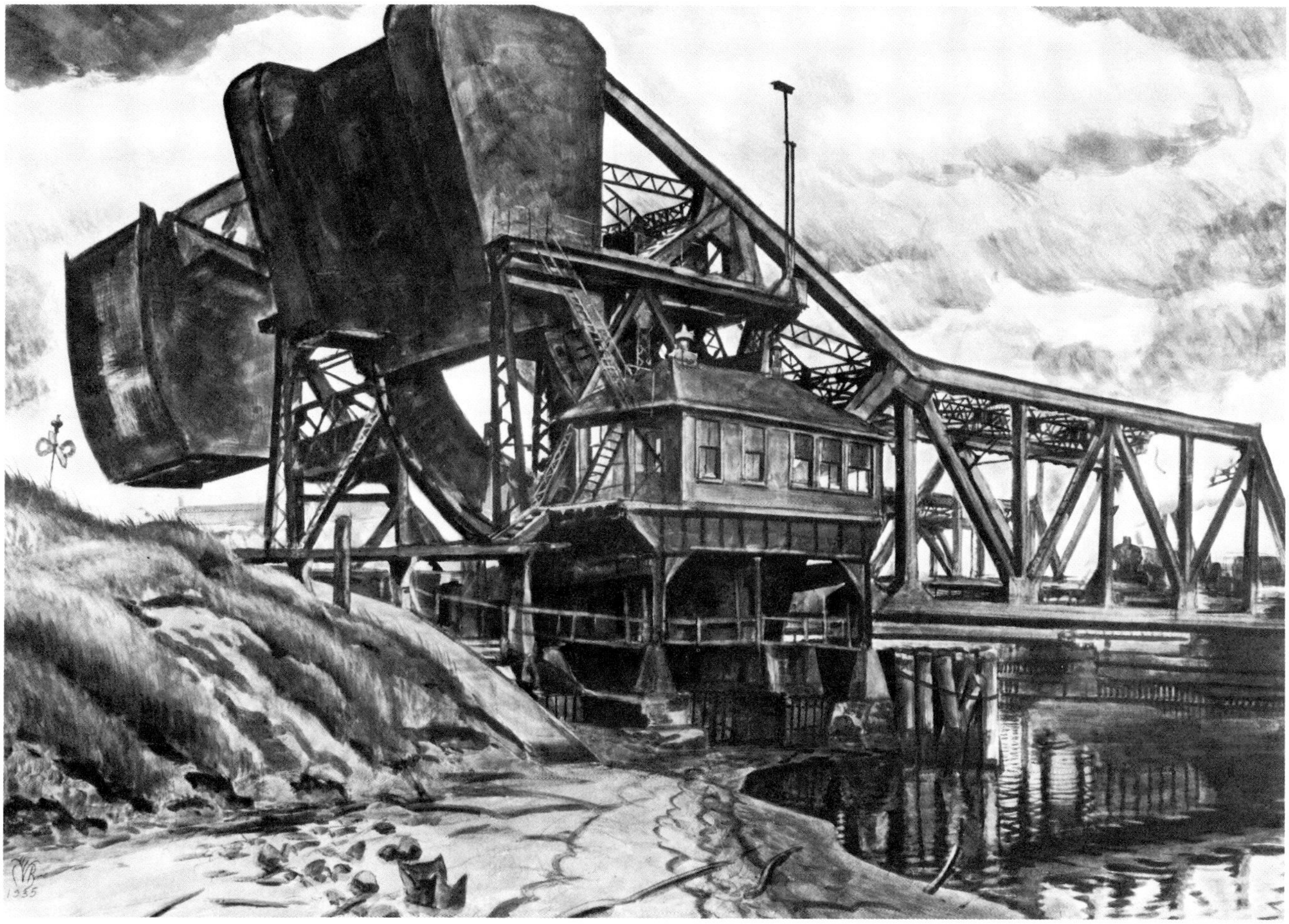

Charles Demuth 1883-1935

No one else has used watercolor quite as Demuth used it. One may think of analogies—the colors of birds' eggs, the clean outlines and exact spacing of a print by Utamaro—yet there are only analogies. He invented his own way. The crisp outlines, delicately exact spacing, the glowing yet transparent colors are unlike anything else.

Demuth was born in the pleasant old city of Lancaster, Pennsylvania, of a family that had come with the first migration of German settlers into that region. He studied under Anshutz at the Pennsylvania Academy of the Fine Arts and immersed himself in the ferment of the first wave of modern painting in Paris. But though he loved the Bohemian life, in the same way that Lancaster was always home to him, his art, though distilled from many influences, was his own creation. He died at Lancaster at the age of fifty-two.

97. *Blue Plums. Watercolor:* 11¾ x 17¾ inches. Signed at the lower left; *C. Demuth 1924.*

98. *Apples. Watercolor:* 11¼ x 13¾ inches (sight). Signed at the lower left, *C. Demuth Feb. 1925 Lancaster Pa.*

97 *Blue Plums* 1924

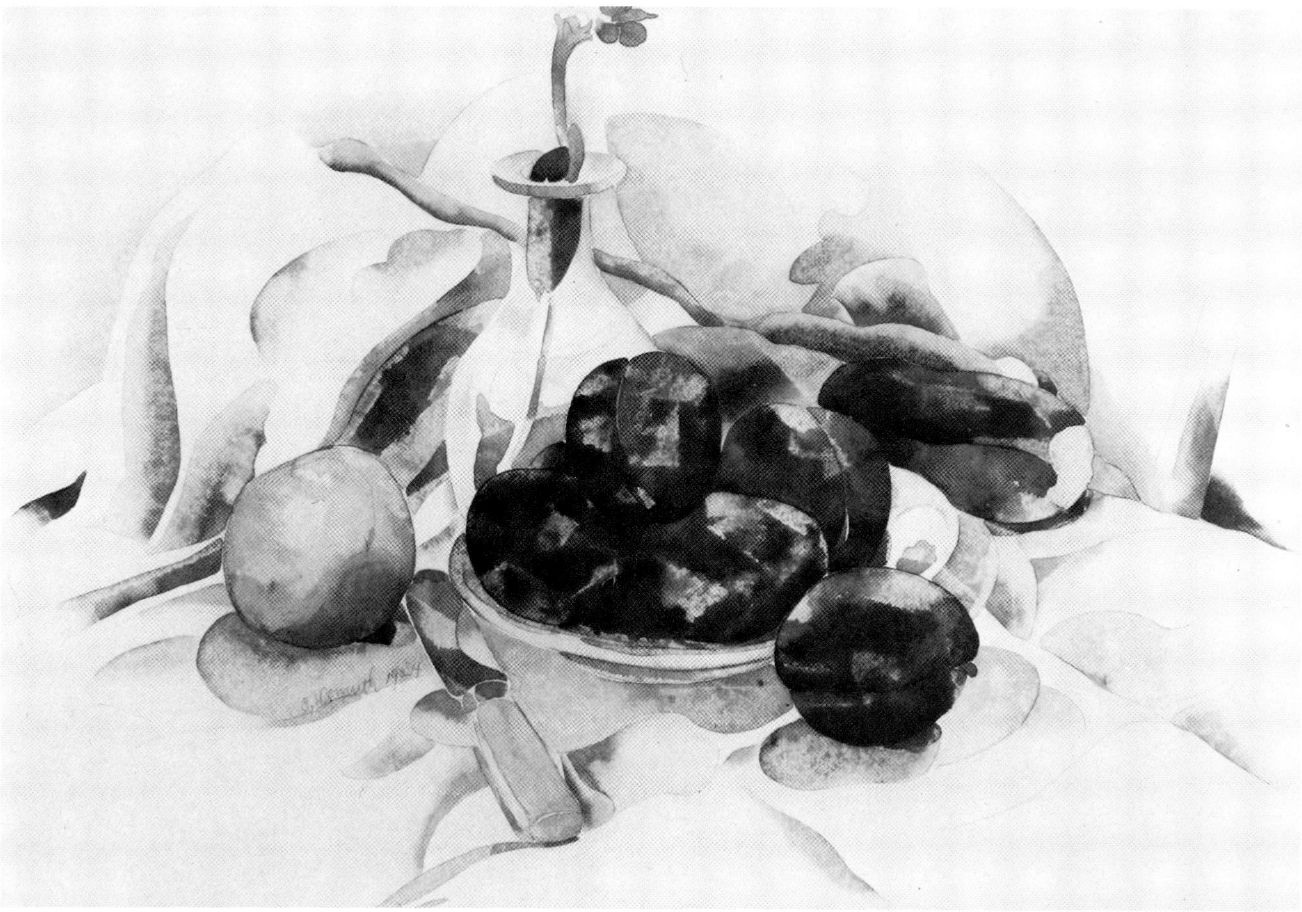

Charles Demuth

98 *Apples* 1925

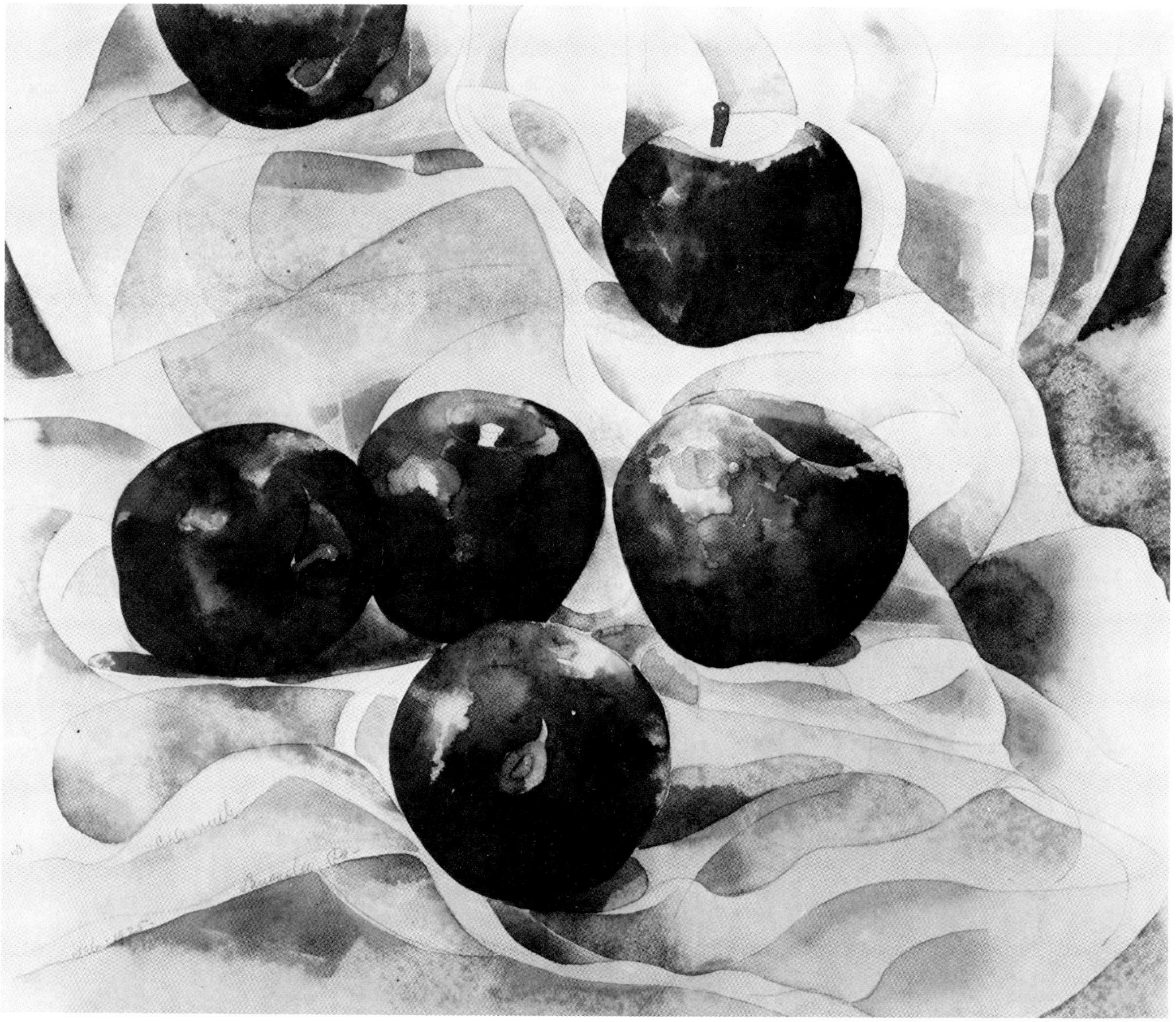

Marsden Hartley 1877-1949

Popular success came late to Marsden Hartley—from the work of only the last ten years of an entire life devoted to artistic experiments. There is a harsh, massive power in his late pictures, painted when he had returned from much wandering to his native Maine. They stood out in the exhibitions of the thirties; by these he is represented everywhere.

This picture belongs to his youth. It was painted in the year of his first exhibition, given him by Alfred Stieglitz at his famous gallery "291" before Stieglitz and Arthur B. Davies financed his first trip abroad in 1912. Alone in Maine, Hartley in 1909 was working out his first vision of the world and his first style of painting under the strangely conjoined inspirations of the Italian impressionist Segantini and the American dreamer Albert P. Ryder. Twenty years later he wrote, "I personally am indebted to Segantini the impressionist, not Segantini the symbolist, for what I have learned in times past of the mountain and a given way to express it—just as it was Ryder who accentuated my already tormented imagination." (Hartley, 1929). This is a lyrical vision: the grandeur of mountain and forest are translated into rushing streams of color and dramatic strokes of the brush. The painting has a quality that I do not find in the later Hartley: one feels the excitement and enthusiasm of a first discovery of the world of color and pigment. It was in Alfred Stieglitz's collection.

Canvas: 30 x 40 inches.

99 *Summer Camp, Blue Mountain* 1909

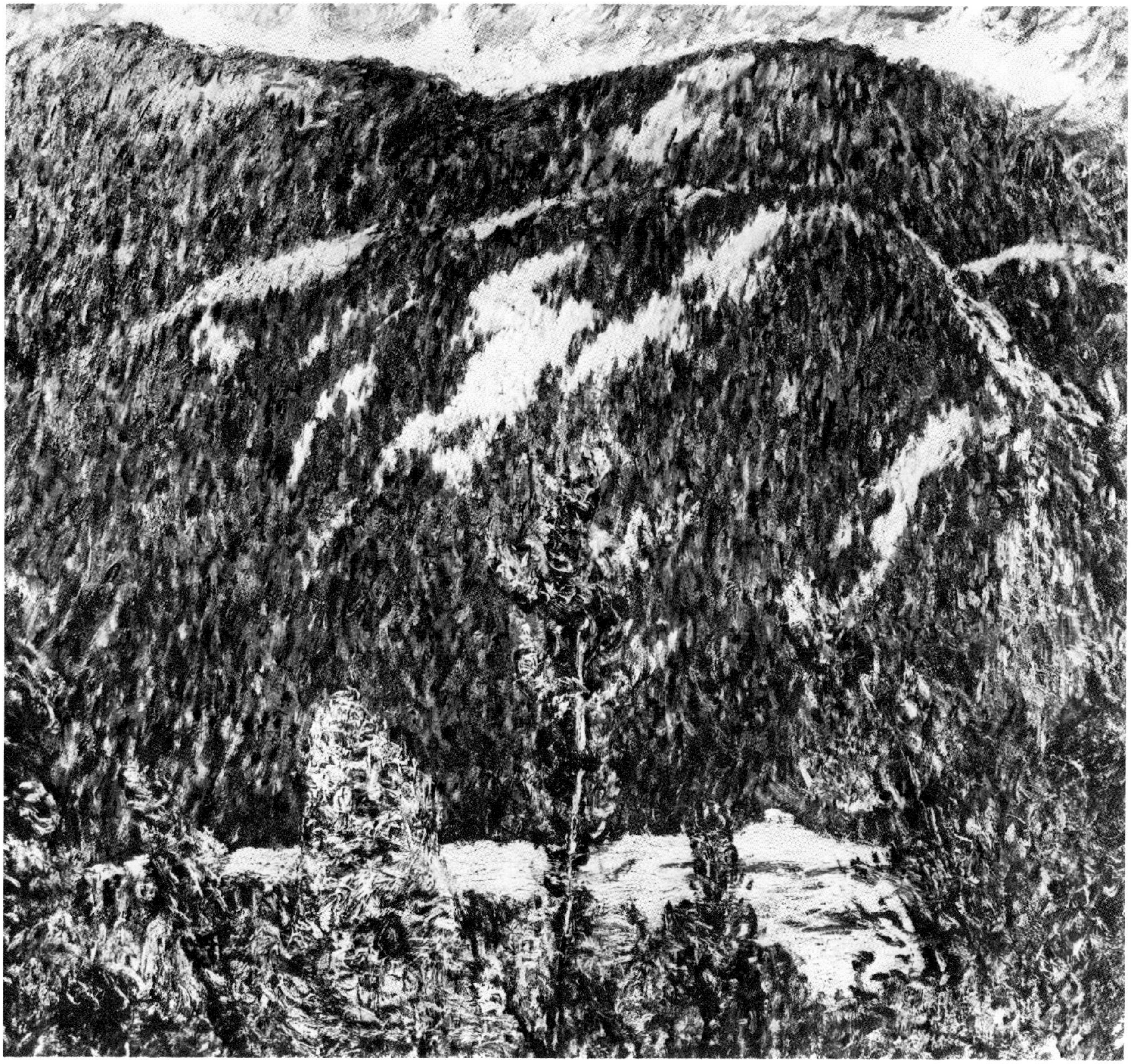

Childe Hassam 1859-1935

Childe Hassam was born at Dorchester, a suburb of Boston, and his first works were city views of Boston in a handsome, tonal style. In Paris in 1888 he came under the influence of the impressionist style, adopting its high-keyed palette and brushwork. There is a vigor and robustness in Hassam's work, a richness of paint and brushstroke, that sets him apart from other members of the group who tend toward more delicate and decorative ways of painting. The bold pattern of light and shadow, the rich impasto and the cheerful atmosphere of this picture of a summer afternoon show Hassam at his best. As the most recent survey of American impressionism characterizes him, "Hassam was a natural-born painter; he enjoyed painting more than anything else and there is a zest and sheer joy in his work that make him, at his best period, the leader of the American impressionists." (Boyle, 1974). This picture was once erroneously called *Afternoon in Nantucket,* but Hassam never visited that island town.

Canvas: 18 x 23 inches.

100 *Afternoon*

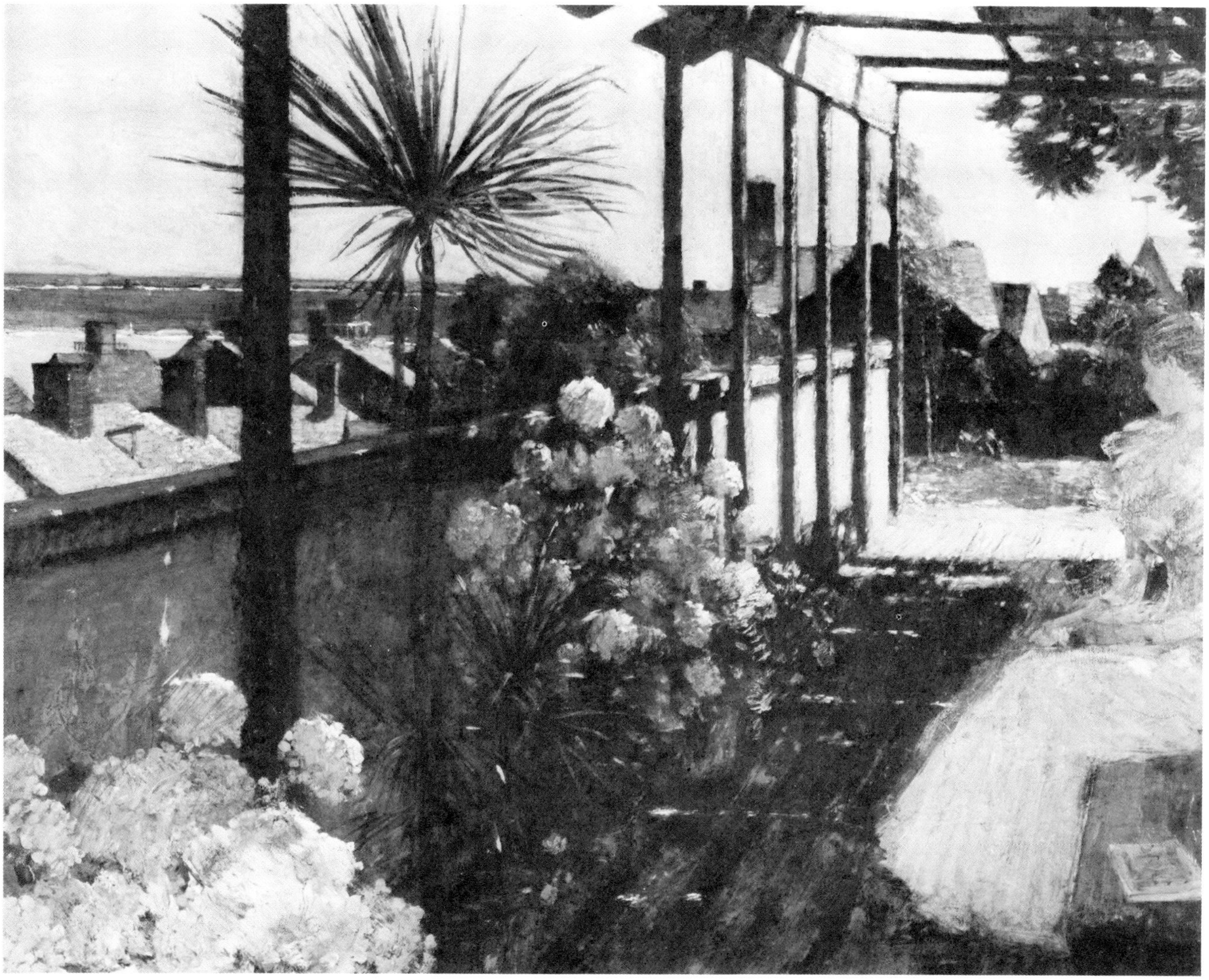

Robert Henri 1865-1929

Henri was born at Cincinnati in 1865 and died at New York in 1929. He studied at the Pennsylvania Academy of the Fine Arts with Anshutz and Hovenden and at the Académie Julian and the Ecole des Beaux-Arts, Paris; but the strongest European influence came from study of Frans Hals and the Spanish realists. He made his home in Philadelphia, with extended stays abroad, until 1900, after which he lived in New York. A magnetic and devoted teacher, he put a great part of his creative energy into teaching. *The Art Spirit* (1923) preserves in book form something of his power to communicate his ideas through words.

By the 1890's the strongest influences upon our painting were the art for art's sake creed of Whistler and the luminous, high-keyed color of Impressionism; but as these became popular, they also became watered down. Henri was the center and inspiration of a group of young artists, products of the Pennsylvania Academy, who brought a fresh impetus. Revivifying the realism and the warm, dark tonality of Eakins' and the Academy's tradition, they returned to the sources of realism in Dutch and Spanish painting. The *Working Man,* in its bold, free brushstrokes and animated spirit, shows what Henri learned from his delight in Frans Hals, whose work he saw in Haarlem that same year. It may illustrate two characteristic sayings in *The Art Spirit:* "The people I like to paint are 'my people,' whoever they may be...the people through whom dignity of life is manifest...I am not interested in any one school or movement, nor do I care for art as art. I am interested in life."

Canvas: 24 x 20⅛ inches. Signed at lower right: *Robert Henri*. The date 1910 is that given by William I. Homer (1969).

101 *Working Man 1910*

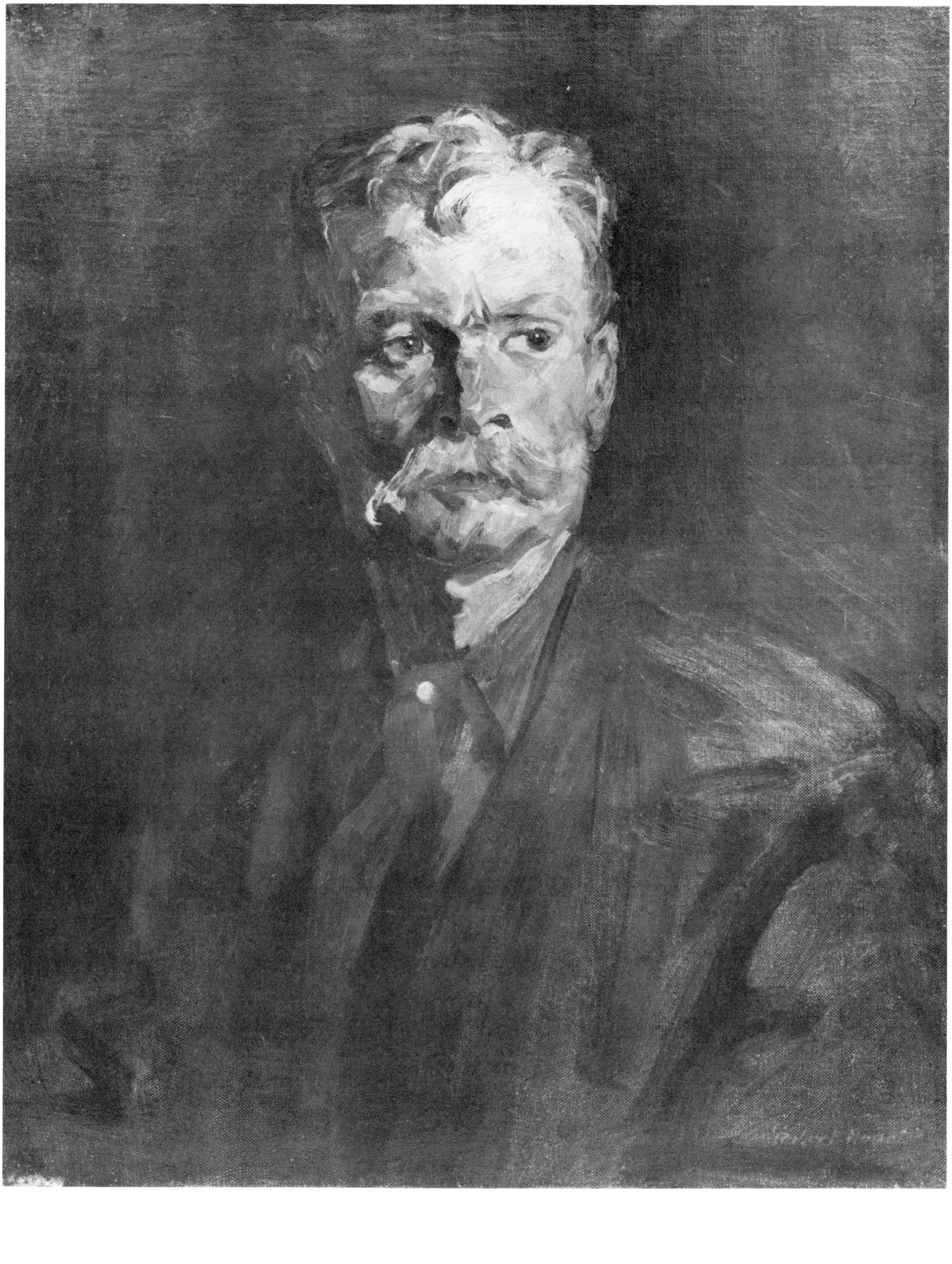

Ben Shahn 1898-1969

There is a power in Ben Shahn's portraits. This drawing illustrated an article on Gandhi written for *Look* magazine by Leo Rosten (*Look*, August 25, 1969). Rosten described Gandhi as "an ugly, skinny, fearless little man (who) was a 'moral genius,' a triumph of sheer character and will." (Prescott, 1973). Although not done from life, Shahn's portrait is unforgettable: it shows more a spirit than a physical being. Part of its power lies in the mental image formed in the mind of the artist, part in the quality of the drawing. Shahn did not draw with a flowing line of the pen or brush; his line is built of short, blunt strokes, each one of which is like a thrust.

Shahn issued afterward three print versions of the drawing: a serigraph (nearly indistinguishable from the drawing), a slightly smaller collotype, and a still smaller broadside. The latter two have an inscription from Mark Twain's *Mysterious Stranger* filling the left background.

Ink and brush drawing: 34 x 25 inches, sight. Signed at the lower right, *Ben Shahn*.

102 *Gandhi 1964*

Grant Wood 1892-1942

Grant Wood's was a late-blooming talent. He was thirty-seven years old when chance took him to Munich to oversee the execution of a large stained glass window designed by him for the Cedar Rapids Memorial Building and City Hall. While the window was slowly executed, he studied the early Flemish and German pictures in the Alte Pinakothek. The people in those pictures, he thought, looked like those he knew in Cedar Rapids. He admired the slow, careful way of painting and the lustrous colors, and he went home determined to paint his own people in similar way. His true life as an artist began then.

Dinner for Threshers shows in its flat, monumental design the influence of the enthusiasm for mural painting omnipresent in the America of the thirties. But it is also straight from the life of the farm on which Wood was born near Anamosa, Iowa, and where he lived to the age of ten, when his father died and his mother sold the farm to move with the four children into Cedar Rapids. In an unpublished fragment of autobiography (Archives of American Art), Wood describes that period of his life vividly and with deep affection. So real is this memory image that after *Time Magazine* reproduced the picture (December 24, 1934), readers wrote to offer corrections: the shadows of the hens are too short for that time of year; one screen door is missing; this or that other detail should be different. Wood defended himself stoutly: "*Dinner for Threshers* is from my own life. It includes my family and our neighbors, our tablecloths, our chairs, and our hens. It was painted with my paint and my brushes, on my own time. It is of me and by me, and readers have no right to force upon me their families and their farms." (Garwood, 1944). His biographer speculates that Wood's father is the man on the piano stool who, as host, took the least comfortable seat; the rag rugs are the kind his mother made; and his mother is the standing woman serving the food on the far side of the table, as she would have appeared thirty-five years before.

Tempera on panel: 19½ x 79½ inches. Signed at the lower left, *Grant Wood/1934* and the copyright mark. Preliminary drawings for the two ends of the composition are in the Whitney Museum of American Art; one for the entire composition is in the collection of Mrs. Stanley Resor, New York.

103 *Dinner for Threshers 1934*

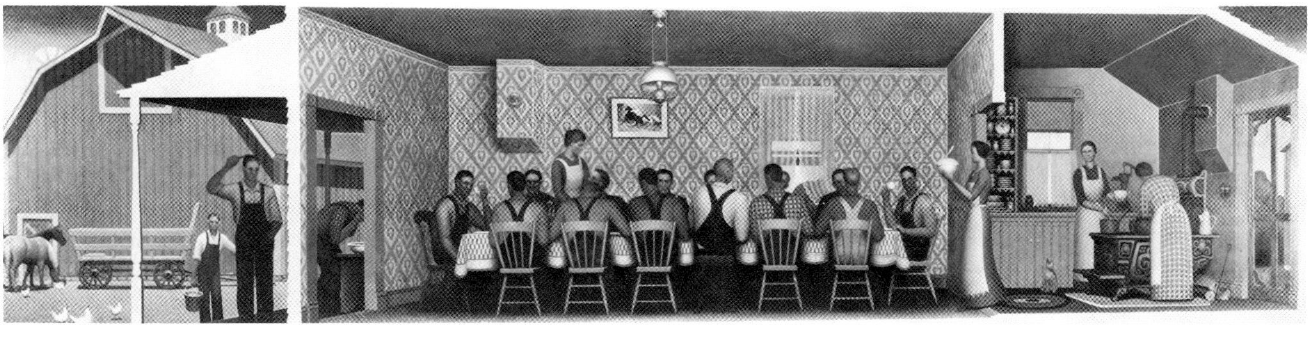

Grant Wood

In 1936 Wood was commissioned to illustrate Sinclair Lewis's *Main Street* for the Limited Editions Club (Chicago: Lakeside Press, 1936). This is one of six illustrations using actual models but converting them into types found in the book: *The Perfectionist, Sentimental Yearner, The Radical, The Good Influence, Practical Idealist*. There were also three additional illustrations: *General Practitioner*, a study of a doctor's hands; *Main Street Mansion,* an old house with a large porch; and *Village Slum.* Wood felt that Lewis's *Main Street* and *Babbitt* had had a liberating effect upon artists of that part of the world, showing them the possibility of finding artistic material in their own lives.

Watercolor and crayon: 20 x 16 inches. Signed at the lower right, *Grant Wood 1936.*

104   *The Perfectionist 1936*

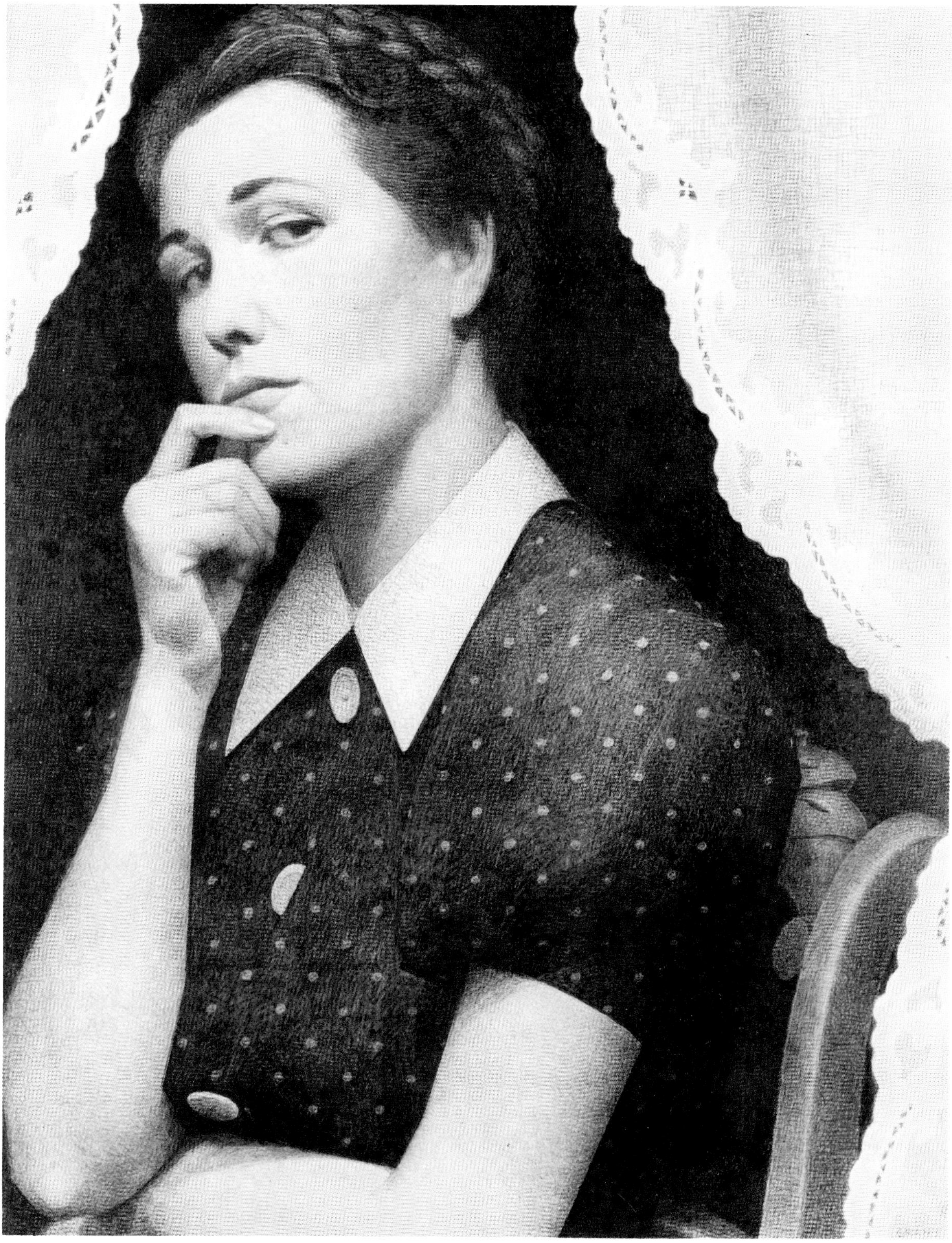
GRANT

Andrew Wyeth 1917-

The place of Andrew Wyeth in the art of our century is a curious commentary upon the incessant striving for novelty that drives so many modern artists. Wyeth paints the simplest, most familiar experiences of his life. His subjects are those he has found at his doorstep. They are all within a mile or two of home, over the hill behind the studio or up the Brandywine valley, in two or three nearby farmhouses, or in only a slightly larger area in Maine. They are familiar things seen a thousand times, yet seen and felt so intensely that they become new. One must go back to the Dutch painters of the seventeenth century to find artists who could see and feel so much in so small a piece of the world.

The Olsons lived near the Wyeth's summer home in Maine. The brother, a fisherman turned truck gardener, did not like to pose; but the sister, crippled by infantile paralysis, and the house itself have been the topics of many pictures. Christina Olson, although so handicapped that she moved about only by crawling or by moving her chair, was a woman of intelligence and strong character, without self pity. There are two earlier paintings of her, *Miss Olson* of 1947 and *Christina's World* of 1948. Here, holding a sick kitten, she reveals her strength.

Tempera on masonite panel: 25 x 28½ inches. Signed at the lower right, *Andrew Wyeth*.

105 *Miss Olson* 1952

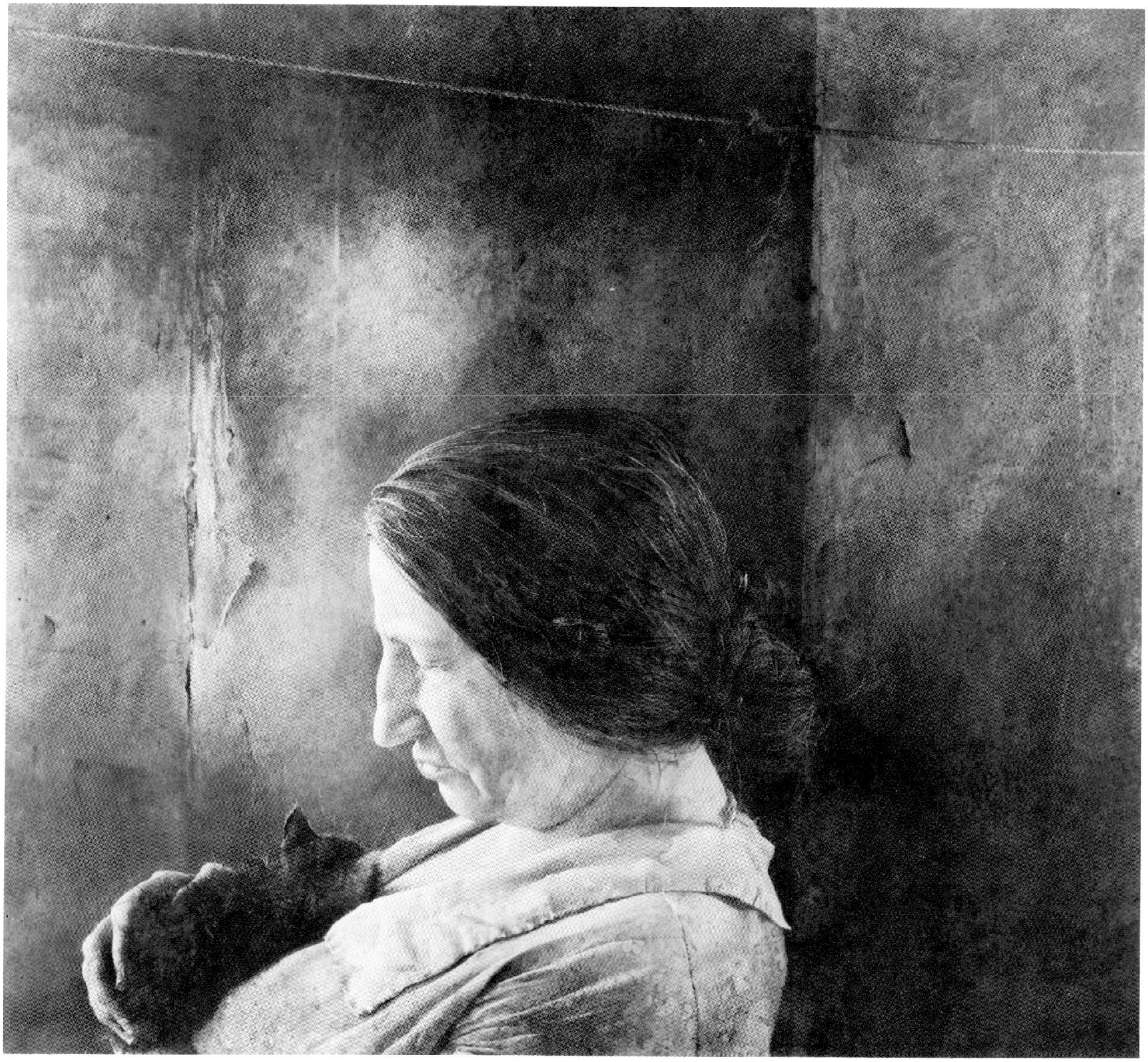

Andrew Wyeth

The orchard on the hill behind the studio in Chadds Ford, on land purchased by N. C. Wyeth, has been part of the artist's life since childhood. The pleasures of autumn days, the fragrance of the apples, the damp cool air, the slanting light of short afternoons, the greys and brown of the November landscape, are part of the recurring cycle of the seasons, remembered and recorded through the vision of an artist. This is a brilliant example of the combined freedom and control Wyeth achieves in what he terms his dry-brush watercolor technique.

Watercolor: 19½ x 27½ inches, sight. Signed at the lower right, *Andrew Wyeth*.

106 *Frosted Apples 1967*

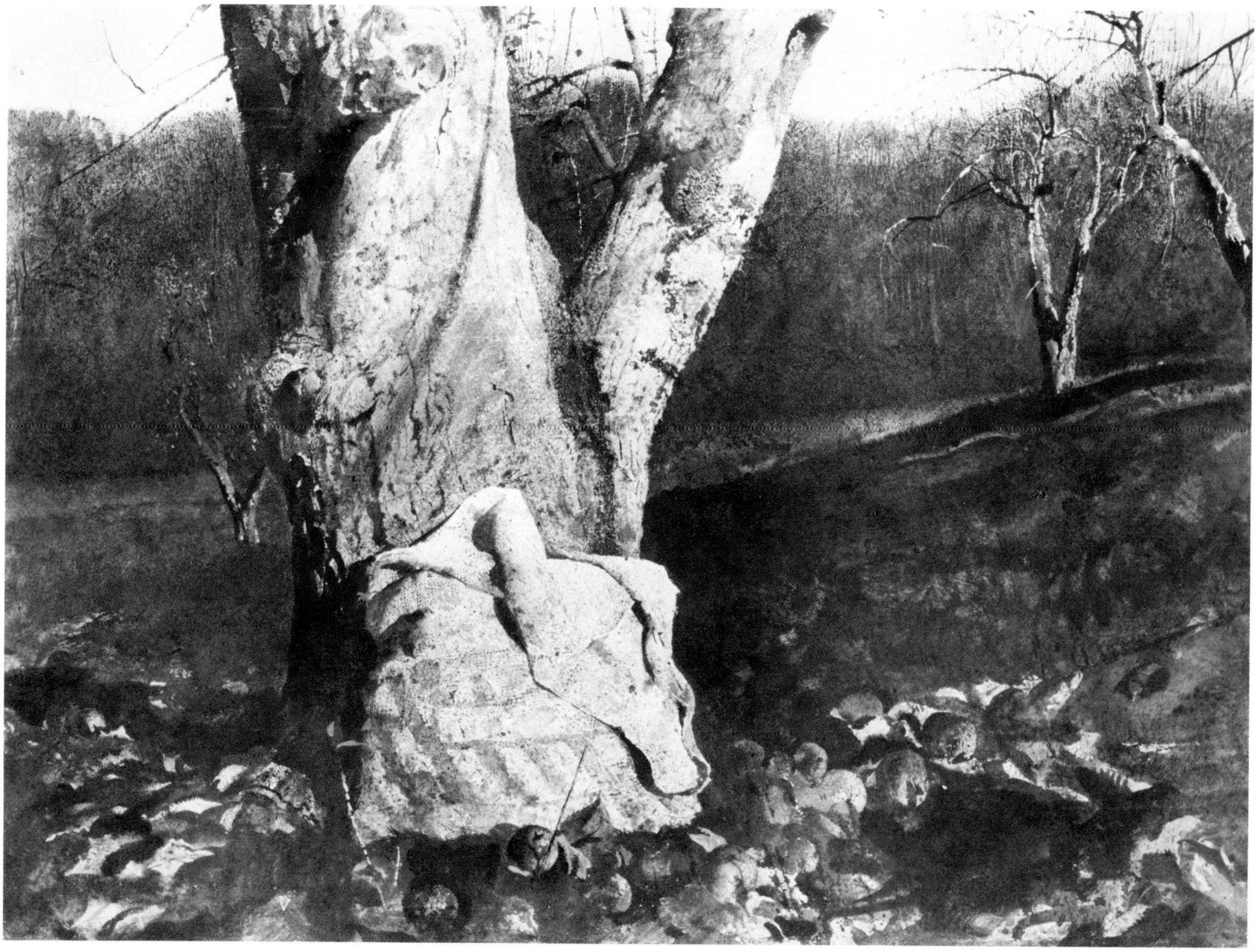

Bibliography of Publications Mentioned in the Catalogue

ADELMAN & CASTERAS
Seymour Adelman & Susan P. Casteras, *Susan Macdowell Eakins*. Pennsylvania Academy of the Fine Arts (1973)

AUDUBON
Maria R. Audubon. *Audubon and His Journals*. New York (1898), 2 volumes

BALL
Thomas Ball. *My Three Score Years and Ten: An Autobiography*. Boston: Roberts Brothers (1891)

BAUR
John I. H. Baur, ed. "The Autobiography of Worthington Whittredge, 1820-1910," *Brooklyn Museum Journal* (1942)

BLOCH
E. Maurice Bloch. *George Caleb Bingham 1811-1879*. Washington: Smithsonian Institution Press for the National Collection of Fine Arts (1968)

E. Maurice Bloch. "A Bingham Discovery," *American Art Review*, I (1973)

BOYLE
Richard J. Boyle. *American Impressionism*. Boston: New York Graphic Society (1974)

BURROUGHS
Alan Burroughs. *Limners and Likenesses*. Cambridge, Mass.: Harvard University Press (1936)

DRESSER
Louisa Dresser. *XVIIth-Century Painting in New England*. Worcester Art Museum (1935)

Louisa Dresser. "Portraits in Boston," *Journal of the Archives of American Art*, VI (1966)

DURAND
John Durand. *The Life and Times of A. B. Durand*. New York: Charles Scribner's Sons (1894); reprinted by Kennedy Graphics, Inc., Da Capo Press (1970)

DWIGHT
Edward H. Dwight. *Audubon: Drawings and Watercolors*. Utica: Munson-Williams-Proctor Institute, and New York: The Pierpont Morgan Library (1965)

FLEXNER
James Thomas Flexner. *First Flowers of Our Wilderness*. Boston: Houghton Mifflin Company (1937)

FRANKENSTEIN
Alfred Frankenstein. *After the Hunt: William Harnett and Other American Still-Life Painters 1870-1900*. Berkeley and Los Angeles: University of California Press (1953); revised edition (1969)

Alfred Frankenstein. *The Reminiscent Object*. La Jolla Museum of Art (1965)

Alfred Frankenstein. *The Reality of Appearance: The Trompe L'Oeil Tradition in American Painting*. New York: The New York Graphic Society for the University Art Museum, Berkeley (1970)

GAMMELL
R. H. Ives Gammell. *Dennis Miller Bunker*. New York: Coward-McCann, Inc. (1953)

GARDNER
Albert Ten Eyck Gardner. *Yankee Stone Cutters: The First American School of Sculpture 1800-1850*. New York: Columbia University Press for The Metropolitan Museum of Art (1945)

Albert Ten Eyck Gardner. *American Sculpture: A Catalogue of the Collection of The Metropolitan Museum of Art*. New York: The Metropolitan Museum of Art (1965)

GARWOOD
Darrell Garwood. *Artist in Iowa: A Life of Grant Wood*. New York: W. W. Norton & Co. (1944)

GOODRICH, LAURENCE
Laurence B. Goodrich. *Ralph Earl: Recorder for an Era*. Albany: The State University of New York (1967)

GOODRICH, LLOYD
Lloyd Goodrich. *Thomas Eakins: His Life and Work*. New York: Whitney Museum of American Art (1933)

Lloyd Goodrich. *Albert P. Ryder Centenary Exhibition*. New York: Whitney Museum of American Art (1947)

Lloyd Goodrich. *Winslow Homer*. New York: The Macmillan Company for the Whitney Museum of American Art (1959)

HARTLEY
Marsden Hartley. "Art and the Personal Life," *Creative Art* (June 1928)

HENDRICKS
: Gordon Hendricks. *Thomas Eakins: His Photographic Works*. Philadelphia: The Pennsylvania Academy of the Fine Arts (1969)
: Gordon Hendricks. *Albert Bierstadt 1830-1902*. New York: M. Knoedler & Co. (1972)

HOMER
: William Innes Homer. *Robert Henri and His Circle*. Ithaca, New York: Cornell University Press (1969)

HOWAT
: John K. Howat & others. *19th-Century America: Paintings and Sculpture*. New York: The Metropolitan Museum of Art (1970)

ISHAM
: Samuel Isham. *The History of American Painting*. New York: The Macmillan Company (1905); new edition with supplementary chapters by Royal Cortissoz (1927)

JARVES
: James Jackson Jarves. *The Art Idea: Sculpture, Painting and Architecture in America* (5th ed.). Boston and New York (1864)

KIRSTEIN
: Lincoln Kirstein. *William Rimmer 1816-1879*. New York: Whitney Museum of American Art (1946)

LAWALL
: David Lawall. *A. B. Durand*. Montclair, New Jersey: Montclair Art Museum (1971)

MARLOR
: Clark S. Marlor, ed. *A History of the Brooklyn Art Association with an Index of Exhibitions*. New York: James F. Carr (1970)

MCDERMOTT
: John Francis McDermott. *George Caleb Bingham: River Portraitist*. Norman, Oklahoma: University of Oklahoma Press (1959)

MERRITT
: Howard S. Merritt. "A Wild Scene, Genesis of a Painting," *Baltimore Museum of Art Annual II*. Baltimore, Maryland (1967)

MILLER
: Dorothy Miller. *The Life and Work of David G. Blythe*. Pittsburgh: University of Pittsburgh Press (1950)

MOOZ
: R. Peter Mooz. "Robert Feke: The Philadelphia Story," *American Painting to 1776: A Reappraisal*. Charlottesville, Va., for the Henry Francis duPont Winterthur Museum (1971)

OLIVER
: Andrew Oliver. *The Notebook of John Smibert*. Boston: Massachusetts Historical Society (1969)

ORMOND
: Richard Ormond. *John Singer Sargent: Paintings, Drawings, Watercolors*. New York: Harper & Row (1970)

PRESCOTT
: Kenneth W. Prescott. *The Complete Graphic Works of Ben Shahn*. New York: Quadrangle/The New York Times Book Company (1973)

QUIMBY
: Ian M. G. Quimby. "The Doolittle Engravings of the Battle of Lexington and Concord," *Winterthur Portfolio 4* (1968)

RICHARDSON
: E. P. Richardson. "Two Portraits by William Page," *The Art Quarterly*, I (1938)

RUTLEDGE
: Anna Wells Rutledge. *Artists in the Life of Charleston: Through Colony and State from Restoration to Reconstruction*. Philadelphia: American Philosophical Society (1949)

SELLERS
: Charles Coleman Sellers. *Charles Willson Peale. Volume II. Later Life (1790-1827)*. Philadelphia: American Philosophical Society (1947)
: Charles Coleman Sellers. *Portraits and Miniatures by Charles Willson Peale*. Philadelphia: American Philosophical Society (1952)
: Charles Coleman Sellers. *Charles Willson Peale*. New York: Charles Scribner's Sons (1969)
: Charles Coleman Sellers. *Charles Willson Peale with Patron and Populace*. A supplement to *Portraits and Miniatures by Charles Willson Peale*. Philadelphia: American Philosophical Society (1969)

SIBLEY
: *Sibley's Harvard Graduates*, vol. 5. Boston: Massachusetts Historical Society (1937)

SIEGL
: Theodor Siegl, verbal communication

SIZER
: Theodore Sizer, ed. *The Autobiography of Colonel John Trumbull, Patriot-Artist, 1756-1843*. New Haven: Yale University Press (1953)

SORIA
: Regina Soria. *Elihu Vedder: American Visionary Artist in Rome (1836-1923)*. Rutherford, New Jersey: Fairleigh Dickinson University Press (1970)

STEBBINS
: Theodore E. Stebbins. *Martin Johnson Heade*. College Park, Maryland: The University of Maryland (1969)

STEGNER
: Wallace Stegner. *Beyond the Hundredth Meridian*. Boston: Houghton Mifflin Company (1954)

SULLY
: Langdon Sully. "Love and Tragedy in Old Monterey," *The American West*, XI (July 1974)

TAYLOR
: Joshua C. Taylor. *William Page: The American Titian*. Chicago: University of Chicago Press (1957)

TUCKERMAN
: Henry T. Tuckerman. *Book of the Artists*. New York (1867); reprinted New York: James F. Carr (1966)

WILLIAMS
: Thurman Williams. *Thomas Moran: Artist of the Mountains*. Norman, Oklahoma: University of Oklahoma Press (1966)

WISTER
: "Journal of Miss Sally Wister," *Pennsylvania Magazine of History and Biography*, IX (1885)

Board of Trustees

EX OFFICIO
George R. Moscone, *Mayor of San Francisco*
Loris de Grazia, *President, Recreation and Park Commission*

HONORARY TRUSTEES
Judge and Mrs. Lucius P. Green
Walter S. Johnson
Mrs. Charles Munn
Mrs. William Lee Olds
Mrs. Alma E. Spreckels

TRUSTEES EMERITUS
David Pleydell-Bouverie
Whitney Warren

DIRECTOR EMERITUS
Thomas Carr Howe

BOARD OF TRUSTEES
Ransom M. Cook, *President*
Mrs. Alexander Albert
James B. Black, Jr.
Joseph M. Bransten
Sheldon G. Cooper
Christian de Guigne
Charles C. de Limur
Mrs. Gunther R. Detert
John B. Ducato
George Hopper Fitch
R. Gwin Follis
Mrs. Edward T. Harrison
Clifford V. Heimbucher
Mrs. Frederick J. Hellman
Mrs. Robert Homans
Mrs. Bruce Kelham
Mrs. Carl Livingston
Cyril Magnin
Mrs. Robert A. Magowan
Peter McBean
Mrs. Robert Watt Miller
Walter S. Newman
Mrs. William P. Roth
Emmett G. Solomon
Charles de Young Thieriot
Mrs. Nion Tucker
Harold L. Zellerbach

Marie S. Jensen, *Executive Secretary*

The Museum Society
William S. Picher, *Chairman*

Auxiliary, The Museum Society
Mrs. Philip G. Green, *Chairman*

Docent Council
Mrs. Charles Martell, *Chairman*

Staff

Administration

Ian McKibbin White, *Director of Museums*
F. Lanier Graham, *Vice-Director for Collections and Chief Curator*
Thomas K. Seligman, *Vice-Director for Education*
Ronald Egherman, *Vice-Director for Administration and Personnel*
Marie S. Jensen, *Executive Secretary for the Board of Trustees*
Charles Long, *Public Relations*
Ann M. Knoll, *Development Officer*
Earl Anderson, *Assistant to the Director*

Curatorial Division

PAINTING AND SCULPTURE

William H. Elsner, *Acting Curator in Charge*
Teri Oikawa-Picante, *Conservator*

DECORATIVE ARTS

D. Graeme Keith, *Curator in Charge*
Anna Bennett, *Curatorial Associate*
Gene Munsch, *Conservator*

PRINTS AND DRAWINGS
(Achenbach Foundation for Graphic Arts)

Robert F. Johnson, *Curator in Charge*
Fenton Kastner, *Associate Curator*
Phyllis Hattis, *Visiting Curator*
Roy L. Perkinson, *Conservator*
Robert Futernich, *Associate Conservator*

AFRICA, OCEANIA AND THE AMERICAS

Thomas K. Seligman, *Curator in Charge*
Kathleen Berrin, *Curatorial Assistant*

ANCIENT ART

Jane Gray Nelson, *Assistant Curator in Charge*

EXHIBITIONS

Thomas H. Garver, *Curator in Charge*
Susan Levitin, *Assistant Curator*
Royal A. Basich, *Exhibition Designer*
Ron Rick, *Graphic Designer*
John Almond, *Acting Chief Preparator*

Operational Division

ACCOUNTING

Marie S. Jensen, *Comptroller*
Josephine Regan, *Recorder*
Patricia Pierce, *Payroll Supervisor*

REGISTRATION

Frederic P. Snowden, *Registrar*
S. DeRenne Coerr, *Registrar*
James Medley, *Photographer*
Harry Fugl, *Registration Assistant*

SUPERINTENDENCE

Sal Priolo, *Coordinator of Museum Services*
Elvin C. Howard, *Chief Guard*
John Cullen, *Chief Engineer*

Educational Division

INTERPRETATION

Thomas K. Seligman, *Curator in Charge*
Lizabeth Cohen, *Assistant Curator*

PROGRAM

Bruce Merley, *Assistant Curator*
Charles Mills, *Assistant Curator*

ART SCHOOL

Elsa Cameron, *Curator in Charge*
Richard Fong, *Associate Curator*
James Stevenson, *Curatorial Assistant*
Eileen Law, *Curatorial Assistant*
John Chiu, *Curatorial Assistant*
Michael Chin, *Administrative Assistant*

LIBRARY

Jane Gray Nelson, *Librarian*

Designed and produced by Adrian Wilson
in collaboration with Jack Werner Stauffacher

Production assistance by Maria Poythress Epes
and James Faris

Photography by O. E. Nelson

Composed by Mackenzie-Harris Corporation
in Spectrum types designed by Jan van Krimpen

Photolithography by Phelps/Schaefer Litho-Graphics
Company

Bound by Cardoza-James Binding Company